"I, JAMES ~~V~~
DO MAKE THE FO

"On Thursday, July 5, 1~~~~~~ ~~~~~~ ~~~~~~~~~ morning hours, I was taken by detectives of the Homicide Squad to Yaphank, where I was told that a guy I know as Gary Lauwers' body was found murdered in Northport. The detectives asked me a lot of questions and I told them some answers but not everything. . . . I made it look like I hadn't done too much during the killing of Gary, that Rick Kasso had done most of it. When I finished telling the first story, I left there with [the detectives] and headed for Northport Village. It was during this time that I realized that I should tell it all, that is, how the murder of Gary Lauwers went down. . . ."

Also by David St Clair

CHILD POSSESSED
MINE TO KILL
THE DEVIL ROCKED HER CRADLE
BLOODLINE

and published by Corgi Books

SAY YOU LOVE SATAN

David St Clair

CORGI BOOKS

SAY YOU LOVE SATAN
A CORGI BOOK 0 552 13532 1

First publication in Great Britain

PRINTING HISTORY
Corgi edition published 1990

Grateful acknowledgment is made for permission to reprint the following:
BARK AT THE MOON by Ozzy Osbourne, Jake E. Lee, and Bob Daisley
© 1983 Virgin Music (Publishers) Ltd.

Corgi Books are published by Transworld Publishers
Ltd., 61–63 Uxbridge Road, Ealing, London W5 5SA, in
Australia by Transworld Publishers (Australia) Pty. Ltd.,
15–23 Helles Avenue, Moorebank, NSW 2170, and in New
Zealand by Transworld Publishers (N.Z.) Ltd., Cnr. Moselle
and Waipareira Avenues, Henderson, Auckland.

Printed and bound in Great Britain by
Cox & Wyman Ltd., Reading, Berks.

For Richard Pine and Robert Mecoy
. . . it's their book.

This is a true story based on events in the lives of three young Americans who let fate spin them out of control. Real names have been used whenever possible. Some names have been changed to protect friends and witnesses and others so fearful they didn't want to be identified. The situations, personalities, events, and conversations found in this book have been reconstructed from weeks of research in Northport and the surrounding towns, from hundreds of hours spent listening, watching, interviewing, trying to understand.

PROLOGUE

SOMETHING HAPPENED

"Say you love Satan!" the curly-headed boy shouted as he plunged his knife into the other boy's chest.

"No! I love my mother!" the younger boy screamed.

"Satan! Say you love Satan!" The long sharp blade dug into the teenage flesh another time.

"My mother! I love my mother!"

"Ricky, what the fuck are you doing?" another teenager, dark-haired and stocky, asked with only slight concern. "You're killing him," he said matter-of-factly. "Christ, man, you're killing him."

"He has to say he loves Satan!" His arm swung, the knife slashed again into the youth's body.

"My mother! I love my mother!"

Shop owner in downtown Northport, Long Island, New York:

"Sure it was a terrible thing and it's been bad for business, but there really wasn't any devil worship or anything like that in it. It was just kids high on dope. They were kids, just punks. It could have happened to any little town. I don't know why the world has singled out Northport. This is a helluva nice place to live."

"You wanna know where Gary is? Gary is dead. I killed him."

"Come on, Ricky. Don't give me that shit, man."

"I did. I killed the little bastard. He owed me for five hits of mesc. He wouldn't pay me, so I killed him."

"You're full of shit, man." The boy, a ninth-grader waiting out the summer to go into high school, stopped and stared into Ricky's haggard face. "You *are* shittin' me, aren't you?"

"You wanna see Gary? I'll show you his body. It's got maggots and stuff all over it, but you can see it if you want to."

"Holy Christ! You're not shittin' me, are you?"

"No. I killed the little son of a bitch. He deserved it."

Northport real estate saleswoman:

"It was awful. Simply awful. The press descended on our town. They wrote all kinds of terrible things about the community. They accused us of having dope here and of permitting devil worship. They even wrote bad things about our school system. I mean, really, our school system here in Northport is the best in the state. People want to live here because the schools are so good. But you know what it did, what that murder did? It lowered property values for a while. For several months afterward we were making deals way down from what we normally do. That was the worst thing about all of this—it hurt property values.

"That Ricky! He's nuts, man. You know what he did?"

The other school student shook his head. He'd wait to see what his friend knew before he said anything.

"He killed Gary Lauwers!" The first boy stood back to see the second boy's reaction.

"I know," the second boy said. "Ricky took me up there. He showed me Gary's body. Really smelled terrible, man. I mean like a hundred people had taken a crap there."

"I saw it too. He pushed back the leaves and there was Gary's face. He doesn't have no eyes no more or any lips. It was a pretty sick sight, man."

"You tell your folks?" the second boy asked.

"Shit no! Did you?"

The second boy shook his head. "I don't wanna get involved. That's Ricky's business. My old man would kill me if I told him. Then he'd tell the police. It would hit the fan."

"Same here, man. I'm gonna keep the hell away from it."

"Me, too. Hey, are you going to Eddie's house tonight? His folks are out of town. They've got a new VCR and Eddie's got ahold of a fuck film. You ever seen one of those?"

The other boy shook his head. "Not yet, man, I'm only fourteen years old."

Detective Lieutenant Robert Dunn, commander of the Suffolk County Homicide Squad:
"This was a sacrificial killing. It's pure Satanism."

No one is sure of the exact date when Satan came to Northport. Local residents pride themselves on its being a small, sleepy, and affluent community. It's always been small and sleepy, the affluence came later.

To find the village of Northport, first locate New York State on the map of the United States. Then go all the way over to the Atlantic Ocean and then along the coast to New York City. On a large map of Manhattan, go north to 178th Street, where the George Washington Bridge spans across the Hudson River from Fort Lee, New Jersey. Go east now, across the factory- and tenement-strewn Bronx. Then when you reach the waters of Long Island Sound, start south through the Borough of Queens with its multitiered nondescript apartment blocks. Suddenly Long Island is right there, like a large fish trying to swallow Queens, its jaws open, its body jutting into the Atlantic, and its tail churning up weeds and sand around the elaborate clapboard mansions of the Hamptons.

Northport sits about a quarter of the way into the Island, on the northern shore, away from the planned congestion of towns like Garden City, Levittown, and Hicksville. The nearest "big" town is Huntington, about ten miles away. The American poet Walt Whitman lived in Huntington. He wrote about freedom, individuality, nonmaterialism, whiskey, and homosexuality. His house is a museum now.

Very few people in the area have read Whitman's work, but there is a Walt Whitman Highway and a Walt Whitman Shopping Center. And the liquor stores and bars and expensive restaurants show that contemporary residents of Huntington approve of at least one of their native son's diversions.

Huntington is the last stop on several commuter trains of the Long Island Railroad. During peak hours the old cars rattle constantly from New York City's Pennsylvania Station in Madison Square Garden. Penn Station has nothing really to do with the state of Pennsylvania and there is neither garden nor square at Madison Square Garden. Passengers can catch the train in Northport, but most regular commuters drive into Huntington and take the train, then return to Huntington Station at night and drive back to their Northport homes. Northport has always revolved around Huntington.

In 1653 European settlers, mostly from England and Scotland, purchased a hunk of northern shoreline from the Matinecock Indians. It went from what is now Cold Spring Harbor eastward to where Northport Harbor is today. About eight miles straight across. Three years later more settlers arrived, so a second deal was made with the Indians to buy all the land over to the next bay, where the Nissequoque River flowed. The new owners, three Puritan gentlemen named Wood, Rogers, and Wickes, paid the Indians with "2 coates, 4 shirts, 7 quarts licker, and 11 ounces powder." The Indians had named their lovely harbor area Opcathontche. Lacking Walt Whitman's sensibilities, the developers renamed it Great Cow Harbor.

In 1790 a man named Ebenezer Bryant, who is described as a citizen-farmer, laid a straight path from his property down to the water's edge. They called it Bryant's Path for a while and then it naturally got changed to Main Street. Bryant wanted to open the area to "communication." He did. Main Street is the vital commercial street of the village, if you don't count Fort Salonga Highway, which connects with Huntington and the town of Kings Park. The highway is lined with supermarkets, restaurants, garages, specialty shops, and—of course—banks. One wonders what citizen-farmer Bryant would say if he could see his "path" today. He would probably like the antique shops, the movie house, the realty agents, and probably even the couple of beer joints along its sides.

A few years after he opened his path, Bryant built two docks at the foot of it. In the old days oyster boats used them almost exclusively. Now the docks are filled with expensive inboard motorboats and fancy yachts. Some of them belong to the citizens of Northport, but many belong to New Yorkers who come on the weekends when the weather is nice.

The docks have a public park around them: old trees, a bandbox, freshly cut green lawns, and benches along the footpaths. Citizen-farmer Bryant would probably like the park too. He probably would not like the fact that marijuana, angel dust, mescaline, and heroin are openly traded here. Anyone willing to sit quietly, or wait on a park bench, can eventually see a transaction being made. Sometimes the seller has come into the harbor on one of the pleasure boats. Sometimes he has driven there from the Bronx or Queens. Ricky Kasso used to do that: drive to the Bronx, buy his stuff, and return to sell it in the park to kids his own age or younger.

It was in this park that Ricky Kasso was the self-proclaimed "Acid King."

It was in this park that Ricky decided to kill Gary Lauwers.

PART ONE

March 29, 1967 to April 21, 1984

CHAPTER ONE

From a bicentennial booklet put out by the Village of Northport:

"Dapper and debonair James J. Walker, former Mayor of New York City, is one of the many famous people who have made Northport or its neighboring communities their home. The list includes, among others, Fiorello La Guardia, Eugene O'Neill, William K. Vanderbilt, the Duchess of Marlboro, Booker T. Washington, and Baron Von Wrangel. Peggy Wood, Broadway actress and of *I Remember Mama* fame on TV, is a native Northporter."

The booklet fails to mention that American poet and Catholic priest Thomas Merton used to visit friends in Northport. At one New Year's Eve party at a house on Church Street (it runs across Main) two pretty blond girls were flirting with Merton as he expounded about the miraculous apparitions of the Virgin Mary. One of them discovered Merton was going to be a priest. She told the other. Merton saw the New Year in by himself.

Another Northporter who rose to fame—though the locals never named a mall or even an alley for him—was beatnik poet and writer Jack Kerouac. He lived there with his mother and escaped to California, yet he kept coming back for visits and hating it. The most visible beer joint on Main Street is Gunther's Tap Room. There is a massive old-fashioned wooden bar on one side of the dark room, tables, a jukebox, and pictures on the other side. In one large frame are Xerox copies of pages from two books about Kerouac. Both books mention Gunther's by name. In his time, Kerouac hung out with the kids in that bar and they all got high on beer and booze. Today's kids bypass the bars. They are mainly for middle-age blue-collar workers and old men. The booze sold at Gunther's doesn't get today's kids high. The dope sold in Cow Park Harbor does.

Richard (Ricky) Kasso, Jr., who was to make Northport more famous than Kerouac, O'Neill, and La Guardia ever did, was born in the village on March 29, 1967. He was the third-generation Northporter. His grandfather had gone through the Northport school system and later became a minor-league baseball player. His father, Richard, Sr., also went to the local schools, was a better-than-average student, and an excellent football player. At the time of the murder Richard, Sr., was teaching social studies and coaching football at Cold Spring Harbor High School, just a couple of miles on the other side of the town of Huntington.

Richard Kasso, Sr., was teaching at Northport Junior High School when he met his future wife, Lynn Barlow, who was also a teacher there. Friends who watched their courtship still smile. Dick Kasso was the rugged outdoor and outgoing male type. Lynn, softer and intellectual. They worked on each other to bring each other around to their standards. The result: a happily balanced couple who became a happily married couple in 1965.

Dick and Lynn Kasso lived typical lives. They didn't make waves that would rock their boat or anyone else's. They are Methodists and seem to fully agree with their church's middle-of-the-road values. They are schoolteachers. They live in a small pleasant community. They are an active part of that community. They bought a small house on Seaview Avenue, just a few blocks from downtown's Main Street. It is a typical red-shingled, two-story house, with white shutters and an attached garage.

Tall trees on each side of the house keep it cool in the summer, and a steady supply of piled cordwood near the patio keeps it warm in the winter. There is a large backyard but no swimming pool. A tall post with a basketball hoop stands on the right of the driveway. It was put there so Ricky would stay home. It didn't work.

23

The Kassos have three daughters, all younger than Ricky and all attractive. Ricky himself has been described as "a good-looking boy" because of his light brown curly hair, angular jaw, and flashing blue eyes. It was those eyes, open and aware and mocking on front pages all over the country, that grabbed America's attention.

The Kassos were typical in another way as well. Each year they would go up to their summer home in Greenwich, New York. It gave Dick and Lynn a chance to escape Northport. It also gave them a little spare cash, for they often rented out their Northport home to summer tourists.

The town of Greenwich lies just east of the wide Hudson River. It sits on rolling hills thick with vegetation. The sky in the summer is incredibly blue and the unpolluted air smells sweet and fresh, as if recently unbottled by the gods.

Little Ricky loved the wooded area around their vacation home. He would spend hours by himself rambling through the woods, making collections of leaves and rocks and dead insects. He liked to find a tree with a large trunk and lots of shade and he would sit on the bare earth, his back against the trunk, and soak up the energy he felt from living nature. Snakes fascinated the boy, and more than once he frightened his little sisters with a live, wriggling specimen he had found in the woods. One of his favorite spots was tiny Lake Cossayuna. He'd fish along its banks, splash his bare feet in its waters, or just sit and watch the play of nature's colors over its surface.

"He told me," recalls a friend, "that once he was

sitting beside the lake and this old man came along and sat down beside him. Ricky must have been about in fifth grade or so. Neither he nor the man said anything. The old guy looked like he might have Indian blood in him, but Ricky wasn't sure. Finally the guy reached into his pocket and took out a small red stone."

"Take this," he told Ricky, "it's got magic in it."

"What kind of magic?" Ricky asked.

"What kind of dreams do you have?" the man replied.

"All kinds," the boy said.

"Those are the best kind." The man closed the boy's fingers over the stone. "You keep this. Believe in its magic."

"My dad says magic isn't real."

"Magic is very real. I don't care what your father tells you. Anything you wish for you can have. Anything you dream you can achieve." Then the old man got up and walked away, into the woods. Ricky watched for him on other trips to the lake, but never saw the man again.

"I asked Ricky if he told his parents about the guy," the friend said. "He told me he hadn't. He said they wouldn't have understood. Anyway, they'd warned him about talking with strangers, especially old bums in the woods. He put the stone on his dresser and a couple of days later it was gone. He figured his mom must have thrown it out when she was cleaning his bedroom. He didn't ask her about it. He didn't tell his parents anything."

One of the things he didn't tell his parents in the

fifth grade was that he had started smoking marijuana.

One would think that something as significant as Ricky Kasso's first cigarette would be surrounded by dramatic intrigue. Considering that drugs and dope became his life-style, indeed his very reason for existing, then his introduction to them should be accompanied by drumrolls and claps of thunder. But it wasn't. Like millions of kids in thousands of elementary school yards, Ricky's first experience with deadly chemical substances came easily and without incident.

"Hey, Rick. How ya doin'?" The older boy was in junior high, Ricky's father was one of his teachers. "I came to give Benny his lunch money." Benny was the boy's younger brother, a classmate of Ricky's.

Benny smiled at Ricky and took another puff of the slim cigarette. He handed it back to his brother.

"Maybe you wanna try it?" The older boy held out the thin hand-rolled cigarette.

Ricky looked from one to the other. The decision he made at that moment affected the rest of his life and the lives of everyone around him. "Sure," he said. "I've wondered what it tastes like."

Astrologers claim they can read a person's horoscope and pinpoint the moment when the stars and planets are in adverse positions. It would be interesting to know what was happening in heaven that day, around noon, in October 1977.

26

* * *

In September 1979, Ricky started junior high. The Northport Junior High School is an imposing two-story building of red brick. Large, well-manicured green lawns slope down onto Laurel Avenue with its prosperous homes. The Northport Public Library is just across the street. A sidewalk runs from the street up to the school's front door, which is in the center of an imposing white wall fronted by four enormous white columns. One almost expects to see Scarlett O'Hara leaning against one of them. To the right of the building is a parking lot (lined with shade trees) and behind it an open sports field for baseball, football, and track. Joining the school property, farther to the right, is a shopping mall. The shops are small and nondescript: bank, grocery, camera, fast-food—the usual. The important part of the mall—as far as the students are concerned—is the back of it, the flat white wall with the loading dock that gives entrance to the rear of some of the stores. The loading dock is where the kids hang out. Where the kids smoke their dope. Where teachers see from their classrooms but where few school authorities ever tread.

"When Ricky was in school," a classmate named Paul remembers, "Northport Junior was a dump." I remember seeing kids sitting in a circle near the football field. I mean it was school hours and these kids were outside, sitting there in full sight of everybody. It was a daily thing. I could see smoke rising from the group. Every one of them was smoking marijuana. Ricky was right in the middle of them. He was the ringleader."

By the time Ricky was in eighth grade, his marks were suffering from too little study and too much marijuana. He had never been more than a C student, even in elementary school, but in junior high he was lucky to get D's. Some students wondered aloud if Ricky was passing because his parents were teachers and friends of Ricky's teachers. The Kassos tried to help him with his homework, spending hours at the kitchen table in an effort to get him interested in schoolwork. It didn't look good for their only son to be a scholastic failure.

They stopped fussing about how he should dress for school. They couldn't keep him in corduroys and sport shirts when the other kids were wearing ragged jeans and T-shirts. He wore deliberately torn blue jeans and a gray sweatshirt with the hood up outside the collar of a patched blue denim jacket. He didn't look out of place. That was the style. All the kids dressed like bums. Even if their old man could afford to buy them clothes from Bloomingdale's or Saks.

Ricky made sure he was at school twenty minutes early each day, so he could smoke a joint with his friends before classes began. The smoking during classes was more unscheduled. You split, went to the football field or the loading dock, and smoked with whoever else happened to be there. At lunchtime the circles appeared again.

"There was a no-smoking rule," recalls Paul, "and another rule that said you couldn't be in that area. I've heard all this bullshit from Ricky's teachers about how they tried to work with him, tried to turn him around. That's crap. They didn't do a damned thing. They couldn't do anything with him, so they just let him sit in the circles and smoke. Sure, there were teachers standing around outside. They called themselves 'monitors.' Kids in the circles called them 'hyenas' because all they did was keep their distance, afraid to interfere. Once or twice the 'hyenas' tried to break up the circles, but they were happening every day. Ricky supplied some of the cigarettes. I don't know if he was selling them yet, but I know he gave some away. He gave me a few.

"You know one time, and this was funny, one time old man Brosnan called the police and they came to the loading dock and chased the kids away. The principal didn't have the balls to do it himself. So the kids staged a walkout at the beginning of the next period. Ricky was one of them. They went on strike like they were working in a factory or something."

In the eighth grade, Ricky decided to dedicate himself to football. Even though he was fairly slight, he was big enough to play against other junior high students. He wanted to get on the team for another reason: It would prove to his father that he wasn't entirely worthless.

"Ricky was concerned about what his old man thought of him," said Eric. "We were on the junior high team together. He played left receiver, offensive left end, or left end on defense. He had a lot of energy until he started smoking all that weed, but after that he didn't have any energy at all when he ran. They say drugs give you speed, but Ricky was easily winded. Sometimes he'd show up for a game and he couldn't perform at all.

"He was having a lot of trouble with his father, because of the dope and his grades and everything. Because his old man was a coach at another school, the coaches at junior high tried to help him more than they helped the rest of us. You know, special counseling and long talks in the coach's office and all that. It didn't seem to work on Ricky. The rest of the Kasso family seems fine. His dad's got a good reputation as a teacher. I've met one of Ricky's sisters. She seems real fine."

Another team player remembers, "One time this other guy, he was a kid going to the school, came into the locker room right after we had played a game. Ricky had just finished taking a shower and the guy says to him, 'There's a girl outside who wants to try some marijuana.' So Ricky says to him, 'Okay, hold on. I'll be finished dressing in a few minutes and I'll meet you out there by the loading dock.' My locker was pretty close to his. I could hear everything that was going on. I said to him, 'Ricky, do you think that's right? Turning that girl onto weed?' He said to me, 'Hey, man, it's what she wants. You only get a chance to go around life once, might as well do what you want when you want to do it.' I didn't argue. Hell, it wasn't my business. I guess this was sometime in the eighth grade. So he must have been peddling stuff when he was only thirteen years old. Jesus! I never thought about it. He was only thirteen, man!"

CHAPTER TWO

In the eighth grade, Ricky and ninth-grader Jimmy Troiano became friends. Again, one wonders where the stars were.

Jimmy was on the football team. He played nose guard and Ricky played end. Coach David Harper remembers them as being good friends but also as "kids who had problems."

Jimmy is described by most of the kids and adults who knew him as "strange." People keep using that word to sum him up. It was this strangeness that kept him a loner, kept other kids afraid of him, kept Ricky fascinated by him.

Jimmy is a good-looking young man today, but when he went to school his peers called him Dracula or Scarface. Both of his eyeteeth were longer than the other teeth in his mouth. They curved down like fangs, so when he smiled the kids were reminded of a late-night TV horror flick. He has a scar, on the right side of his face, running from just below his eye down to the corner of his mouth. He says he got it by falling off a swing set when he was five years old. Others claim he was on the swing set, all right, but he put the S hook of the swing into his mouth and jumped from the top of the A frame. That daredevil stunt is what gave him a scar for life, they say.

Jimmy was a year older than Ricky but had been smoking marijuana two years before Ricky ever tried it. Where Ricky was tall and thin, Jimmy was short and stocky. Ricky had light hair, Jimmy's was dark. Ricky's eyes were blue, Jimmy's a deep brown. Opposites attract.

Jimmy Troiano was adopted and brought to Northport when he was four and a half years old. He knows almost nothing about his real parents except that his father had light brown hair, blue eyes, and was five feet six inches tall. His mother, he has been told, was of French descent. He often wondered if he had any brothers and sisters. As an only child, he used to fantasize about having brothers and sisters to play with. "Sometimes when my folks would take me up to Saratoga and places, I'd see other kids and say to myself, Hey, I wonder if that boy is my brother or those two girls look like they could be my sisters. Maybe I bumped into my real family one time and I never knew. That bothered me, the fact that I never would know."

The couple who adopted him, Vincent and

Mary Troiano, were like the Kassos. They wanted security and respectability and no one rocking their boat. Vincent Troiano is an art director with Fawcett Publications in New York City. His wife, Mary, is a registered nurse at Huntington Hospital . . . in the psychiatric ward. They are both good Protestants who attend Trinity Church in the heart of the village. Their home is even simpler than the Kassos'. It is in East Northport. (East Northport is not considered as chic or desirable as Northport Village.) It sits on a small lot on Barry Drive, facing Clare Drive. It has a sloping roof, white trim, and no front porch. There is a narrow manicured lawn and then three rounded steps forming a platform to the front door. Every house on both sides of the street looks exactly the same. Owners who want to demonstrate their individuality can only landscape or decorate the front lawn with concrete elves or flamingoes.

Jimmy went to Dickenson Avenue Elementary School, just two streets away from his parents' home. He was a poor student, just managing to squeak through the system. Dave Condit, a former teacher in Northport, remembered him. "Jimmy was a student of mine all through elementary school and even in junior high. I taught music and he played in the band. He played the trumpet but he didn't play very well. That's okay, I know a lot of kids who aren't very good trumpet players. He was always a strange kid. [There's that word again.] He always wanted to go out in the parking lot after school and fight. He'd take on kids twice as big as he was. He frightened kids, he frightened everyone around him. I knew one kid who was twice as big as Jimmy was, yet he would ask me to drive him home sometimes because he was afraid Jimmy would beat him up. Troiano dropped out of the band in the eighth grade. I've heard the stories about him being into devil worship. I don't buy that. Jimmy was too independent for that. He wasn't afraid of anything. Not even the devil."

Ricky and Jimmy had a bond that went beyond football: They both loved to smoke pot. The two, after practice, out of their shoulder pads and cleat shoes, would sit in their ragged blue jeans and denim jackets and tell each other tall tales as they watched the smoke curl up around their heads.

One of their favorite spots was a secluded area in Aztakea Woods. It is a privately owned area of close trees, bushes, shrubs, and a couple of hills. Kids went there, climbed to the top of the biggest hill, smoked their pot, and looked down at the village below. The harbor, with its boats and clammers, was on one side. Main Street could be seen from the other. It was a quiet spot, with no adults and lots of space.

"You know what I wanna do one day?" Ricky had his eyes closed, talking in the direction where he knew Jimmy was sitting against a tree stump.

"What? Get some pussy?"

"No, not that. Yeah," he laughed, "that *too*, but what I really wanna do is get away from here. Go out to California. I talked with a dude who has a friend out there. He says there's sunshine all the time. None of this snow shit like we have here. And there are beaches, man, fantastic ones with sand and stuff and all kinds of weed. This guy said there were parties every night."

"Yeah?"

"Yeah. Parties and free beer and nobody does anything but sit around and get high." As if for emphasis, he took another pull on his cigarette.

"Sounds like a good idea. Better than this dump." Jimmy nodded. He had heard about California and the girls with the blond hair and the deep tans. "So when you goin'?"

"Soon, man. Soon."

"You gonna wait till you graduate or what?"

Ricky spat into the leaves. "Graduate? I ain't gonna graduate. I ain't gonna hang around here until then. That's a long time, man. Too fuckin' long to wait."

"How you gonna get there?" Jimmy, at times, was the practical one. "You gotta have bread to get there, man. You can't walk it."

"I'll steal a car when I'm ready."

"You don't know how to drive yet."

"I'll learn. Any asshole can learn to drive a car."

"You'll still need bread, man. I mean you may be able to steal a car, but you can't steal gas. You need money to buy gas and shit like that."

"I'll sell dope. There's money in dope."

Jimmy laughed. "You get a large stash and you'll smoke it all yourself. Won't be nothin' left to sell." He grinned and the scar stretched. "Anyway, takes bread to buy a stash of weed and the supplier got to have his bread up front. Ain't no credit with the main man. No cash, no stash." He had heard that phrase on television a few nights earlier. He'd been waiting for a time to use it. He grinned again, but Ricky still had his eyes closed, didn't see the very white teeth.

"If you don't say anything, don't rat on me, I'll tell you something." He waited. Jimmy grunted agreement. "Me and some other guys know about a place that'll be empty soon. People that live there, they're going away for a while. One guy says he's been in the place. They got silverware and stuff. We're gonna get the stuff and sell it in the Bronx and buy some *real* dope." Now he opened his eyes. "You wanna come in on this with us?"

Jimmy shook his head. "No thanks. I don't wanna give the cops any reason to come lookin' for me. My old lady would kill me."

"How'd they know?"

"They'd know. With my bad luck, they'd know." He took another drag on the joint, held his breath, then exhaled slowly. "My old lady would paste my ass to the wall."

"Well, we're gonna do it," said Ricky.

"Shit," replied Jimmy.

A week later, acting on a report from another junior high student, the Northport police came to the Kasso home with a warrant for Ricky's arrest. He and five other youths the same age had burglarized a house while the occupants were away. The other five were also charged. Lynn Kasso refused to believe it and she went through her son's bedroom looking to see if there was any evidence for the police charges. Hidden behind a stack of schoolbooks, she found a water pipe and other drug paraphernalia. Up until that moment the Kassos had not faced the reality that their son was into drugs. The few times they had questioned him about it, he had denied it.

"How could he *do* it?" his mother asked a close friend. "I've explained to him how dangerous these things are. I thought he was listening. I guess he was just pretending to listen. He told me he had tried marijuana once in the fifth grade and didn't like it. He said he would never put those poisons into his body. He told me a football player had to keep clean. He lied to me. My own son lied to me. I thought I knew him better than that."

"She seemed more upset over the drugs than she was over the arrest," the friend recalled. "If it had been my kid, I would have belted him."

There is an agency in an old building on Main Street called The Place. It is a nonprofit, government-funded counseling center, mostly for kids who are on drugs or who are contemplating suicide. The Kassos took Ricky there for several sessions with Tom Fazio, a dark-haired, intense young social worker who is genuinely interested in kids. Ricky would listen, nod his head in agreement, occasionally even add something to the conversation, then leave and immediately light up a joint.

"He told me once," a friend remembers, "that he and Fazio sat across a table from each other and he tried something he'd read about in a yoga book. You keep your eyes open but you block off your mind. You keep doing it until you have shut off all the sounds around you. He said he could see

Fazio's lips move but he couldn't hear the words. He tried it once with me and claimed he didn't hear a thing I was saying even though he was wide awake and staring straight at me. I don't know if he could do that or not. He was such a bullshitter. Who could believe him?"

Tom Fazio decided Ricky needed more professional help, so the Kassos started paying a psychiatrist. Those paid sessions went exactly like the ones the Place gave for free.

"You threw away another seventy-five dollars," Ricky said to his parents after a visit with the professional shrink. "That guy's a real jerk, but if you want me to, I'll go back and play the game. I'm good at games."

Soon after that Fazio ended the sessions completely. Fazio had to admit that Ricky had a sharp mind, even an intelligent mind, but he was deliberately wasting it. At the final session he accused Ricky of not wanting to get off drugs.

"That's right, man. Why should I? It's you and my folks who want me to quit, not me myself. I like me, man. I like what I'm doing."

That year Jimmy Troiano did something at junior high school he was proud of. He enrolled in a class that dealt with various aspects of the media: newspapers, radio, and television. The teacher divided the class into groups and held a contest to see which group could make the best documentary. It was to be in black and white and could be only fifteen minutes long.

Jimmy jumped wholeheartedly into the project.

"Why don't we do one about the loading dock?" he suggested.

"The loading dock?" a girl replied. "That's boring."

"No it isn't," Jimmy insisted. "What we'll do is film a kid getting high on the dock. Get one of us to pretend—"

"Yeah. *Pretend.*" The others laughed.

"To pretend he is smoking some weed and getting high. He can't really be smoking because that'd be against the rules"—he grinned—"and we don't wanna break the rules."

"Not here at Angel Junior High," a girl said with a laugh.

Jimmy continued excitedly. After all, this was *his* world he was talking about. "We can show him going over there, sorta hanging around, then bumming a joint. Then we can show him lighting it up, getting mellow, then getting high."

"Then we can show him floating back to school and sitting in his next class," another kid suggested.

"Then show the teacher being pissed at him and throwing him out," offered another.

"Yeah," agreed Jimmy, eager with the first project outside of football that had excited him. "Yeah. That sounds great!"

They made the film with Jimmy as assistant director and acting coach. After all, who knew more about getting high than he did? The film was completed and edited. Then it, along with all the others made in that class, was shown at special assembly to the entire school and put to a vote. The

Northport Junior High Academy Award for Best Picture went to Jimmy Troiano and his group. It was the high point of his scholastic life.

In June of 1980 the Northport school system promoted Jimmy Troiano into high school. "I don't believe it," he said to Ricky that afternoon when both of them got their report cards. "They know I deliberately didn't take the final exams. Shit, I was absent from class more than I was present. What the hell is this?" He laughed. "All those other kids bustin' their asses and sucking up to the teachers for grades and I pass right on through without doing a frigging thing. Who says there ain't no God? Huh?"

"Yeah. Me, too," Ricky replied. "Look, I got all D's and a couple C's. Shit, I should have gotten F's. I should have failed half my classes, but they passed me too. I'm going into ninth grade. You"—and his voice lowered a little—"you are going to go to high school. I still have another year in this junior high dump. We're not going to be on the football team anymore. Not together."

"That's okay," Jimmy replied, "we'll still be buddies. You'll be at high next year. We can be together again over there next year. Anyway, we still got this summer. We got lots of time yet."

"Maybe I'll go to California," Ricky said. "Maybe now's the time to go."

"Graduate from the ninth grade first," Jimmy advised. "Get that piece of paper."

"What good is a fuckin' piece of paper saying I

graduated from junior high? Shit, you can't even smoke it!" Both of them burst out laughing.

"Wait till you get your high school diploma," Jimmy said with a grin. "Think of the expression on your old man's face."

"I won't be here to see it," Ricky said, and shook his head. "My old man will get that paper in the mail. From California."

That summer was the last one that either of the boys would worry about school. It was to be their last summer vacation.

That summer was also another turning point in Ricky's life. It had been a hot July afternoon. His parents and sisters had gone to Greenwich and so had he, for a few days; but he had gotten restless, wanted to see his buddies in Northport, and needed to buy some grass. The stash he had taken to the summer vacation home was gone. He bought some marijuana from a guy standing in front of the Midway.

The Midway is a teenage hangout place, specializing in posters, biker regalia, and drug paraphernalia. Concerned citizens' groups have picketed it. Kids know, if they hang around long enough, someone will be there with dope to sell. That afternoon Ricky waited and made a purchase.

He walked down the street, openly puffing his illegal cigarette, but while he met a few school friends, he didn't meet anyone he really wanted to rap with. Main Street had started to fill up with city people—tourists—with alligators on their shirts. Most of the women were in khaki-colored skirts that hung past the knees (some of the older and fatter ones wore khaki-colored shorts that stretched across their hips). They wore thong sandals, sunglasses, and carried either Gucci or Louis Vuitton handbags. The men, all very pale and most with love handles and sagging bellies, wore the same kind of alligators, the khaki or cotton striped trousers (there were a few knobby knees draped with madras), and blue deck shoes without socks.

Ricky watched them watching the boats in the harbor, watched them admiring the quaintness of Main Street's facade, watched them admiring and taking pictures of each other admiring the view. None of them noticed this scruffy-looking teenager, but a few did turn and sniff the smoky air he trailed behind him. There was nobody at the wooden gazebo along the harbor shore and no one who mattered in the Phase II pizza shop, another teenage hangout.

He walked back up Main Street, past the police station, the city hall, the post office, and the one movie theater in town, then decided it would be cooler in the public library. It was up past Church Street. He took a right on Laurel, waved at the silent junior high school up ahead on the left, then entered the Georgian doors of the library. It was much cooler in there, and much quieter. None of the clerks paid any attention to him. He thought he would find the books about sports, maybe read up on some of his father's football heroes. He stood for at least two minutes staring in fascination at an enormous Christmas cactus on top of the card cabinet behind the librarian's desk. His mother had one like it, but not as goddamned big as this one was. The plant was enormous, with thick stalks and broad swordlike leaves. In his grass-hazed brain, the plant looked like a giant tree. A tropical tree. A California tree that somehow had had the bad luck to get permanently potted in Northport. He made a mental note to tell Jimmy about the tree. Maybe he could free it from its captivity. Maybe he would take it back to California when he split.

He walked slowly down the aisle, wondering where the football books were, when one section seemed to jump out at him. He stopped, stared, then looked around, then back at the dozen or so books that had so attracted him. They were still doing it. They were glowing. They were shifting nervously on their shelves. The reds and the greens and the yellows of their jackets pulsated like neon. He stopped and smiled. He knew he was high. He knew other objects besides books came alive when he smoked real good weed. He was glad he had another cigarette in his pocket, another of the same smooth stuff.

He started slowly, carefully, with measured steps, toward the section of living volumes. The other books on the other shelves just sat there, mute and dead, but these books were something else and he was sure they had something to tell him. He reached out and took one of them in his hand. He could feel it vibrating. He looked down at the title:

A History of Satanism.

"Son of a bitch!" he said aloud.

The book that sat beside it was also about Satan. So were the books on either side of it: *The Devil, History of Witchcraft, Demons and Possession, Spells, Magic and Incantations.* He ran his hand slowly over the backs of the books. They seemed to settle down, as if his touch were the calming influence they had been seeking, the stroke of friendship they needed.

He carried the book reverently over to one of the reading tables. They were divided into cubicles, with two-foot walls separating one reader from another. He sat down, opened the book slowly—that was always the way he read, slowly—and he began with Chapter One.

A hand touched his shoulder. "I'm sorry, young man," a female voice said, "but we're closing now. You'll have to go."

Ricky looked startled, then glanced out of the large windows. The day had gone. Night, with its shadows, had taken its place. He stood up, amazed that he had spent the entire afternoon and evening with that book. Indeed, with *any* book.

"You can check it out if you'd like," the woman said.

"No"—he shook his head—"I'll leave it here. That way, I know it'll be safe."

"Safe?"

"Yeah. My folks wouldn't . . ." He paused and shook his head. "Never mind. I'll be back and read the rest of it another day. It knows that. It knows I'll be back."

The librarian watched him place the book, respectfully, she thought, back in the spot where he had found it. Then she watched him leave the building and disappear in the summer darkness. "I remember thinking, what an unusual young man. What unusual eyes. I was fascinated by his eyes. They seemed to sparkle as if they had made an incredible discovery. In light of what was to come, I now know they had."

Late that night Ricky and Jimmy sat in the round sheltered area at the extreme end of the dock. The built-in benches had been put there for yachtsmen and tourists, not teenage dopers, but the two paid no attention to that.

They each had a lit marijuana cigarette in their hands and they chatted easily as they watched the few still-glowing lights bobbing on the boats anchored in the harbor. Farther off, on the other side of the bay, the hills, stretched out like rising bread dough, could barely be seen through the night's darkness.

"It was fantastic, man," Ricky was saying. "I mean those books just came alive for me. They almost called my name out loud. Shit, I was looking for football books. Shit, I wasn't really looking for anything at all. Just someplace air-conditioned."

"The library's okay," Jimmy said. "I been in there couple times."

"But what I'm trying to tell you," Ricky insisted, "is the way these books just jumped off the shelves at me. It was weird. Just like I was supposed to read them."

"You were high, man."

"Yeah, I was. In the beginning. But I didn't stay high all afternoon. Not on just one joint."

"That's true. Takes more than one joint to keep you high all afternoon."

"Right. I'm tellin' you, I started reading this book and I couldn't stop. I just kept going from page to page. I didn't even get up for a leak, man, that's how firm it grabbed me."

"You musta pissed a poolful when you got out of there."

Ricky ignored him. "It was the weirdest thing. Here I am reading all these things about Satan and the devil and hell and all that and yet it was like I already knew what I was reading. You understand what I'm sayin'?"

"No," Jimmy answered, knowing that Ricky wanted to tell him anyway.

"It was like I was understanding things *again*. I can't explain it right, but the things I was reading I already knew. Just that I didn't remember them." He paused, searching in the shadows for his dark-haired friend. "Does that make sense to you?"

"You mean like you get introduced to a girl at a party and when you hear her name you remember that you've already met her? Like that, you mean?"

"Yeah, something like that. But in this book it tells about ways to make *contact* with Satan. How to light candles and what kind of necklaces and shit you gotta have on. That kind of stuff. Well, I

47

know all that stuff. I don't know how I know, but I *know.*"

"Maybe it was from another life," Jimmy said easily, "maybe when you lived before. Maybe that's when you did all that Satan shit."

Ricky was about to take a drag on the cigarette and stopped. He stared at Jimmy. "What the fuck you talkin' about? Lived before?"

"Sure." The street-wise fifteen-year-old nodded his head. "Everybody has lived before."

Ricky was still staring at him. "Before what?"

"Before they were born into this life, asshole."

"You sayin' that before I was Ricky I was somebody else?"

"Uh-huh."

"Who? Who was I?"

"How the hell should I know? I don't even know who *I* was before this life, but I know this isn't the first time I've been here."

"Here?" Ricky was interested. "You mean here in Northport?"

"No, man." Jimmy spat with mature weariness into the waters below. "Here on earth. As a person."

"You believe that shit?"

"Sure."

"I never thought about it before." Ricky paused and took a long pull on the thin, pungent cigarette. He held the smoke for a while in his lungs, not breathing. Then he exhaled. Slowly. He let his eyes wander over the darkened boats and his ears caught a rift of music coming from one of the yachts. Five minutes of silence—like the bay

48

breeze—drifted past, unnoticed. "At church they say that's not possible," Ricky finally said.

"What's not possible?"

"Coming back again. When you die your soul stays with your body. In the ground. Only when Jesus comes back will you come back. We had that in Sunday school once. It's called the Resurrection. That's what the Church says."

"C'mon," Jimmy said simply. "What do they know?"

Ricky thought about that for a few silent moments. "Yeah," he said after a while, "What do they know?"

CHAPTER THREE

Ricky went to a Main Street bookshop the next morning, a dark and dreary holdover from the sixties called the Avitar New Age Books and Records. He had never been in there, but he knew from other kids you could buy things about astrology there, and get tarot cards, and magic potions. He leafed through a copy of Anton Le Vay's *Satanic Bible*. It was in paperback and came highly recommended by the clerk behind the counter.

"This got spells and stuff in it?" he asked. He almost added that he had never bought a book before but he didn't want to appear un-cool.

"Whatever you need." The clerk thumbed the pages. "Here's candle burning. Here's a chapter on chants and incantations. There's one in here on the Black Mass."

"What's that? Something for Velcro heads?"

"No. A Black Mass is like a Catholic Mass except things are done backwards and chants are said in reverse. This shows you how to use a living altar."

Ricky scowled. He had no idea what the man was talking about.

"A human altar. A woman. You get a woman to take off her clothes and you stick candles in her openings."

"Yeah? That's heavy shit, man." Ricky was impressed. "I'll take it."

He went back to his parents' vacation home and in the days that followed he'd disappear for hours into the woods or over by the lake, reading his treasured volume and smoking marijuana. He would read a paragraph or two, take a puff, close his eyes, and turn the printed words into moving pictures. Pictures far removed from his life in Northport and his parents' ideas about morality and Christianity.

If what this book said was true, if what this book promised could be realized, then nothing was impossible. Nobody should have to put up with the shit they were born into. If the guy that wrote this really knew what he was talking about, then Satan was the way to go. The devil had the answers for life on earth. The devil was the one to contact, the one who would do things for human beings who wanted to achieve.

Jesus was fine, he supposed. Christianity was okay for when you died and went to heaven and all that crap, but what about *now?* What about when you were fourteen years old and going into the ninth grade? Jesus wasn't interested in helping a kid with his football game. Jesus didn't give a damn about rock music. The Savior wasn't there to boost you up in your chemical high. Jesus wasn't going to let a kid have fun. He demanded sacrifice. Ricky had never liked the idea of Jesus anyway. A middle-aged Jew in a robe who walked around ordering everybody to do goody-goody things, to obey Him, to not have any fun in life. Don't enjoy yourself, Jesus seemed to be telling the kids of today. Put your fuckin' noses to the wheel. Be standard and plastic. Don't have any thoughts and don't do anything I wouldn't do. Pass up all the fun while you are on earth for a promise of a harp and a cloud in heaven. Shit! He had been spreading that stuff for almost two thousand years and the world was more fucked up than ever before. Things needed to be changed before they would get better. Kids had to be the ones to change things. Old people sure as hell didn't make changes. Old people, like his parents and his teachers, wanted everything to stay the same old boring way. Well, he wasn't about to go along with them. He never had, but he never understood why.

Now he understood. He was meant to walk in the path of Satan.

An oddly "different" Ricky showed up for the first day of ninth grade that September of 1981. Few noticed in the beginning, but he seemed more sure of himself, more in command of who he was and what he expected of others. Some might have put it down to just being in the senior class at junior high. That fact alone inflates many young egos. But the aura around Ricky Kasso was oddly changed. He knew he could do whatever he wanted. He knew nothing was impossible. He knew he didn't have to live the life other jerks his same age had surrendered to. He was somebody. He had power. He had Satan.

"In ninth grade," remembers Paul, "Ricky was a son of a bitch on the football field. He didn't give a goddamn how hard he hit somebody, couldn't care less that another kid got pounded. There were three kids who got so bruised by him that they had to take time off from the team, and shit, they were guys on *our* team!"

Ricky was on the first-string team, playing both offensive and defensive ends. Often his doper friends would come to the practice sessions and jeer from the sidelines. They'd yell at him, "Nice play, you jock!" and "Head of smoke, balls of steel!" Ricky wouldn't pay attention to them, didn't even glance in their direction. He enjoyed football and he was proud that he had made the first string. Just being on the team in ninth grade smoothed things over at home. He had to make good on the field; he had promised he would study hard and play great. Everyone wanted to believe it.

He went to practice, even when he was stoned, even when somebody over at the loading dock had a new rock tape. Music had become of major importance to him. Like teenagers everywhere, he made music a part of his life. But the sounds he liked were those of heavy metal: clashing notes, howling lyrics of protest, screaming instead of singing.

His favorite group was Black Sabbath, with Ozzy Osbourne.

"He really dug Osbourne," remembers Norma, a slim girl who went through junior high with him. "He used to tell me, 'Ozzy is God!' and when Ozzy bit off the head of a chicken, right on stage, that really turned him on. That's all he would talk about for days, Ozzy and that poor chicken. That and Satan, of course, Ricky never stopped talking about Satan."

By Thanksgiving Day the football season was over. Northport Junior High didn't do so great. But for Ricky, it was a relief. He'd kept his promise to his folks. He'd shown his old man that he could stick with something, even if it was a kids' sports team. By Thanksgiving he was into heavy drugs.

"He was into LSD," Norma says. "It wasn't no secret. Everybody else knew about it."

"I saw Ricky go downhill," a boy recalls, "and it wasn't nice to watch. The first time he ever tripped out was in the seventh grade. The *seventh* grade! He was high on something, God knows what, in art class, and he drew a dragon on the blackboard. Colored it all in yellow and red and put fire and smoke coming out of its mouth. He made it bigger than he was, bigger than life-size. All of a sudden there's this scream from him and he starts to back away from the blackboard and starts shaking and stuff like that. The teacher, she don't know what to do, and meanwhile Ricky is

54

standing there crying and yelling that the thing's moving, that it's alive and it's gonna eat him. Us kids just sat and stared. We couldn't believe it, couldn't make any sense out of it. Finally the teacher put her arm around Ricky's shoulders and got him out of the room. He didn't come back for the rest of the class. I don't know where she took him or what they did to him. I don't know if they told his folks or not. Probably not. That was the first time I ever saw someone get spooked by being on drugs. In a way, I owe Ricky a thank-you. From what I saw that day, I decided *I'd* never get hitched to drugs. I haven't. Not even a drag on a marijuana cigarette. Kids used to make fun of me, but at least I knew where my head was all the time. Hell, half the time those kids didn't know where their *asses* were!"

Ricky moved into his rightful position as "King" of the loading docks. He was in command. He had been around. He had both marijuana and acid for his friends. His main man would meet him in front of the Midway, supply him with enough for the day, and then Ricky would use some himself, sell some to other kids or, more likely, just give it away.

"He didn't need the money then," a boy remembers. "He was still living at home and his folks gave him pocket money. So he didn't need to sell the stuff for profit. By handing it out free to other kids, it got them hooked on it. Then when they wanted more, and Ricky wasn't around, they'd go to the man in front of the Midway. There were other pushers around town too. They'd hang out in the park down near the harbor. Sometimes they'd be sitting in a boat at night, waiting for a kid to come along after midnight to make a purchase. It wasn't unusual to see a kid out after dark, not in this town. Kids have always done their own thing here. Most parents don't give a damn what their kids do anymore. As long as they don't end up in jail or get pregnant, the parents don't give a fuck. Sometimes the pushers would just be hanging around on the sidewalks in front of the school, or parked in cars on Laurel Avenue.

"Now, I don't mean they were *only* at the junior high school. They were at all the schools from the high school down to the elementary schools. Yes, that's right, even the elementary schools. I know kids in the fifth grade who go to school stoned. Why don't their parents do something? Shit, most cases the parents don't even know. The father takes an early train into New York and the mother drives to her job in one of the little towns around here. The kids get their own breakfasts and pack their own lunches. That's called a two-income family. Wonderful! They leave the house to make all that money so they can buy all those *things* and their kids get flushed down the toilet!"

Jimmy Troiano went into tenth grade at Northport High School as expected. As expected, he hated it. He wasn't in the top-dog senior class anymore. He was a sophomore and there were two classes of older kids ahead of him—lording over him—before he would be a top-dog senior again. He cut classes, he never did his homework, he swaggered through the halls trying to be Mister Tough Guy and getting laughed at by the older kids.

"Jimmy's friends at that time were all dirtbaggers," a girl recalls, "they were real scum, the pits. You know what I mean? They weren't kids from our school, they were other kids, older kids mostly, who had dropped out of school or were from other towns here on the Island. They looked like hell. They didn't wash their blue jeans for months and their hair was pulled back with a rubber band or tied down with a real scrungy bandanna. They stank too. Under their arms and when they breathed down at you, it was like a garbage disposal unit was leaning over you. They were always high or else talking about getting high. I don't know what Jimmy saw in them. He was a bright kid. He had a brain when he wanted to use it, and these dirtbaggers had nothing between their ears. Oh, sure, over their ears they might have had a cigarette, but *between* their ears, *nothing*."

Jimmy imitated his new friends. Wore the same kind of clothes, swore the same oaths, smoked the same weed, and headed down the same twisted path.

The Troianos received a registered letter from the school board. Their son was incorrigible. Their son wasn't doing himself any good at high school. Their son wasn't doing anybody else any good at high school either. It was the board's recommendation that Jimmy be sent to a special school: Woodbury High at Wyandanch. It was over a thirty-minute drive, south from Northport, but

Mary Troiano gladly did it because she thought it would help her son.

It didn't.

The second day there, Jimmy tried to establish his territory, tried to be the big shot in an entire building of other big shots. He was pushed against the wall, kicked in the groin, and left on the floor. A week later someone broke into his locker, stole his winter jacket, and that night he rode home with his mother almost blue from the December cold.

"These are the goddamnedest bunch of shitheads you've ever seen," Jimmy told Ricky. It was almost Christmas and downtown Northport was hung with festive blinking lights, wreaths, and sparkling tinsel. The two friends had met at the magazine rack inside the Midway. "There is this one black mother with only one eye. I don't know where he lost it. Probably somebody gouged it out of his fuckin' head. Well, he had the balls to tell me I was going to give him five dollars a week and I was going to do his English homework for him! Just like that! Five bucks and his homework!"

"Did you tell him to fuck off?" Ricky asked.

"Hell no, man. Not to his face. I told him I'd think about it. Then that night he grabbed me as I was leaving the building and he wanted to know where his fuckin' money was. I said, 'What money?' He said, 'The five you promised to give me!' Well, the son of a bitch is a giant. I mean that mother is a *tall* Watusi! I couldn't spit in his face. It was too far away."

"What'd ya do?"

58

"I let him talk and I kept smilin' at him and then I let him have a fast one right in the balls. He yelled like he was killed, then grabbed his balls and doubled over. When his face came down to my level, I hit his black jaw with a sharp right and he went backward and over and flat on his ass."

Ricky was fascinated. "What happened to you? What did his buddies do?"

"I jumped into a Bruce Lee pose and gave a Kung Fu yell and I said to all those other black faces around me, 'Okay, which one of you suckers wants a free lesson?' "

"Then what? They all jump you?"

"They parted like Moses parting the Red Sea, man. They stepped back and I walked out of the building and got into my old lady's car."

"Looks like you got it made there."

"Yeah." He nodded his head. "I suppose so, but what the hell for? Why should I have to be on my guard all the time? I didn't ask to get sent to that damned place."

"You gonna stay?"

"I promised my folks."

But just after Christmas he told them he was going to quit school entirely.

"You said you'd give this place a try," his father said.

"That dump is for the incorrigibles. For the impossibles," he shouted. "For Blacks! And I ain't none of the above."

"I want you to stay on," said his mother. "Everybody needs a high school diploma. You can't get a decent job without one."

"I don't need no piece of paper to make it on my own," he said flatly. "I got brains and I got some ideas. I'll make it."

"Life is tough enough out there even if you are prepared," his father added.

"I'm prepared," he said. "I can make it. They can shove their school."

"What will you do?" his father asked.

"Don't worry, I'll do something. I won't starve."

"We *do* worry," his mother said. "We worry a great deal about you."

"I've got plans," he said, and he saw the image of a friend of his selling drugs in front of the Midway. "I know what I can do."

"Whatever it is, you still need our permission," said his father. "We are still your parents, you know."

"You may be my parents—my adopted parents —but I don't need you to *permit* me to do nothin'. I am sixteen years old. I am of legal age to drop out of school on my own if I choose, and goddamn it, I *choose.*" He started for the front door.

"I don't know why you're so ungrateful," his mother said, her voice choking. "We've tried to do everything for you."

He wheeled around. "Jesus Christ, Mom! Who said anything about being ungrateful? You took me in. You gave me a home. You lived up to all your promises to take care of me as a kid. Well, I ain't a kid any longer. I'm sixteen years old and I'm a *man.* You took care of the kid, now let me take care of the *man.*"

"They let you quit?" Ricky couldn't believe it. "Just like that?"

"Had nothing to do with 'let,' man. I'm sixteen. I told them and they bought it. Wasn't no 'let' involved."

"What did the school say when you left?"

"Who gives a fuck? My mother called them and told them. I didn't ask her what she said or what they replied. Who needs them anyhow?"

"Yeah. You didn't learn nothin' over there."

"Fuckin' place was filled with potential thieves and killers. I had to have my guard up all the time. Pot, speed, and acid everywhere."

"Yeah?" Ricky grinned.

"Yeah." Jimmy grinned back. "About the only *good* thing I can think to say about that place." He grinned again.

"Wish I was sixteen," Ricky said sadly.

"You will be. In March."

"Then I'll quit too. Just like you did."

"Then it'll be me and you," Jimmy said.

"Not quite." Ricky was grinning again.

"What d'ya mean, 'not quite'?"

"It'll be me, you, and Satan. He's my number-one man. Can't do nothin' without *him*."

CHAPTER FOUR

Whether it was drugs or the fact that Jimmy wasn't going to school anymore or his study of Satanism, Ricky became impossible to keep in junior high the second half of the school year. Now he *never* had his homework. Now he skipped classes more often than he attended them. Now he sat with virtually every group who made a circle near the football field or congregated at the loading dock. He was smoking marijuana. He was taking regular doses of LSD. He always had enough for himself and enough to hand out to other kids.

"You gotta trust in Satan!" he'd tell his smoking buddies. "He's the only one that can free you from all this crap the teachers lay on you."

"Oh come on, Ricky. You're full of shit."

"Satan is the only way, man. I'm tellin' you."

"Satan is an asshole!"

"What? What the fuck did you say?"

"I said Satan is an asshole."

"You take that back! Take it back right now or—"

"Or what? And you're another one. You're another asshole!"

"Fight!" the girls screamed and clapped their hands. "Fight! Fight!"

Or:

"My checkbook was in the top drawer of my desk, Ricky. I saw you come out of my classroom. I looked in the drawer. The checks are gone."

"So?"

"So where are they? I know you took them. I know you did, Ricky."

"Prove it."

"You can't cash them. I'll call the bank and have them stopped."

"Go ahead."

"I don't make so much money as a teacher that I can afford to let you rip me off."

"You got no proof."

"I'll tell your parents. I know your father."

"So do I."

"I want that checkbook!"

"You got no proof."

"I'll call the police."

"It's in the boys' toilet. Inside the paper-towel dispenser."

When Ricky's parents decided he was going to Camelot School—when North-East Northport

63

school system designated Ricky an "emotionally handicapped," "anti-social" student—the fight started and finished with Ricky running away. He was gone for seventeen days and the school refused to consider him after that.

Ricky stayed with a friend named Eddie. Eddie's parents were Italian and they were shocked when Ricky told them his folks had kicked him out of his own house. Eddie's mother fussed over Ricky, cooking him platters of spaghetti and lasagna, making sure the guest room had clean sheets and there were fresh towels laid out every day for "this poor little boy who had been abandoned by his family." Ricky talked about going to California and they said they had some people out there who would take him in for a while, until he got a job and enrolled in a good high school. Ricky tearfully explained that he really wanted to get his high school diploma. He needed it. Life was tough enough even with a diploma. The family nodded their heads and passed him more fried chicken. They thought it was terrible what the Kassos were doing! Denying their son a home. Denying him an education.

"If my folks had known Ricky had left on his own and that he was starting to sell acid and dope for pocket money, they would have had a fit," Eddie says now. "If my old man had known Ricky was taking LSD in the guest bedroom, he would have thrown him out immediately. But he didn't know. He never suspected Ricky of doing anything wrong. Only when he saw Ricky's picture in the newspaper because of the murder did he suspect anything. Then he couldn't believe it. Neither could my mom. Ricky had them both conned. He could do that. Ricky could have conned the whole world if he had had the time."

When spring of 1982 came to the Long Island Sound, Jimmy Troiano was a bona fide street person. His parents finally were forced to throw him out. He was disrupting their lives. He would come home high on drugs, he would fall asleep with a lit cigarette, he had weird people knocking on the front door wanting LSD, mescaline, and marijuana. Neighbors had complained, the cops had visited more than once. Vincent and Mary Troiano both worked, they couldn't be there all the time, they worried about what would happen to their house and their hard-won possessions. They loved their adopted son—their only child—but they couldn't manage him, couldn't outguess him, couldn't trust him.

Jimmy always had money in his pocket, his parents noted. Not just change and a few singles, but twenties and folded fifties. All the time. Once they joked that he made more than both of them did from their combined jobs. He just grinned that toothy grin and patted his back pocket.

They believed throwing a kid out of his own home was wrong, but so was selling dope to minors. Tensing every time the phone rang, every time there was a knock on the door, flinching each time they heard a police siren, was gnawing at their nerves. When the weather got warmer and Jimmy stayed away several nights in a row, they told him it was time to leave. Vincent Troiano was the one to put it into words, while Mary sat pale and dry-eyed on the living-room sofa.

The sixteen-year-old boy wasn't upset. He stood with his hands in his pockets, his eyes firmly on his father's face. "I don't blame you," he said. "I understand. It ain't easy havin' me around. I'd probably do the same thing if I had a kid like me."

"It doesn't mean," said his mother, "that we don't love you. You can come back for visits."

"Sure," he said. "I will. Christmas is in December this year."

CHAPTER FIVE

"Okay, here's what we are gonna do. I'm gonna draw a pentagram on the floor here—"

"A what?" a boy asked.

"A pentagram," Ricky said again. "That's a five-pointed star. Looks like the star but it's not the same thing."

He had rolled up the rug on the floor of Billy Evans's recreation room. It was in the basement and had been remodeled a few years previously, with paneled walls, an acoustical tile ceiling, and a smooth cement floor. It had a sofa, a bar, television and stereo, the middle-class works. The Evanses encouraged their kids to use it, urged them to bring their friends there. They were at a dinner party that night. The friends their son brought in were dopers. Ricky "the Acid King" Kasso was going to hold a séance.

He had been reading up about séances all winter and was anxious to try one. It wasn't going to be the kind held by little old ladies, or turbaned mediums, or Spiritualist churches. This was going to be black magic—Ricky was going to summon his old friend Satan. There were five slightly high kids, all in their mid-teens, in the room. They had been smoking and washing the taste down with bottles from old man Evans's well-stocked bar. Name it and it was there: gin, whiskey, vodka, scotch, whatever. The room was filled with the vibrations of a loud tape called "Metal Massacre." The picture on the cassette was that of skulls floating in white smoke over an ocean shoreline. There probably had been that much smoke over Northport's shoreline that night too.

Ricky was on his hands and knees, drawing in red chalk. Even though he was high, he moved carefully so as not to muss the lines of the star. When he completed it he was standing in its center. His rightful place. "Each of you get one of those black candles over there. In that paper bag." Dutifully, the candles were distributed. "Give me the extra one," Ricky ordered. "Okay, now each of you come and sit in one section of the star. Be careful not to fuck up the lines. Billy, turn the lights down real low. This is your house. You know where the control is." While the others, carefully holding their unlit candles, chose a star point, the lights dimmed. "I want boy girl, boy girl here," Ricky said. Two kids got up and switched star points with each other. "Now everybody sit down. Okay. Now I'm going to sit in the center here." He sat down. "Now reach out and put your candle inside the circle. Just in front of you. They'll stand up. That's what those flat holders on 'em are for."

"You sure this is gonna work?" one of the girls giggled.

"Sure," he replied confidently. "If we do it right."

"I don't understand what we're trying to *do*," a boy complained.

"Pay attention, asshole. You will." Both girls giggled. "Okay, now I'm gonna light those candles." Ricky took a disposable cigarette lighter from the pocket of his denim jacket and lit the black candle in front of him. The wick took the fire immediately. "Good sign," he murmured. He picked up his candle and lit the wicks of the other five candles inside the circle. When they were flaming to his satisfaction he put his candle back down on the floor, inside the circle. "Now don't anybody say anything," he ordered. "Just sit there and give the circle energy."

"We don't have to hold hands or chant or anything?" one of the girls asked.

"Just sit," he said. "Don't do anything."

No one asked if the ear-pounding music was too loud.

Ricky closed his eyes, took a deep breath, and put the palms of his hands together, as if in prayer, under his chin. "O great Satan," he intoned. "O great, horned god. O leader of the darkness. Hear

69

me. Hear me as I call you. Hear my prayer to you. Hear me and be with us. Come to us and bless us. O great spirit of death and destruction, I ask for your presence here in this room. I ask for your presence among us. Here in this room."

"I didn't know you were going to call up the *devil!*" Barbara complained audibly.

"Shut the fuck up," Ricky said without opening his eyes. "This is serious." He took another deep breath. "We love you, Satan. We adore you, Satan. We are here to do your bidding. We are here to serve you. We love you, Satan. Give us a sign. Give us a sign, O great destroyer of the universe. Let us know you are here with us."

The other kids kept their eyes on Ricky's face. It seemed to glow more than the other faces did. They didn't know whether it was from the drugs, from the candles, or from Satan himself. In fact, the whole room looked like it was glowing . . . but it could be from the good weed and the fine booze as well as from what Ricky was trying to pull off.

"Please, Satan, give us a sign. Make yourself known to us. We love you. We really love you. All of us love you." He opened his eyes and looked at the others. "Don't you love Satan?"

None of them said anything.

"Sure you do! Say it. Go on, say you love Satan."

One boy mumbled something, but the others remained silent. They hadn't expected to play this game. It had all been Ricky's idea.

"Say it!" he ordered. "Say you love Satan!"

"I love Satan," one of the girls said in a soft voice.

"You others. Come on!" Ricky said louder. "You all have to say it. If not, Satan won't show up. Come on now, don't fuck this thing up. Say you love Satan!"

They looked at each other over the candle glow. A couple of them smiled, a couple of them shrugged. Sure, if that's what Kasso wanted. Why not? "I love Satan," they said. Then repeated it louder: "I love Satan."

"Great." Ricky closed his eyes and smiled. "You hear that, O great demon? You hear that? We all love you. We all really do. We all really want to see you. Please make an appearance. Please make yourself known to us. Give us a sign. Anything," he pleaded, "let us know you are here."

The candle in front of Barbara fell over, its flame pointing straight at her. The girl screamed and jumped up, almost colliding with the boy next to her and smudging the chalk marks on the floor. "The hell with this!" she yelled. "I'm getting the fuck out of here!" She fumbled her way across the darkened room, managed to find the steps leading upstairs, and they could hear her over them as she ran across the living room and out into the hot summer night.

"Shit!" said Billy. "Just when it was gettin' interesting."

"Hey, Rick," another boy said, "can we do this without her?"

But Ricky still had his eyes closed, still sitting with his hands under his chin.

"Rick?" the boy said. "Are we going to go ahead with this?"

"He ain't breathin'," the remaining girl whispered. "Rick, you okay?"

Billy got up and went over to Ricky. He touched him on the shoulder, but Ricky didn't move. "I think he's passed out," Billy said.

"Sittin' up?" the other boy asked.

"He's stoned," the girl said.

"Probably," Billy replied. "I never saw him like this."

"I never saw *anybody* like this," one of them added.

"Do you guys think maybe it's something else?" the girl whispered.

"What? He's stoned. That's all."

"What if he ain't?" The girl was still whispering. "What if Satan really did show up? What if he's inside Ricky *now?*"

It was a few days later, inside the gazebo in Cow Harbor Park. This rustic wood structure, with its natural wood beams and roof, had been erected by the town of Huntington and then given to the Village of Northport. It sits very near the edge of the water, with a view across the bay. Its main purpose is to give shade and rest to senior citizens and to parents when they bring their children to the newly installed playground right beside it. The playground has a maze of boxes and platforms for the kids to crawl in, around, and under. There is also an area of rough unpainted wooden pillars, some round, some square, some angled, that sit in a bed of hauled-in sand. Northport's small children are supposed to enjoy this collection of lumber, which resembles an unfinished construction site. In actuality, small children rarely visit the place, and the senior citizens prefer the shade trees in the grassy park.

So the play area became the haunt of the teenage and older dopers. They all agreed, as they sat in the gazebo, leaned against one of the pilings or perched up on the wooden maze, that it was awfully nice of the village to build them a smoking area, something just for them. During the night it was ideal. There were no streetlights to shine on their illegal smoking parties. Ricky had just finished spray-painting the words "I Love Satan" on the main beam across the inside of the gazebo when Pat Touissant walked into the structure to join him. There were three other kids in there with Ricky, younger kids, and though it was just past midday, the younger kids were almost high on the cigarettes they had bought from him.

"Hi, Rick. How ya doin'?" The white-haired man in the dirty jeans and khaki jacket stepped carefully over to a wooden bench and sat down. The smell of gin was suddenly everywhere under the wooden roof. The man reached inside his shirt and brought out a fresh bottle. He put the cap between his teeth and twisted. Then he spat the red plastic cap as far over the gazebo railing as he could. He waved the bottle in a gallant gesture toward the kids, who were watching him, then he took a long drag from its neck. At least a glassful poured down his throat before he set the bottle securely on the bench beside him.

"Pat," Ricky asked, "are you drunk?"

"I hope so, man" was the reply. "If I'm not, then I'm gonna sue that fuckin' liquor store on Main Street."

The kids laughed.

"You get your check today?" Ricky was grinning.

"Yep. Right on time. Ronald Reagan sends it to me every month, just like he was my brother. Hell, man, better than a brother. My brother doesn't even know I'm alive." He laughed and picked up the bottle. "To Ronnie," he said, and took another long swig. He wiped his mouth, then pleased that he had an audience, put the bottle back to his mouth. "And to Nancy too! Long may she wave." The kids watched, fascinated, as he almost drained the bottle.

One of the kids, a thin blond boy, took a pull on his cigarette. "How come the government sends you money, man? You on some kind of pension?"

"Social Security," the man replied. "They want me to be social and mingle with the public. They want me to be secure so I don't have to worry about the rent. So I'm paid to be social and secure."

"He was in 'Nam," Ricky said. "He gets that bread because he was over in 'Nam."

"In 'Nam?" the blond boy questioned. "Vietnam? With that white hair? You sure it wasn't that war with Hitler? He's too old to have been in 'Nam."

74

Pat reached up and brought some of his long white hair around to where he could see it. It hung down past his shoulders. Sometimes he wore it pinned up, under a bandanna. Sometimes he pulled it back with a headband or a Navaho comb. On that day, it just hung down. It was check-cashing day and he didn't have time to fuss with his hair. "Don't let the color fool you," he said to the blond youth. "It didn't used to be white. When I first went to 'Nam it was black, real black. Then one day, after my outfit went through some real shit, it turned white. From one day to having black roots to the next day having white roots." He laughed and took another hit from the bottle. "Hell, don't let this hair fool you. I'm still a young man. I'm not an old fart. Not yet."

The slim blond boy got a little bolder. "You're not that young," he said. "Look at the wrinkles you got in your face."

"That comes from clean living," Ricky said, and laughed.

"Right," Pat agreed. "I've lived a real clean life. Ricky knows. Ricky understands where I've been and where I'm at. Me and Ricky, we understand the same things." He managed a drunken wink and Ricky gave a theatrical wink in return.

"Understands what?" the youth asked.

"Stuff like what Rick was paintin' when I came in. Stuff like that."

They all glanced at the words, dry now, that Ricky had sprayed: "I Love Satan."

"You into that too?" another youth questioned.

"You know what my nickname is? You know what they call me?"

"What?" said the boy.

"Pat *Pagan.*" And he laughed, showing nicotine-stained teeth. "Pagan's my name, Satan's my game." He laughed again.

"Oh, that's bullshit," the blond boy said, and spat on the ground.

"You wanna see? Look at this." Pat opened a couple of buttons on his soiled plaid shirt and brought out a medallion on a leather cord. "Here. See this?"

"Is it a saint's medal?" the blond boy asked.

Both Ricky and Pat burst out laughing. "Go on," Ricky said, "look at it. It's a medal from my main man. Me and old Pat here, we got the same protector. We got the same vibes."

The boys came closer, trying to avoid the gin-laden breath of the Vietnam veteran. What they saw was a brass medallion, about two inches across, engraved with a five-pointed star with some strange symbols around the edge. "It's a penta-gram," said Pat. "I got it in 'Nam. We had a coven over there, some of my buddies and me. We all wore one of these. Had them made by a 'Nam art-ist who was also into Satan. This is the last one left," he said proudly, pleased that their eyes were wide and interested in his story. "Last one left. There were thirteen from my outfit in the coven. Everyone else got wasted. I am the only one left."

"Why you?" asked the blond boy.

"Don't know." He shook his head and put the medallion back inside his shirt. "I've wondered

76

about that. Probably was spared because I still have work to do." His voice started to slur. "When I was in 'Nam, it wasn't my time."

"You and me," said Ricky, "we got unfinished business. We got things to do together."

"Right." He nodded his head, closed his eyes, and then jerked himself back awake. "Old Rick is one of the few people in this town who knows where I'm at. Old Rick and I, we have long sessions. We *do* things together."

"What kind of things?" the blond boy asked.

"Things with our main man," Pat said thickly. "Things we can't tell about."

The blond boy looked at the almost unconscious drunk and then over at Ricky. "What kind of things, man? Rick, what the fuck is he talkin' about?"

Pat opened his eyes and his lids fluttered quickly. "Things that little kids like you can't know. Not yet." He tried to raise his head, tried to fight off the effects of at least two full quarts of gin since the bank had opened that morning. "Gotta get older," he said huskily, "gotta get wiser too. Secret's in being wise. Like Rick." He gestured feebly in Ricky's direction. "Rick's my man. He understands. He . . ." But the rest of the words were lost as his chin rested heavily on his chest.

"He's out," said the blond youth. "Fucker's drunk as a skunk."

"Yeah," laughed Ricky. "Once a month when his government check comes, he gets bombed out of his skull. Here, let me show you guys somethin'." Ricky went over to the sleeping man and lifted up one edge of his jacket. He reached his hand into the man's front pocket and took out a wad of money. "Look. Here's the rest of his cash." He peeled off a twenty-dollar bill and extended it to the blond boy. "Take it," he said. "He won't miss it."

The boy pulled back. "Come on, Rick! I don't want that old guy's money."

"Go on," Ricky insisted. "Here you guys, take some." He unrolled two more bills from the wad and held them out to the two other boys. "Don't be saps, it's real money. Take it."

One boy looked at the other, then shrugged and silently took the offered bill and shoved it in his pocket. Then the other youth did the same.

"Here," Ricky said to the blond boy, "you wouldn't take twenty. So take forty." He added another bill and extended it to the boy.

"Well"—he hesitated—"I don't think it's right, but . . ." His small hand closed over the green paper. "I can use it," he apologized.

"We all can," Ricky said, and with that he put the entire wad of Pat's pension check into his own pocket.

"Rick!" the blond boy exclaimed. "You can't do that!"

"Why not?"

"What's he gonna do? He *needs* that money."

"Fuck him. If I don't roll him, somebody else will."

"But he's gonna know it's you that took it. He's gonna come looking for you. And us too," the boy added. "He's gonna know we were the ones that took it!"

"He's not gonna know shit," Ricky said. "When he sobers up he won't even remember talking to us. I know this guy. His mind is shot. His brain is full of holes."

"But he said the two of you are friends." The blond boy could feel the two bills burning in his jeans pocket. "You don't steal from your friends."

Ricky came over to the boy and grabbed him by the lapels of his denim jacket. "You've got a lot to learn," he said in a low voice. "Gary Lauwers, you've got a helluva lot to learn."

CHAPTER SIX

"Freeze!" the police officer shouted.

Jimmy turned to run, to get out of the house before the cops came in the front door. To get into the house, he had broken a back window. Maybe he could reach it in time.

"Freeze!" shouted another cop through the shattered back window. "Stay right where you are! Don't move even a finger or I'll blow your head off."

Jimmy twisted, ready to go upstairs or down cellar or anywhere.

"Didn't you hear me, punk?" The officer's voice came from the outside darkness. "I said don't move!"

"Shit!" said Jimmy, and he let the portable television he was carrying fall to the floor. "Shit, shit, shit!"

It was all over before he was really aware it was happening. He had been high on LSD, had decided he wanted to watch television, and knew he needed to have a set to do that. So, with his head a mile up past his shoes, he broke into the unlit residence and grabbed a set. In his haze, the sound of the breaking back window wasn't any worse than someone turning on a faucet—a gush and then the tinkling. He couldn't see the glass shards as they fell, but he imagined them tumbling over and over into the air, falling to the deck of the sun porch and being absorbed, like rain drops.

The neighbor next door was not high. She knew what breaking glass meant in an empty house. She called the police, they came quickly, and Jimmy Troiano was taken away in handcuffs.

His parents hadn't seen him in weeks. The only reason they knew he was in Northport was because one of their friends had seen Jimmy down along the harbor a couple of times.

Jimmy grinned at them when he was brought before the judge. It was his large toothy grin, the one with the dog fangs at each corner of his mouth. The wide grin stretched his scar, giving his face a lopsided look. He waved at them but didn't go to them. He had told the police he was "of age" and didn't need his folks' permission for anything, yet he was glad when he saw them in the hearing room. He didn't actually *see* them. It was more their outlines, their impressions. He was still high from last night.

The judge had spent a few minutes alone with the Troianos. He'd heard them tell of Jimmy's drug problem, his dropping out of school, his leaving home. They tried to convince the judge that their son needed medical help, not a jail sentence. Putting him in a jail cell would not do him any good. They told the judge that, now that summer was coming, Jimmy would be spending it with disreputable influences like Ricky Kasso. If His Honor would take him off Northport's streets for the summer, put him in a health-care unit for those crucial months, it would indeed be a blessing. The judge saw they were concerned, that they still loved their son, even though they could no longer do anything to help him.

The judge gave Jimmy a lecture on disobedience and the civil rights of others while the boy stood with his hands in his pockets, trying to focus on what the man up there on the platform behind the desk was saying.

"I will give you another chance, young man. I won't put you behind bars. What I will do is parole you into the custody of the South Oak Hospital in Amityville. You are to undergo their drug detoxification program and their behavior modification program. You are to spend a maximum time of eight months there. That should be plenty of time to clear your body and your mind."

As Jimmy was led away he could hear his parents saying thank-you to the judge.

The first two weeks they kept Jimmy in a room by himself. They watched him come down off his high, sat with him while his body ached for another hit, smiled with him when he spent an afternoon calmly reading or looking out the window. Then they opened his door and let him wander through the halls.

"At first, it was weird," he recalls, "seeing all those people together in the television room or the sun room or the dining room. Some of them talked to me and some of them didn't talk to anyone. A lot of them talked to themselves. Most of the patients were kids my age, a little older or a little younger, but mostly my age. They hadn't all gotten into trouble with the law, like I had. Some of them had been put in there by their families. A couple of them even put themselves in there. Volunteered to go in and get help beating the habit. Most of them were dopers. A lot of them were Black. Oh, yeah, and all of them were men. All I saw for the first few months were other guys."

There was breakfast, something healthy with cereal and fresh fruit, more than any of them ever ate on the outside. Then came the distribution of morning medication for those who required it. Then there was room detail: making their own beds, sweeping in front of their doors, getting laundry done. Then there would be a group session, from three to a dozen mostly school-age youths talking about addiction and the problems that came from them. Then would come a light lunch, followed by a rest period. Sometimes there would be another group session in the afternoon, but more often it would be an educational class: history, English, current events, whatever. It was as close to high school as they could get. There was a recreational room with card tables, Ping-Pong tables, and lots of reading material. Patients could use it when they weren't expected at a counseling session. Dinner was always meat, a green vegetable, a yellow vegetable, rice or potatoes, bread, butter, milk, and a dessert. After that the nighttime medications were handed out and there was TV or card games until lights out.

Once a week Jimmy had a one-on-one session with a counselor.

"I got into the routine," Jimmy says, "and it wasn't so bad. I missed Ricky and the guys on the streets at Northport and I *told* myself I didn't miss the dope. I missed it like hell at first, in spite of their pills and all their bull sessions, but after a while I realized that I felt better. I had more energy, I slept better, and I seemed to think better. I had a place to sleep every night. I didn't have to worry about food. Being in that place wasn't so bad. After a while I couldn't think about it being 'punishment.' They weren't trying to 'punish' me, they were trying to *help* me. It had been a helluva long time since anybody, including my folks, had tried to *help* me."

After five months, and much medical and psychiatric testing, they moved Jimmy to another wing. This one was more open, with more recreational facilities and with less obvious supervision. There was another plus: girls mingled with the boys in the reading and television rooms.

At Christmastime each of those rooms had a decorated tree. The patients helped hang wreaths on

84

windows and ropes of tinsel around the walls. Jimmy's parents had come to see him often during the previous months, and when they arrived with wrapped gifts and cards they reminded him, "When you left home we said you could come for visits, but *we* are the ones doing the visiting." His mother laughed. "Remember 'Christmas is in December this year'?"

That Christmas was memorable for another reason. Lucia came into Jimmy's life.

He was in the rec room, reading a magazine about deep-sea fishing. He sensed someone sitting in the chair next to his but he didn't glance up. Then he stopped reading. In the air, near him, around him, was the scent of floral perfume. He sniffed several times, then turned to her.

"It's lilacs," she said with a smile, "my favorite."

Jimmy stammered, then blushed that he had stammered. "Smells good," he said. He laughed. "At least it's different from what I *have* been smelling in here!"

The dark-haired girl lifted the sleeve of her arm and breathed in the scent that was on her buttoned wrist. "It was a Christmas present. My sister brought it to me. She knows how I love it."

"Where you from?" he asked her. "I'm from Northport."

"Oh, I have a real good friend who lives in Northport. Sharon Annunzio. You know her?"

Jimmy beamed, delighted he had someone in common with this pretty girl. "Sure, I know Sharon. Doesn't she go with Ralph Bedelia?"

"Yeah," Lucia replied. "That's right."

Jimmy shook his head. "Ralph's a real jerk. No offense, but he's kind of a wimp."

She laughed. "Oh, no offense. I agree. I don't know what Sharon sees in him"—she paused—"unless it's his daddy's money." She laughed again.

"That'll do it," Jimmy said with a grin. "The rich guys always get the pretty ones."

"I know. I'm waiting for a rich guy myself."

"Oh?" Jimmy felt something deflate inside his chest. "That leaves me out then. My old man doesn't have any bread."

"What does he do?"

"He works for a publishing house in New York. He's an artist."

"Artists don't make a lot of money." She shook her head.

"My mom's a registered nurse," he said with a little more animation. "Nurses make pretty good."

"What do *you* do?" She gazed at him, her brown eyes locking with his vivid blue ones. "Do you go to school or what?"

"Or what," he replied, and that full feeling started building again in his chest. "I dropped out last year. I went to Northport High."

She scowled. "Sharon tells me that place is a bummer."

"She's right. It's the pits. That's why I left. I couldn't put up with their shit."

"What were you on?" She asked it as naturally as a teenager asking a friend what dress she wore to a party.

"Acid. Mesc. Weed."

"Booze?"

He shook his head. "Not really. It messes my stomach up too much."

"Who do you like?" Another no-frills cryptic question.

"Ozzy Osbourne. Def Leppard. Motley Crue. Pink Floyd's my favorite."

"Really? You like the Floyd?"

He grinned, amazed that they had something else in common. "You like 'Money'?" She nodded. "Fantastic!" He started to beat time on the arm of his chair with the fishing magazine. He closed his eyes, shook his head a couple of times, and started to sing the song softly.

As he finished the first verse Lucia joined in, her voice rising slightly above his. When they hit the final line there was a quiet, almost embarrassed moment as the two smiled at each other.

"That really is a great song." He grinned and wondered at the pleasure that was washing over him.

"It's real fine," she agreed.

So are you, he wanted to say, but he didn't. "Why you in here?"

"Booze and Mary Jane," she replied simply.

"Couldn't handle 'em?"

"Didn't want to."

"Didn't want to?" He looked at her. "What's that mean?"

"I just didn't give a fuck about things. You know how that is?" Jimmy nodded. "So I drank too much and smoked too much and when my old man or my teachers started bitchin' about my life, I told 'em I didn't want to handle their shit either. But they never shut up about it. You know what I mean?" He nodded again. "So about two months ago I had all the shit I could take and I tried the big S."

Jimmy scowled. He had just met her, he didn't want her to be damaged in any way. "How?"

She unbuttoned the cuff of her blouse that circled her right wrist. There was a bandage under it. "I dug deep enough on this one but not enough on the left one. I should have bled faster. My mother found me. It was her idea, and my shrink's, to put me in here."

He put out one of his hands, lightly touching the white bandage as if his touch would heal her. "Did it hurt?"

She shook her head. "I was high. I didn't feel anything. I remember taking the knife and doing it and being amazed that there were stars and comets and things coming out of my wrist with the blood. I mean they were just riding in it, like what you see fireworks in the sky do on the Fourth of July."

"I'm sorry," he said.

"What about?" she laughed. "It wasn't your fault. It was mine. I won't do it again. I know better."

He sighed. "I wish I had money."

"For what," she said. "What do you need money for?"

"You said you were waiting for a rich guy. I'm not rich."

"Don't be silly." She smiled at him. "I don't need a rich man in here. Only things I need money for in here are the cigarette and the Coke machines. I don't need a rich guy in here. I'll settle for a poor one. If he's a friend." She flashed him one of her dazzling smiles and he felt high again, high without drugs.

"How old are you?" he asked.

"Real old," she said. "I'll be seventeen my next birthday."

"Me, too. That's another thing we got in common. We're both gettin' real old. I still have lots to do."

"Me, too. We'd better hurry up and do them," she said. "Not got much time."

"That's why we have to do them *fast!*"

"That's the only way, Jimmy. Do them fast, then get out even faster."

CHAPTER SEVEN

For the first two months of 1983, Jimmy Troiano continued to walk on air. He was in love. No doubt about it. He had all the symptoms. This wasn't just a crush: He'd been through those before and he knew what they felt like. No, this was love. It was like in the movies and like on TV. He went to bed at night thinking of Lucia, and when he awoke in the morning he was still thinking of Lucia. It was the best thing that ever happened to him, of that he was sure. He didn't have any brothers and sisters. His parents were distant. His friends were all scumbags or dirtbags. He didn't even have a dog. There was nobody in the world to love and nobody who loved him. Suddenly, thanks to a nosy neighbor, a cop, a judge, and a hospital, he had been given someone. He had been given Lucia.

They spent as much time as they could together. The staff encouraged it. In their weekly meetings the nurses agreed it was the best therapy for both these young people. Jimmy, who had been morose and aloof when he arrived, now was outgoing and active. He was joining in group games and discussions willingly. He didn't look for a fight. He didn't try to scare younger kids, to frighten them away from his own territorial boundaries.

Lucia was smiling more. After she had arrived, she didn't take care of herself, didn't comb her hair, didn't want to fraternize. Now she had her parents send her nicest blue jeans and tops, her favorite sweaters and her makeup kit. She had a good voice and it could often be heard in group sing-alongs and in discussions on all kinds of subjects. She and Jimmy walked the corridors, hand in hand, and the staff smiled, all agreeing that the dark-haired teenage couple was "sweet."

Jimmy began to make plans. "When I get out," he told Lucia, "I'll get a job. I don't know at what just yet, but there has to be lots of things I can do in Northport to make money."

"You won't go back on dope? You promised me."

"I won't. I promise. I can make lots of bread with it but"—he shook his head—"it's not for me. That's not the way I want it to be. For us. I'll get a job. I've got lots of contacts, they'll help me."

"You'll move back in with your folks?" she asked.

"Sure. Why not? They want me back now. They

told me. I can stay there for free while I get started in the job. Once they see that I'm clean, they'll help me." He smiled at her and passed his finger-tips lightly over her cheek. "And when they meet you, you'll win 'em over." He laughed. "You know who's gonna blow his mind?" He didn't wait for an answer. "My best buddy, Rick Kasso. He's gonna shit when he hears I'm gonna settle down. When he meets you he'll try and con you. I'm warning you in advance. Be careful. He's a real smart fella, but once you get to know him, you'll like him."

"Is he the one they call 'the Acid King'?"

"You know him?"

"Who doesn't know about *him?* You want some? Ricky will get it for you. That's what they say. I've heard lots of kids from Northport say that."

"He was dealin' a little when I came in here," Jimmy said, "but I didn't know he was gettin' famous, for Christ sake."

"I might have even met him once," she said after a moment's reflection. "I went down by the harbor with some friends a couple weeks before I tried to kill myself and there was this supplier who was tall and thin and had long curly hair. That must have been him. About our age."

"His eyes. Did you notice his eyes?"

"Shit yes. They were strange, man. I mean weird! You saw them first, like they were made out of shiny glass and stuck in a mask or something. They looked right through you. They looked out of place, like they belonged to somebody else. The kids I was with said this guy was into devil wor-

92

ship, that he did things to call up Satan. I mean this guy was far out!"

Jimmy grinned. "You met him. You met Ricky. He's my best friend."

"And you want him to be our best man?" Lucia was shocked at the idea. "Come on, Jimmy!"

"We're not going to get married right away," he reminded her. "Not till you're eighteen and don't need your folks' permission. By that time, Ricky will change. He'll have time to outgrow all this dope and devil shit. He'll straighten his ass out by then, you'll see."

She shook her head. "The way he's going, by that time his ass is liable to be dead."

By mid-April Jimmy had crossed all but ten days off his calendar. Just ten days remained for him in the hospital. He had mixed emotions about how fast his release date was approaching. He'd be out, he'd be free, and of course he was glad of that. There would be Northport and old friends and a new spring and summer coming around. But there was Lucia, he would leave Lucia. He was going away from the hospital and she was going to stay. It was her parents' idea. They had finally come to visit her (not just her sister but her Italian-born mother and father as well) and they had had an argument. Her father had started in on her, laying down rules and regulations as to how she was to act when she returned to *his* home. A litany of what she could not do, where she could not go, who she could not see. Lucia had started screaming at her father, unraveling emotional threads that had taken months to be correctly knitted. A nurse was called, a tranquilizer administered, and her father signed a paper to commit her for an extended period of time. When Lucia awoke and realized what her father had done, she tried to pry open the almost healed scars on her wrist with a nail file.

The nurses explained to Jimmy why he couldn't see her, why they had decided it best for her. It was difficult for the teenage boy to understand their reasoning. He was the one person in the world who loved Lucia, who could help her just by being beside her, yet he was forbidden to see her. "It's fuckin' injustice!" he yelled at a nurse. She agreed with him, but wasn't permitted to say so.

So in mid-April Jimmy sat in the rec room alone, trying to read a magazine, his feet up on the windowsill in front of him. There was no view from this window. Unless the wall and windows of another wing of the hospital could be called a view.

He flipped the pages of the magazine and glanced up occasionally at the sunlight that came through the wire-mesh glass. He read that way, a few paragraphs at a time, then looked away to chew and digest what he had just read. At one point he glanced up, closed his eyes, and then he opened them immediately.

"What the fuck . . . ?" he said aloud. He jumped up, got as close to the window as he could without crashing through the glass, and stared. Across from him, sitting with his back to the window, was a boy with a familiar head of hair. Jimmy stared, then squinted, sure but not sure it was who he thought it was. "Turn around," he said softly, "come on, turn around. Let me see your face." He stared at the boy's back, took in the thinness of the shoulders and the color of the hair. He put all his effort into a mental message, a command: "Turn around, buddy. Let me see your face."

As if the ESP had been transmitted and received, the boy turned his body slowly around and the face could now be seen.

"Ricky!" Jimmy shouted with delight. "Hey, Rick! Over here! Look at me! Look over here!" The window was closed, there was no way Ricky could hear him.

"Okay, Rick. You always said this stuff works. I'm gonna try it. I'm gonna try it, you fucker!" He looked again, making sure it was really Ricky sitting in that window across the way. Then he closed his eyes, took a deep breath, and said to himself, "I believe in Satan. I love Satan. I love you, Satan, and because I do, I want you to do this for me. Please, Satan, contact Ricky Kasso over there. Make him turn and see me. Make him *see* me!"

Jimmy opened his eyes. The boy had turned into the room, only his back was showing. "Shit!" Jimmy said aloud. "Fuckin' Satan!"

At that moment the boy turned around, raised his glance, and looked straight into Jimmy's eyes. There was no doubt about it. It was Ricky Kasso.

Ricky grinned and waved. Jimmy waved back, grinning just as broadly. Ricky made a motion for Jimmy to come over to his wing. Jimmy put up the palms of his hands and shrugged. Ricky made another come-on-over gesture. Jimmy nodded and grinned. Ricky put up his right hand, making an okay sign with his thumb and forefinger. Then Jimmy saw an attendant's hand grab Ricky's shoulder. He shook it off, made a face, waved good-bye at Jimmy, and left the window.

"Son of a bitch!" Jimmy whispered aloud. "What's he doin' in here?" Then he remembered: "Thank you, Satan! Thanks a lot."

All that afternoon Jimmy worried the nurses and counselors with his request to talk with Ricky. It was impossible, they told him, Ricky was in a special-care unit. Ricky was undergoing psychiatric examinations. It was suspected that Ricky had a severe suicidal tendency. He had to be watched at all times. No, there was no way he could be permitted visitors.

"But I'm an old friend," Jimmy insisted. "I *understand* him. Maybe I can help him."

They informed him the *doctors* were the only ones who could help Ricky. Thanks but no thanks to his request.

Two days later a nurse came for Jimmy. "Let's go see your friend," she said.

Jimmy looked at her. "Why'd they change their minds?"

"Your friend tried to hang himself last night. He says he'll do it again if we don't let you guys get together."

Jimmy grinned. "He's crazy!"

The nurse looked at him. "We know," she said.

They had Ricky in a small room, with just a single bed and mattress. There wasn't a chair or a toilet. Jimmy had heard of these rooms. They were maximum-security rooms where everything dangerous was eliminated. There was a one-way window in the door. The staff could look in, the patient couldn't see them doing it.

The teenage boys stood staring at each other for a moment, unsure what to do with their hands. Then Jimmy stepped closer, put his arms around Ricky's shoulders, and hugged him. "Good to see you, man," he whispered.

"You, too," Ricky said, "but shit, man, I almost had to kill myself to get you over here." He laughed, and Jimmy, when he pulled away, saw that the glitter in his eyes was even stronger.

They sat on the bed, feet folded under, facing each other. "So what the fuck are you doin' in here?" Jimmy asked. "Man, was I blown away to see your face in that window!"

"I knew you were in here," Ricky said. "Everybody heard about the cops bustin' you and you gettin' sent here. A real bummer, man."

"Oh, it ain't so bad," Jimmy said. "They treat you fair if you're fair with them."

"Can you get any dope here?"

"Sure," Jimmy said, "but I never tried. I got that shit out of my system, man. I'm clean. I'm gonna stay that way."

"Shit!" Ricky spat on the wall and watched it run down the painted bricks. "What you wanna stay clean for? Dope is where it's at, man. You know that."

"I *don't* know that," Jimmy replied. "I've been

97

off it for almost eight months now. I don't miss it. I did at first, I won't shit you, but I don't need it now. I'm clean."

"What ya gonna do when ya get back out, back on the street? Gonna wear a white shirt and fag shoes and only piss Coca-Cola?"

"I don't know what I'm gonna do yet," he said. He knew it was too soon to tell Ricky about Lucia. "I'll survive. Probably get a job."

"A job?" Ricky clutched his sides, pretending he was dying from laughter. "You? With a job? What the fuck do you know how to do?" Before Jimmy could answer he added, "What can you do that pays more bread than pushin' dope? You can make a hundred dollars a week at McDonald's. You can make a hundred dollars a *day* on the street."

"I know all that," Jimmy said. "Look, it's my life. Let me do with it what the fuck I want."

"You do that, and when I drive past in my black Mercedes I'll honk when I see you cookin' a Big Mac to go."

Jimmy decided to change the subject. "Look, I already asked you, what ya in here for? You get busted?"

"Can you believe it? My fuckin' parents put me in here!" He unfolded his long legs and strode angrily across the small room. "My own people! They went to some judge and put me in this fuckin' place. Slapped me in here! I didn't have no say at all."

"But ain't you sixteen?" Jimmy asked. "Ain't you legal now, where they can't tell you what to do? You remember I quit school when I was six-teen and my old man couldn't do a thing."

"Course I remember." Ricky paced from the door to the back wall, from the back wall to the door. "But those fuckers got my ass while I was still fifteen! I mean just one fuckin' week before my sixteenth birthday, man! They got me just seven days before I was legal. And that shithead judge knew it too. He didn't care. He didn't care if I was going to be sixteen in a week. Bastard!" Jimmy saw the glow in his eyes. "I'll get that fucker when I get out. I swear by Satan that I'll get that fucker!"

"But what'd ya do?" Jimmy questioned further. "You get high and beat up some kid? The cops catch you making a deal?"

"Nothin'," Ricky almost shouted. "That's what pisses me off! They went to a judge, they had pa-pers from a couple of asshole shrinks, and the judge ordered me here. They called me a manic depressive and they've been shootin' me full of some shit every day."

"How long ya in for?"

"Until they finish with their damned tests." He stopped pacing and grinned at Jimmy. "I'm gonna make damn sure they complete those tests in a hurry. I'm gonna be real good and cooperate with everything they ask. I'll tell 'em anything they want to hear. Will I stay off drugs? Oh, yes, sir. Will I go to church every Sunday? Oh, yes, sir. Will I be good and go to school every day? Oh, yes, sir. Will I stop playing with myself? Oh, yes, sir! I've been through this scientific shit before. Find out what they want and then give it to 'em. Beat 'em at their own game. They're all so *stupid!* They think having a degree on their fuckin' wall makes 'em smart. Shit! *I'm* the one that's smart, and I don't have no degree. I got my smarts by being on the street, man. That's where you get an education. On the fuckin' street. Not in some schoolroom. Havin' a diploma doesn't make you smart. Havin' it up *here*"—and he touched his forehead— "and having it down here"—he grabbed his crotch —"that's what makes you smart! If you've got it up here and down here, ain't no fucker with a degree that can touch you!"

CHAPTER EIGHT

Jimmy had to smile as he tied the brown apron with the gold arches logo around his waist. Just as Ricky had predicted, here he was at McDonald's and frying up Big Macs. Ricky must really be psychic.

It hadn't been too difficult getting this job. It was in nearby Huntington and his mother knew a lady who knew the manager and she explained that Jimmy wasn't into drugs anymore, that he had paid his dues to society. Now all he wanted was to straighten out his life, get into the mainstream, and become respectable. And he was talking about getting married. That fact alone convinced his parents, the friend, and the manager that Jimmy had reformed.

Jimmy believed it too.

He moved back into his parents' home after he had been released from the hospital. He had a clean bill of health but was expected to continue his counseling once a month. The Northport Police Department also let him know they would be keeping an eye on him. They hoped now that he was clean he would stay that way.

Jimmy promised he would.

Frying up Big Macs wasn't all that bad. There were kids his age working there. The place was air-conditioned. Several of his old school chums came in as customers (most of them couldn't believe that "Dracula" Troiano had gone legit) and he had pocket money again. It wasn't the hundreds of dollars he used to make pushing dope. In fact, it was only three dollars and seventy-five cents an hour. Not a helluva lot of bread, but his folks kept telling him it was "a start." And it was, he supposed. If this was the way the straight world did it, then it would have to be his world too. If he was going to make it as a husband and a provider, he would have to abide by "their" rules. In a way it was a new experience, a different challenge, another way of looking at life, and like everything new, it was interesting. At least that's what he kept telling himself.

One night in May, it was after 3:00 A.M., Jimmy was awakened by a scratching on his bedroom window. He sat up in bed and peered through the darkness. The noise came again. He got up and looked out the window. It was Ricky.

Jimmy opened the window. "What the hell are

you doin' here, man? I thought you were in South Oaks."

"I was," Ricky whispered hoarsely, "but I busted out. Somebody left a side door open and I used it."

"You escaped?" A still groggy Jimmy couldn't believe it.

"Escaped. That's the word. That place is a fuckin' prison, man."

"Well, how'd you get here? To Northport?"

"Hitched. Some guys in a pickup were headin' this way. They wouldn't take me for free, man. I paid with some dope."

"Where'd you get dope?"

"In the hospital, man, where else would I get it?" Ricky grinned. "It costs, but my folks send me money for cigarettes. It's just that I buy another *type* of cigarette."

Jimmy was awake now. "Come on in," he said. "Through the window. My folks are asleep, so be quiet."

"Can't stay, man. They must be looking for me. I've been gone several hours now. I need some cash, man, some folding stuff. You got any?"

"Uh . . ." Jimmy's mind raced. He had about two hundred dollars in the top drawer of his dresser, but he was saving it. It was going to be a down payment on an engagement ring. "Not very much, man. I don't make that kind of bread any-more."

"Not at fuckin' McDonald's, you don't," Ricky sneered. "How much can you let me have?"

"What do you need money for? Why don't you

just lay low? Maybe over at Billy's place. His folks are away for a couple weeks. In Europe."

"No." Ricky shook his head. The tight brown curls shimmered in the moonlight. "I gotta split. This place is death city. Cops find me here and it's back to South Oaks in a wagon and with cuffs on my sweet wrists." He shook his head again. "No, man, I'm going to California. That's where it's at. A guy can be happy in California."

"You don't know anybody in California." Jimmy was stalling for time, trying to figure out how much he wanted to give Ricky. "All your friends are here."

"Friends? I got no friends here, except maybe you and Billy and a couple others. Nobody came to see me in the hospital. Nobody even sent me a fuckin' get-well card. Nobody sends Ricky Kasso a Hallmark, man. That's why California looks so good. I've been thinkin', *any* place is better for me than Northport. This place sucks, man."

Jimmy sighed, the full weight of his seventeen years on his shoulders. "I know, man. I know where you're comin' from. Look, I don't have a lot of bread here, but I can give you a hundred bucks. Is that okay?"

"You mean *loan* me a hundred bucks. When I get out to California I'll pay you back. I'll send you back double that amount." Ricky came closer to the window, extending his open palm toward Jimmy. "I'll send you double, man. I promise."

"I believe you," Jimmy said, and handed his friend half of Lucia's ring money. "Sure you will. I believe you."

104

A night watchman at a Northport lumberyard saw the thin young man crawl between two piles of rough-cut planks. He waited for a few minutes, and when the intruder didn't come out he telephoned the police. They found Ricky, drugged into semiconsciousness. He still had three small purple dots of mescaline in his pocket. He had no money. True to his own psychic predictions, the officers returned him to the hospital in handcuffs.

Ricky escaped from the Amityville hospital four more times after that. Each time he was discovered and returned. He also tried to kill himself again. He took a sweatshirt into the shower stall and tied it over the shower rod. They cut him down in time.

He couldn't believe it. He was actually holding her, actually kissing her. She was actually there. With him.

Lucia had been released from the hospital the first week in June, and after a couple of days with her folks, she got some friends to drive her to Northport. She lived in Floral Park, in the borough of Queens. Floral Park is a busy area of single-family homes and high-rise apartments that sits on the line dividing Queens and Long Island. A ride from her place on the Long Island Freeway and then up on Walt Whitman Avenue and over to the shore in Northport took only three quarters of an hour. Yet to many of the working-class residents of Queens, northern Long Island is a lifestyle away.

Homes in Northport are two or three times as expensive as those in the borough of Queens. Borough parents believe the schools are better "over there" and borough kids believe there is more freedom "over there." Residents from the Bronx, Brooklyn, and Queens consider a trip to Long Island a holiday. Residents on Long Island never mention it if they have to go into one of the boroughs. Even New York City is looked down upon by the Islanders. The most they will say, if they must go into Manhattan, is that they went into "the city." Some residents of Long Island brag that they never go into "the city" at all, for anything. "Harry and I haven't been into the city for over twelve years" is the sort of thing one can overhear in a northern Long Island restaurant. "His business is on the Island, so there's no need for him to go there at all. I have no reason to go there. It's so crowded, don't you know."

Lucia now sat in a park on Long Island Sound, at the foot of the village's central—but terribly chic—Main Street, holding hands with a boy who actually lived there, a boy whose parents owned their home there, and he was talking about marrying her and the two of them living there. Permanently! Forever! She knew all of her friends would be jealous. That's why she told so many of them about Jimmy even before she came over to visit him.

"Do you want to have a boat?" Jimmy gestured broadly at the dozens of small yachts and fishing craft in front of them.

"Is one of them yours?" Her eyes widened.

"Not yet"—he shook his head—"but we could get one. I know a guy that has one for sale."

"Don't they cost a lot of money?"

"Sure, but I know I could buy one if I decided on it."

"That'd be real nice." She smiled. "It would sure piss some of my girlfriends."

"Anything you want." Jimmy waved expansively at the expensive boats bobbing on the blue waters. "You wanna go out in one?" She nodded. "Okay, next time you come out here, I'll get a friend to take you onto the Sound. He owns one of those big ones out there."

She squinted. "Which one?"

"Ah"—he paused, unsure which of the boats to give his imaginary friend ownership—"that one. With the two red flags."

"That *big* one? You know the guy that owns that big one?" She snuggled closer to him. "He'd take us out on it?"

"Sure. Anytime. All I have to do is ask. He's my buddy."

She kissed him lightly on the cheek. "It's so good to be with you, Jimmy," she said softly, "and so good to be out of that damned hospital." She gave his hand a squeeze. "When my old man came for me I didn't know if he would let me out of there or sign me up for more tests. He spent almost a half hour in the office talking to my counselor. I almost plotzed when they said to go get my suitcase."

"Your father sounds like a son of a bitch," Jimmy said.

"Oh, he's not so bad," she said. "He's just old. He doesn't understand me."

"How old is he?"

"He's gotta be almost forty-five. I mean he's *old*."

"I hate to have to deal with old people all the time," Jimmy sighed.

"They always think they know what's so fuckin' good for you," the girl said. "I mean all the fuckin' time. They never ask a kid what *he* wants or how *he* feels about something. They just *tell* a kid. I talked that over with my counselor and he said old people usually know best, because they been around longer and seen more, but, shit, my old man gets up in the morning, goes to work, comes home, watches television, and goes to bed. Six fuckin' days a week, man. I mean, what has *he* been around? I mean, what has *he* seen that I haven't seen? Shit, I mean, you know I've done lots of things and seen lots of things that my old man can't even imagine being real. Yet he is allowed to tell me what to do because he's lived longer!" She sighed. "It's a bummer, man, a real bummer being a kid today."

Jimmy was about to agree when two kids stopped in front of the bench where he and Lucia were sitting.

"How ya doin', Jimmy, my man?" The thin blond boy kept his hands in his pockets and shrugged his shoulders in greeting.

"Yeah, man," the other boy, taller and with auburn hair, said.

"How ya doin', guys?" Jimmy replied. "What's happening?"

"Nothin'," the blond said. "Just walkin' around." He smiled at Lucia. "Who's your lady, man?"

"This is Lucia." Jimmy blushed so slightly, none of them saw it. "She's from Floral Park. We met when I was at Amityville."

"Bill Evans," the auburn-haired youth said.

"Gary Lauwers," the blond replied.

"Guys." Lucia smiled and nodded.

Gary came a little closer to Jimmy and lowered his voice. "Hey, man, you got some weed on you? Just one?"

Jimmy shook his head. "I'm not into that shit anymore."

"Come on, man," Gary insisted. "I know you got one on you. Let me borrow it. I'll pay you back."

"He's not into that stuff anymore," Lucia said a little loudly.

Gary ignored her. "Come on, Jim. Sell me one. I'll pay you when I get some bread next week."

"I said I don't have any," Jimmy replied.

"It's not like I'm asking for your whole stash," Gary said, "we just need *one*. Billy and I don't have any cash on us right now and none of the regulars will give us credit. Come on, man."

"You didn't hear me?" Jimmy started to get up off the bench and the two boys backed off slightly. "I said I don't have anything on me. I'm clean. What the fuck's wrong with you? Can't you understand English?"

"Okay, man. Okay," Gary said, and put his arm

on Billy's shoulder, pulling him away. "If that's what you say. Play your game, whatever it is."

"It's no game," Lucia said quite loudly, "it's for real!"

"Uh-huh," Gary said dryly. "Pussy will do that every time."

"You little punk!" Jimmy jumped up, ready to fight and defend Lucia's honor, but both boys took off across the park, laughing and leaping into the air and making faces at the couple back at the bench. "Little scumbag," Jimmy said as he sat back down. "Never did like that little fart."

"Why do you let him hang around you?" she asked.

"I don't. Shit, he's no friend of mine. I barely know him. He and Ricky hang out together. He's Ricky's friend. That's how I know him."

"Ricky still at South Oaks?" she asked, glad that Gary and the other kid were out of sight.

"Yeah," Jimmy replied. "I guess so. I haven't seen him around. The word on the street is that he's gonna get out soon."

She looked at him for almost a half minute before she spoke. "And you, when he does get out, are you gonna hang around with him again?"

"He's my friend," Jimmy said quickly.

"He's bad news," Lucia said just as quickly.

"Maybe he's changed," Jimmy wished aloud.

"People don't change," she said, "not that much. Not as much as Ricky needs to change."

"I did," Jimmy said. "I changed in there. Even my folks say I ain't the same guy that went in there."

110

"Well, you had me," she said, and she squeezed his hand again. "You changed because you had me. Ricky don't have anybody. When he comes out it'll be the same old shit again. It'll be drugs and the street and the cops and back to the hospital. Or maybe this time, the jail."

"I hope not," he said, "but you're right, I have you and you have me and that's what's important. That's where it's at."

"Ricky's like lotsa kids. He don't have nobody. That's why he's gonna always be in trouble. You and me are real lucky. My counselor said two people together can do anything they want, but one person all alone don't have the ambition to do nothin'. I mean, we have it *together*, and as long as we have it together, nothin' bad can come to us."

"I know that," Jimmy agreed, "nothin' bad can come to us at all."

CHAPTER NINE

Gary Lauwers and Billy Evans sat in the gazebo, blowing the smoke from the shared marijuana cigarette into the night. The soft June air carried it out across the water that slapped against the stone retaining wall. Sitting in the dark, only the glow from the tip of the cigarette gave the two teenagers away. That and the scrambled, slamming, metal sounds of Judas Priest that filled the gazebo like smoke from a damp bonfire. Their lyrics were great, man, great to listen to when a kid was high. They told a story, man. They told a truth. A kid's really gotta listen to the lyrics, 'cause a kid's really gotta understand the truth. There's a lotta shit out there, but the lyrics of Judas Priest are the truth, man. And when you're sixteen, the truth is where it's at.

"Mmm." Gary's eyes were closed as he slowly let the sweet-smelling smoke drift up and out of his lungs. "This is okay stuff, man. Really fine."

"Primo," Billy agreed, and reached for the cigarette now that it was his turn to take a drag on it. "Must be Colombian," he said slowly. "It ain't that Mexican junk."

Gary shook his head, his eyes still closed as he subconsciously listened to the familiar rock music, absorbing it without mental effort or thought. "I had some of that Mexican shit last week. Thought my throat was gonna catch fire. Had to drink a quart of orange juice just to make it feel right again."

"Know what you mean," Billy said softly.

"This stuff here, this is super-fine." Gary was smiling into the darkness. "I like the stuff from Jamaica, too, man."

"Yeah."

"And the stuff from Venezuela. That's cherry stuff."

"Yeah."

"Know what I'm gonna do someday?"

"No, man."

"I'm gonna go down to Colombia and buy me a farm and I'm gonna plant acres and acres of this stuff and bring it back up here and sell it."

"You better be careful you don't get caught." Billy handed back the cigarette.

Gary took it. "Hell, man, I'm too smart for that. Anyway, if you slip a few thou to the Feds, they look the other way." He took some of the smoke into his body. "I won't live here, of course. I'll probably stay most of the time on my ranch down there."

"You said a farm, first," Billy reminded him.

"Well, it can be called a ranch or a farm. Why not? Anyway, I'll live down there most of the year and come up here only in the summers to see all you guys and I'll bring some of the stuff with me and give it to all of you. For free." He inhaled more smoke.

"That'd be great, man," Billy said.

"And then I'll get a huge car, maybe a Cadillac, I don't know yet, but it'll be huge and I'll have any chick in Northport that I want. I'll just drive that fucker down Main Street and all the chicks will shit to get in it with me."

"Sounds great, man."

"That ought to show that fucker Jimmy Troiano too!" Gary scowled, but Billy couldn't see it. He had closed his eyes as he leaned back against the rough wooden pilings of the gazebo. "He'll be sorry he didn't give us anything tonight. If my man Ricky was here, he would have told Troiano where to shove it." Billy didn't reply, he was listening to the great music. "My man Ricky's getting out soon. That's what I hear. Then there'll be weed enough for everyone. And when I have my ranch down there in Colombia, Ricky can come and stay there. For free. I'll even have girls there for him. All he wants. Jimmy won't be invited. And then I think I'll get me a penthouse in New York City. One of those places with a balcony that has a view of the whole town. I won't let Troiano in there either. Oh, yeah, I might let him visit, but

only once, and then to rub his fuckin' nose in it."
He paused and let himself be carried off momentarily by the music. "Maybe I'll get me a jet plane
too. Like those Texans fly all over the place. That
way when I want to go to my ranch, I won't have
to go only when some airline company says I have
to go. Know what I mean?"

Billy nodded, then glanced at his watch. It was
one of those novelty watches that glowed in the
dark. "Hey, man, you better bring that jet back
from South America. It's gonna be midnight
soon."

Gary opened his eyes and quickly stood up.
"Shit! I gotta get my ass home. My mother will kill
me if I come in late again!"

Jimmy smoothed back his straight dark hair one
more time before he rang the front-door bell. He
wasn't sure he wanted to be here, but Lucia had
insisted. Jimmy had to meet her folks if they were
going to continue to go steady. He had started to
argue with her but she said it was important. She
had made three trips to Northport and, her mother
pointed out, her young man had yet to make one.
They were a close Italian family, Lucia reminded
him, with strong ties to tradition, religion, and social structure. That plus the fact that Lucia was
still under observation because of her suicide attempts. Her parents wanted to make sure whoever
she was seeing would not unhinge her again.

Jimmy had expected to see the living room decorated with oil paintings of Roman landscapes, a
picture of the Pope, and lamps with crystal beads

hanging from them. He wasn't disappointed. Lucia's mother was a small woman. Jimmy had expected her to be bigger, like someone in a pizza commercial. Her father, Jimmy guessed, would be large, with a potbelly and a five o'clock shadow. He had been correct.

They sat Jimmy in a single chair by the television and the others, Lucia, mama, papa, one sister, and one brother sat on a sofa on the other side of the room staring at him. Jimmy wondered if they knew he was alive or just an extension of the TV set. Lucia fussed with glasses of iced tea and some crispy fried things with jam baked in them.

The conversation had been about the weather, traffic Jimmy had encountered on the Long Island Expressway, and whether the Yankees or the Mets had a chance this year.

"Lucia tells me your father is in publishing," the father said.

"He works for a book company in New York," Jimmy replied. "He's an artist."

"He paints pictures?" The man gestured to a painting on the wall that was mostly trees, mountains, and small fishing boats.

"Not like that," Jimmy said. "Book covers and advertising layouts and things they put in bookshops to catch a person's eye."

"Oh." The man was slightly disappointed. "Then he's not so much an *artist*. He's more like a drawer. He draws things."

Jimmy nodded. "I guess so. I haven't been to his office in a long time. I don't know what he's doing now."

"And your mother?" This from Lucia's mother. "She works?"

"She's a nurse. An RN. In a hospital in Huntington. She's in charge of her whole department," Jimmy added quickly, hoping to make up for the fact that his father didn't paint old masters for living rooms. "She is very good at what she does."

"Which one do you favor?" the mother asked. "Him or her?"

Jimmy glanced quickly at Lucia, unsure what she had told her parents. "Neither one," he said. "I was adopted."

There was a long silence in the room. Lucia's brother crunched another pastry.

"Do you know who your *real* people were?" the father asked.

Jimmy shook his head. "I think they were from somewhere around Saratoga. Upper New York State. My mother was French. That's about all I know. But they were married," he added quickly. "They had to give me up because they were poor, not that I was illegitimate." He glanced at Lucia again, hoping her folks would believe that last one. He had made it up at the spur of the moment. Like Ricky, he was starting to let people hear what they wanted to hear. "It must have been pretty sad for them," he said, and lowered his eyes.

"I'm sure," said the sister, who was short and dumpy and looked nothing like Lucia. "We have a cousin in the Bronx who had a baby and she—"

"Don't need to tell that story," her father said quickly. "He isn't interested."

The sister shrugged. "Sorry," she said.

"You and Lucia," the father continued, "you met when she was in the hospital? Right?" Jimmy nodded. "Okay. We know why she was in there, but what were *you* doing in there? Same thing?"

"You mean did I try to kill myself?"

The father shook his head. "No need to mention it," he said. "We promised Lucia we wouldn't talk about it—out loud."

"No," Jimmy said slowly, trying to decide what to tell these people. "I was in there for another reason."

They stared at him, like they stared at the television screen, waiting for further developments in the plot.

"I did a stupid thing," he finally said in a low voice. Still they stared, waiting for more dialogue. "I broke into a house."

"Like a burglar?" the sister asked, her voice rising with interest.

"Like a burglar," Jimmy confirmed. "They caught me."

"They put you in a hospital?" The brother was interested now.

"It was for examination," Jimmy mumbled, wishing he had never come for this visit in the first place.

"You were hurt?" asked the mother. "Wounded somehow?"

"No, Mom," Lucia spoke up. "It was for dope. They put him in the hospital because Jimmy was high on dope when he pulled the burglary."

"Dope?" The father's dark eyebrows raised. "You mean like marijuana?"

"Yeah," said Jimmy, "something like that."

"You take that stuff?" the mother asked.

"Mom," the brother said, "you don't *take* marijuana. You smoke it."

"Whatever." And she waved her hand aimlessly in the air. "You were high and you got caught. That's what you're saying?"

Jimmy nodded. How soon could he get out of there?

"This the first time?" the father asked.

"That I took dope? No. I used to take it all the time." He couldn't look at Lucia.

She spoke up for him. "But he doesn't use it anymore. He kicked the habit in the hospital. Didn't you, Jimmy? Tell them."

"Yeah," he said, not looking at any of them, "I did. I went through the programs in there. I learned my lesson. I'm clean."

"It costs money, doesn't it?" the father was speaking.

"What does?" Jimmy stared at the flowered pattern in the carpet.

"Marijuana. Dope. That stuff you take."

"Yeah, it does. It cost a lot of money."

"Where did you get the money to finance your habit?" the man wanted to know. "Ripping off houses?"

"I said I never did that kind of thing before." He tried to keep his voice from rising. He was still determined to make a good impression on these stupid people. "My folks gave me the money," he lied.

"Your folks gave you *all* that money?" the

brother said loudly. "Your old man's an artist. Doesn't make a dime. You expect us to believe that?"

Jimmy's blue eyes squinted at the pastry-munching jerk on the sofa but kept his cool. "He makes enough," he said. "I could buy the stuff I needed pretty cheap."

"How?" the brother kept up the attack. "Buy wholesale and sell retail?"

"Lenny!" Lucia said loudly. "That's not fair!"

"Figures," Lenny continued. "If he got it cheap, that means he was selling it later. Hell, I know how that works. I've seen it right here in Floral Park."

"That true?" said the father, his voice suddenly louder. "Did you sell dope? Are you a—what do you call it? A *pusher?*"

"Oh, God!" the mother said shrilly, and put both hands to her bosom as if to protect it from a sudden attack.

"What do you want me to say?" Jimmy asked them. "Lucia? What do you want me to say?"

"Try the truth," said Lenny.

Jimmy looked at Lucia. Her face was ashen, her hands were trembling. "I blew it with you people, didn't I?" he said, and his gaze went from face to face across the room. "I should have told you I was studying to be a priest and that I was in that hospital to spread the Gospel. You would have liked that. I am what I am and I've done what I've done."

"He's just trying to be honest." Lucia was almost in tears. "You would have found out later, anyway."

"Later would have been too late. Good thing we found out now," said her brother.

"Oh, Lenny," Lucia yelled, "shut the fuck up!"

"Lucia!" Her mother pretended to be shocked. "Such language!"

Jimmy stood up. "I'll call you," he said, and gave a slight wave in Lucia's direction.

"No, you won't," her father put in loudly. "You won't call my daughter. Don't you dare!"

"It's a free country," Jimmy replied loudly.

"This isn't a country in here. It's my house and Lucia is my daughter. I'm not having any scummy shit of an illegitimate dope pusher calling on my daughter."

"My Lucia's a good girl," the mother said loudly.

"I know she is," Jimmy said.

"Too good for you," Lenny put in.

"Lenny, shut the fuck up!" Lucia screamed.

Her father whirled around, took a couple of steps, and slapped Lucia noisily across the face. "Young lady, you don't use language like that! I've told you more than once! Not in my house! You get to your room and don't come out." He turned back to Jimmy. "And you, you creep, you get back in your car and you drive back to wherever it is that you sell your drugs and don't you *ever*—I mean *ever* —come around here or call this house again! You hear me?" He advanced on Jimmy and the boy took several steps backward, toward the door.

"And if I do?" Jimmy replied bravely.

"If you're smart, you won't cross an Italian father!"

Jimmy opened the front door and stepped outside onto the small cement porch. "The only one in this whole family that's worth a shit is Lucia!" And he slammed the door before they could grab him.

He barely recalls the drive back to Northport. He must have made all the right turns and avoided collisions with other vehicles, because he was able to arrive safely and pull up across the street from the Midway. "Hey, man," he shouted at a guy standing under a tree. "What's happening?"

The ragged-looking man walked slowly across the street and stuck his head in the car window. "Jimmy, baby. Haven't seen you in awhile. How's it goin'?"

"What have you got?" Jimmy reached into his pocket and brought out a hundred-dollar bill. It was part of the cache he was going to show Lucia's parents when they asked about her engagement. "Anything good?"

"From Colombia!" the man purred.

"Real fine," Jimmy said as the money and the merchandise exchanged hands.

"I thought you was clean, man. Didn't I hear something about that?"

"Lies," Jimmy said loudly as he turned the ignition key, "those were fuckin' establishment lies!"

CHAPTER TEN

When Ricky got out of the hospital the last week of May, he and Jimmy rented an apartment together on Cherry Street. It was a tattered-looking place with sad furniture and walls that were long overdue for a paint job. It was on the second floor of an old house that had once been—in the twenties and thirties—a first-class single-family residence. Its history had been, since the fifties, like its tenants: scruffy, on its way down and out.

But it was a perfect location. Just a few yards down the hill was Main Street, and a few steps more and you were at the Midway.

Neither boy wanted to live at home. Jimmy left his folks when they found out he had quit the McDonald's job and was doing dope again. He didn't actually quit, he reassured them, he just never went back to work. When they blamed Lucia he told them to leave her out of it. That girl is sick, they said. The whole world was sick, he replied. It would never have worked out, they said. Because adults never gave them a chance, he replied.

Ricky had decided while he was still in the hospital that he couldn't live with his parents any longer. They didn't understand him and they didn't bother to try. "They have this idea of what they want their only son to be and I'm not it," he told a patient on his floor. "They've got this mold of the perfect kid and they've been trying to squeeze me into it. Well, I don't go. I don't fit. Shit, man, I don't know *where* I fit!"

When Jimmy was asked where the rent money came from, he'd reply, "From selling dope. Ricky and me made enough money in the couple of days after he got out of that hospital to pay a full month's rent. It couldn't have happened on the salary I was getting from McDonald's, man."

He and Ricky knew if they waited long enough in front of the Midway, someone would come by to buy some dope. It wasn't the owners' doing, and after the murder the family that ran the Midway made sure the reporters understood that they had a legitimate business. They couldn't help what went on *in front* of their store, they complained. Nor could they help it if kids sold and smoked dope in the run-down area *behind* the store. They ordered Ricky Kasso out of their place, they said. He never was permitted inside it.

"I used to see Ricky and Jimmy selling dope all

the time," an employee of Home Sweet Home Deli told everyone who would listen. "I used to look out the window and see them in front of the Midway, on the sidewalk, selling to junior high school kids."

"The owners of the Midway like to say Ricky never went inside their place," another boy laughs. "Hell, that's like saying the Pope never goes inside a church."

A thin girl with long legs and much blond hair remembers the Cherry Street apartment:

"Sure, I was there a couple of times. They only had it a month or so. I forget why they didn't keep it longer. Jimmy got arrested again, I think. Anyway, there was always dope there and music and there was always a couple of kids that you knew. School was out and there was nothin' to do and no place to go. Kids that don't have cars are pretty limited in Northport. Kids that do have cars get the hell out every chance they can and they drive to Huntington or Kings Park for some fun. *Any place* is more fun for kids than Northport.

"Anyway, one night I was there, in their apartment, and Ricky decided he was going to do some of his Satan stuff. I had heard about it but never seen it. There was me and a couple of other girls and Ricky and Jimmy and Gary Lauwers too. I was surprised to see Gary there because Jimmy didn't like him very much. Ricky didn't like him that much, either, but that kid must have been made out of glue! You could never get rid of him. He was always there. You know what I mean?

"Anyway, that night Ricky had had several hits

of mescaline. Those little purple dots? You know, they come on a piece of paper and you pull them off with your teeth? They're real convenient. Especially if the cops come around. With a marijuana cigarette, you have to worry where you're gonna throw it or step on it in a hurry or somehow get rid of it, but with a hit of mescaline you just swallow it. No fuss and no evidence.

"Anyway, Ricky decided he was going to work the Ouija board. I don't know where he got that thing. It must have been something he borrowed or got at a garage sale because it was kind of scratched and dirty. It didn't have one of those wooden things that scoot along the letters . . . yeah, a planchette . . . so Ricky brought out this cat's skull! I mean it was a real skull from a real cat! A dead cat! I asked Ricky where he got it but he just smiled. I didn't ask no more. Ricky liked having his secrets. He enjoyed being mysterious. Jimmy used to say it was part of Kasso's image. This skull had been boiled and cleaned. I suppose Ricky had boiled all the skin and crap off of it. It didn't have no lower jaw, so it was kind of flat on the bottom. Just like that planchette thing was. So it could move around easier.

"Anyway, Ricky didn't ask us if we wanted to do the Ouija board. He just *told* us. We all figured what the hell, why not. It was his place and his dope. I don't remember what group was on the tape deck. Probably something with Ozzy Osbourne. Both Ricky and Jimmy *love* Ozzy Osbourne. Did you know that Jimmy has Ozzy

Osbourne's name tattooed on his right arm? In big letters right across his muscle?

"Anyway, Ricky put the board on a coffee table that was in front of their junky old sofa and we all got down on the floor. Not all of us, not Jimmy. He was in the bedroom with one of the girls. I forget her name. I never saw her before. She wasn't from around Northport. So Ricky lit about six black candles and put them on plates around the room. Black! I asked him where he found them and he said there was a Puerto Rican spirit place in the Bronx that sold them. He got his dope from the same neighborhood over there, sometimes.

"Anyway, he had these candles lit and all the other lights in the living room out and he started in to call up the devil. He looked real weird bent over that table, his hands like he was in prayer and his eyes closed and everything. He kept saying 'We love you, Satan. Please come to us, Satan.' You know, stuff like that. Stuff you see them do in the movies. Oh, yeah, I forgot to mention, one of the girls didn't want to do this Ouija board stuff, so she sat over in a big chair in the corner. She said she was a good Catholic. Ricky said the only good Catholic he knew was Martin Luther. He laughed but she didn't get it.

"Anyway, after a few minutes of this 'Satan, we love you' and 'Satan, are you here?' stuff, Ricky told us to put our fingertips on the poor cat's skull. We all did that. I was sitting next to Gary and I remember how our fingers touched each other's. I mean, there wasn't a lot of room on that little skull. Ricky had his fingertips on it, too, and he

127

told us not to push, not to try and influence the skull. He said we didn't need pressure and that Satan would use our energies when he decided to move the skull.

"Anyway, we must have sat like that for five or ten minutes and I began to wonder what the hell I was doing there. I mean, I know why I went there in the first place, but why I was sitting in that uncomfortable position on the floor saying I loved Satan when I really didn't. I don't even believe in Satan. Well, not really. Not until maybe that night, I didn't. I was getting tired and wanted a drink. There was an open vodka bottle in the kitchen and some orange juice in the refrigerator. I kept thinking about how great it would be to have a full glass of that stuff when I heard Gary beside me say, 'Oh, wow!'

"Anyway, I looked and that damned cat skull had started to move. I mean it moved by itself! I wasn't putting any pressure on it and everybody said afterward that they weren't either. So Ricky asked if it was a spirit. And it went up to the 'No' word in the corner. Then he asked if it was Satan, and back again it went to the 'No' word. Then Ricky asked if it was a demon, a kind of representative from Satan. The skull went straight to the 'Yes' word in the other corner. Again Gary did his 'Oh, wow!' almost in my ear.

"Anyway, Ricky got really into it and he started asking all kinds of questions and getting all kinds of answers. He asked about an ex-girlfriend and he asked about making money and all kinds of things. Then I asked a couple questions about my future. I was worried about making the cheerleader team the next semester and the skull said I would get it. I also asked about this jerk of a boy I was going with at the time. The skull said he didn't really love me. Of course I was devastated, but a few months later, when I got a new boyfriend, I couldn't even look at that jerk.

"Anyway, Gary said it was his turn and Ricky said it was okay. So Gary asked about school and about his mom's health and if his sister was going to marry the guy she was living with. Things like that. I didn't pay them too much attention. I was upset about my then boyfriend and I wanted that vodka and orange juice more than ever.

"Then Gary asked, 'When I graduate from high school, am I gonna go on to college?' Well, my God! I mean, all of a sudden the cat skull went *crazy* under our fingers and started zipping across the board from one corner to another. Ricky tried to talk to it, tried to get it to stop and answer the question, and then . . . nobody believes this when I tell them about it.

"Anyway, the damned cat skull goes all the way *off* the board, goes all the way to the edge of the table and flies across the *room!* I mean like there was somebody that tossed the thing! It flies across the room, bounces off the wall and lands, kerplop, in the lap of the Catholic girl in the corner.

"Anyway, she starts screaming and screaming and screaming, just staring at that skull in her lap. The screaming was so bad that Jimmy came out of the bedroom to see what the noise was all about. He only had his shorts on. And he yelled at Ricky to shut the girl up. Ricky went over and grabbed the skull and took it into the kitchen. He came back with a glass of water and the girl drank a little. Then she calmed down. She and her friend left right after that. I never saw either of them again.

"Anyway, the thing that bothers me about all this, the thing that I remember, is that the skull only started going bananas when Gary asked if he was going on to college! Gary never went to college, you know. Gary never had a chance. Ricky killed him before he could even finish high school. I mean, now that's *weird!*"

"I can get the stuff real cheap down there," Jimmy told Ricky. "It's right off the plane from Colombia. With about five hundred dollars I can make three thousand dollars here on the street, if I play it right."

"You sure this guy knows what he's talking about?" Ricky asked. He had only heard Jimmy talk about the young man he was going to Florida with—a friend of a friend from Kings Park.

"He does it all the time," Jimmy assured him. "He makes the run to Orlando, buys the stuff, and drives back to Long Island. He's already done it about a dozen times. That's how he got his car. You saw it when he dropped me off yesterday."

"It's a neat car," Ricky had to admit. "It came from dope?"

Jimmy nodded. "We can get a neat car too," he said. "We gotta play it right, that's all."

"So how long will you be gone?" Ricky asked. "The rent is due in four days."

"Three at the most," Jimmy assured him. "We ain't gonna take time out to get a suntan. We're going down there to work. One day to go down, one day to buy the shit, one day to get back. With me and him both driving, we won't need to stay over in a motel. Piece of cake."

"You sure you trust this guy?" Ricky wasn't so sure.

"Course I do."

"I got a funny feeling," he said.

Jimmy shook his head. "You and your feelings! Don't give me that crap. We stand to make a bundle. I'll be back in three fuckin' days. I told you."

"Okay, but I still got this feeling."

"Then keep your feeling," the dark-haired youth replied. "If it makes you happy, keep it."

The ride down was uneventful. Jimmy and Mark drove to Orlando without incident. They reached the supplier's apartment just before dawn. They parked in the condo parking lot and slept, one in the front and the other in the backseat.

The deal took just minutes to arrange. They paid their five hundred dollars and received a bulky pack of what the kids call Angel Dust. It's a white powder that also goes by the name of PCP. It's popular because it's the cheapest high of all and it doesn't have a taste, doesn't smell up fingers. Jimmy and Mark had enough to make six times their original investment. Once they sold it on the street in Northport, they would drive back down for more. Once they made their second six hundred percent profit, there would be another drive to Florida, and then another, and soon they would have so much money they wouldn't know what to do with it all. Hell, they might even start selling heroin. Or even cocaine. There was a market for both those drugs in Northport. Older people, adults and parents, bought those items, though. Jimmy and Ricky and Mark would have to expand their clientele if they were going to get into those drugs. They weren't too sure how to find adult clients, but once word got out, the older dopers would find them.

Mark had a friend in Orlando and this friend was having a party that day. Around his pool. Actually, it was his parents' pool, but they were away for the week. Why didn't Mark and Jimmy come by for a drink? Around two or so? Great. Lots to drink, lots to smoke, and some truly smooth females.

The party lived up to its advance billing. There was a well-stocked bar right beside the pool and well-stacked girls beside the bar. There was dope, too, and heavy-metal music on the stereo and lots of sunshine. Jimmy borrowed a bathing suit, and as he had hoped, the girls admired his broad chest and his muscular legs.

Jimmy was small in stature and, like many small boys, dreamed of having a great build. He enjoyed working out, and two of the things he missed by living away from home were the barbells and bench press his father had installed for him in the basement. He knew he looked good in the bathing suit, but he also knew someday he'd look even bet-

132

ter. When he built his mansion, one room would be nothing but gym stuff.

He awoke the next day lying naked on a waterbed. There was a girl beside him. He didn't remember how he got there or what had led up to it. He shook his head. Hell, he didn't even remember *doing* it to her. He must have, though, for why else would both of them be naked?

He stumbled into his blue jeans and found it difficult to put one bare foot in front of the other as he walked down the hall looking for Mark. He found him sitting on the toilet in one of the guest bathrooms. He was snoring.

They breakfasted on a lemon pie they found in the refrigerator along with a bag of chocolate-chip cookies. They washed it all down with a quart of milk. Then they left without bothering to find their host or even say good-bye to the naked girl on the waterbed. They just got into the car and headed north.

Mark drove and Jimmy, still high and still hung over, climbed into the backseat and fell asleep.

He felt the prodding in his side, then the slapping against the soles of his tennis shoes. "Okay! Get out of there! Come on! Now!"

Jimmy opened his eyes and looked into the face of a Florida State highway patrolman. "Shit!" he said aloud. "Oh, shit!"

Mark was already out of the car, wearing handcuffs, standing on the side of the road as an officer read him his rights. The officer had their bag of angel dust in his hand. "Oh, shit!" Jimmy said again.

Once they got to the police station, Jimmy learned what had happened. The car they had been driving had blown a tire. Mark had pulled over and discovered there was no spare in the trunk. But there was a car parked a few yards away, parked in a driveway leading to a house. It was the natural thing to do, Mark thought. So while he pried the tire off the wheel of the parked car, someone called the police.

Mark, still high, couldn't see what he had possibly done that was wrong. He needed a tire. That car over there had one it wasn't using.

Jimmy and Mark were flown back to Long Island (where they both were still on probation) and an unsympathetic judge gave them both eight months at Riverhead Correctional Facility in Suffolk County. Mark never considered the bag of angel dust illegal and repeatedly told the judge he thought eight months was a long time to serve just for wanting to borrow a tire.

CHAPTER ELEVEN

With Jimmy in jail, Ricky didn't want to keep the apartment by himself so his father tried to get his son to return home and be part of the family. Ricky agreed, but let them know it was against his will.

The Kassos went to their upstate summer place, hoping that the familiar woods and the little lake that Ricky loved so much would snap their son out of his downward spiral. His mother hoped she could put some meat on the boy's bones. He had always been thin, but he'd lost weight in the past few months. Maybe they could get him to cut his hair and wear something besides blue jeans and T-shirts. And there was that cough. Ricky swore he didn't have a cold, yet there was a cough that suddenly seized his lungs and shook his body. The air was fresh in Northport, but the Kassos hoped it would be even fresher in Greenwich.

It was a time of strain for them all, in spite of the flowers and the nature walks. Once when Dick Kasso got angry with his son, he shouted that one day Ricky would wind up in jail.

The boy shouted back, "If I'm ever put in jail, I'll kill myself! I promise you. I'll kill myself!"

That was just about the time that Gary Lauwers —on his own and without Ricky or Jimmy to blame—was arrested.

Gary and a group of kids his age were sitting in a secluded area smoking hashish pipes when another boy came by. Nobody in the group liked this boy, and Gary, on the spur of the moment, decided to play Mr. Macho. He ordered his friends to grab the boy, which they did, and they started punching him. Then Gary took his pipe and pressed it against the intruder's bare flesh some ten times.

"He gave him circles, like a tattoo," one of the boys who was there recalls. "It was real sick. The kid screamed for mercy but Gary wouldn't stop. He was acting like he was out of his head. You know what he was acting like? He was acting like Ricky!"

The attorney who represented Gary in court later told a reporter, "He wasn't really bad. He was just acting out." And she said the Lauwers were "a caring family who loved their son and worried about his future." Was the youth involved with drugs? Oh, no. Not Gary. It was just bad company.

In the middle of August 1983 the Kasso family returned to Northport. It was almost a relief to get back to the normal routine. Being isolated up there with Ricky had taken a toll on them all.

One afternoon Ricky started screaming from his upstairs bedroom. His mother stopped what she was doing and ran up the stairs. At the top stood her son, great slashes of red across his wrists, running down his open palms and fingers.

"See what you did?" he yelled at her. "See what you made me do by keeping me here?"

Lynn Kasso screamed, "Oh, my God! Oh, my God!"

Ricky waved his wrists near her face. "You see? You see? I told you I needed my freedom! Now it's too late!"

His mother wheeled around and started back down the stairs. She had to get to a phone and call the paramedics. Then she heard him laugh. She stopped, turned back toward him, and saw him licking at the wounds.

"This is not bad catsup," he said with a grin. "It'd be better on a hot dog, but at least it's nice and red. Catsup's fun, isn't it, Mom?"

Mrs. Kasso sat down on the steps, her face ashen, still shaking from the scare.

Ricky stood there, over her, laughing loudly.

Not even his father insisted he remain living there after that.

* * *

There was a spot that Ricky claimed as his very own. It was in Aztakea Woods, that overgrown area of trees and bushes and hillocks that rose right downtown, right beside the harbor, surrounded by expensive homes. It was a perfect spot to smoke some dope, listen to heavy-metal tapes, and get real high. Sometimes a guy, if he was lucky, could get laid there too.

Ricky often built a bonfire there at night and would sit up until morning smoking, talking, playing his guitar, or just staring at the flames through acid-glazed eyeballs. Kids walked to the spot easily from Main Street. Even though it was private property, no one lived in the woods so no one ever stopped them. Cars couldn't drive up there, and that made it all the better because adults and outsiders couldn't just happen by. On the rare occasion when someone called the cops complaining of loud music and a fire, they would be told that it was private property.

They had to have a warrant was the cops' cop-out.

It was early September and still warm. A few of Ricky's cronies had joined him on a Saturday night around his bonfire.

"He held court there," one boy recalls. "He really did. He was the Acid King and that spot in the woods was his throne room. Kids would buy a little dope from him, smoke some bags of angel dust, and get mellow with the music and the glow from the fire. Gary was there a lot. He had dropped out of school, just like Ricky did. That's probably why

138

he did it, because he was imitating his idol. He said he had helluva fights with his folks about not graduating from high school, but there was nothing they could do. He had turned sixteen. He must have learned that from Ricky too."

"Ricky would sit there and talk to the devil," a girl remembers. "I mean, he was *of* the devil, and when he was high, he really believed the devil could hear him. He'd sit there with those big eyes of his and say things like 'Satan, you're my main man. I really love you, Satan. I really need you in my life. Without you, life has no meaning.' You know, shit like that there.

"He used to play a guitar up there some nights. I think it was his guitar. Probably he stole it. Wouldn't surprise me. When he wanted something, he just took it. Know what I mean? Anyway, he composed songs to the devil and played them on this guitar. I remember one—

> *'I'm a child of the devil,*
> *Just a child of the devil.*
> *You know I'm on the level*
> *Cause I'm a child of the devil.'*

"It went something like that. I don't remember exactly because I was usually stoned too. But he was such a nice guy, Ricky was. He could be so sweet and sincere when he wasn't high. There wasn't anything he wouldn't do for a person. I wanted to be his steady girl, one time, and he told me no. Flat out, just like that. I told him he hurt my feelings and he apologized. He said he didn't

139

get into relationships because they never lasted. He didn't want to get hurt. I used to think it was a waste. I mean he was so cute and so full of feeling. It was the dope that did it. That fuckin' stuff became his whole life. I told him once that if he kept taking all those drugs, he would be dead. You know what he said? He said, 'That's what I want. I want to be dead.' What he needed was someone to love him. But he would have had to love back, in return."

There was one girl, a dark-haired teenager named Debbie, who did manage to get to Ricky. She was in tenth grade at Northport High and she had admired him from afar for several semesters. Finally, much to her delight, he stopped her when she was coming out of the five-and-ten store on Main Street one Saturday afternoon. He asked her if she wasn't the girl he used to see with another friend, Margie. She said she was. He asked about Margie. She said Margie's folks had moved to New Jersey and Margie was going to school over there. He said it was too bad, because he thought Margie was neat. She agreed that Margie was neat. Then he asked her if she was in a hurry. She said no. He suggested a cheeseburger in a nearby upper-class cafe called the Northport Feed and Grain. She accepted.

Several kids saw them in there that afternoon, and kids who would never have spoken to Ricky came by the table and said hello to Debbie. Debbie was popular and a good student. Debbie's father was an executive recruiter in Manhattan and Debbie's mother had a fabric shop in a Manhattan design center. Debbie saw her parents in the evenings and sometimes on weekends. Her father was usually flying off to interview a client and her mother usually spent the weekends inside expensive homes selling advice along with her special materials. Debbie was an only child and the Northport home/house she lived in was expensive but empty.

Ricky and Debbie walked to her place, talking about "old times" back in junior high. She brought him up to date on what was happening in the high school. What kids had moved, what teachers had transferred, who was going steady with whom. When they got to her front door she reached up and kissed him, lightly, on the cheek. He smiled and said he'd see her later. She went into the house feeling good. He walked back downtown feeling good.

He phoned her about midnight. Things down at the park were dead, man, and what was she doing? Did she want to come down to the park with him? She couldn't because her mother might call for her messages at any time. Her father was in Boston and her mother was in New Haven at a seminar. No, she couldn't leave the house, not at that hour. He suggested, so why didn't he come over to her place? She paused, then relaxed. Yeah, that was a good idea. Why not? Come on.

Debbie had several hard-rock tapes and she put them on the player in the rec room. There was a completely stocked bar down there as well, but Ricky didn't want a drink. He had some acid. He'd take that. He tried to get her to try some but she refused. She had seen what it did to other kids and, anyway, if her mother found out . . .

They sat on the sofa, with the lights down low, and Ricky talked to her about his dream of moving to California and how he'd like to have a boat out in the harbor and how he was going to buy a big car and how that math teacher in junior high was an asshole and which of Led Zeppelin's songs were his favorites. They sat close to each other and occasionally she stroked his head of curly hair and he purred contentedly. Someone was giving him affection. Someone was showing that she cared. When the sun came up and its rays finally managed to get past the oak trees in the side yard and through the tulips and lilac bushes planted alongside the house, they illuminated the basement rec room and there were the two kids, still on the sofa, fully dressed, asleep in each other's arms.

Ricky stood before the altar and stared at the images atop it. Pat Pagan had often told him about it, but this was the first time he had actually been invited into the old guy's apartment.

"Some people collect stamps or old dishes"—the white-haired Vietnam veteran smiled—"but I prefer Satan and voodoo things. Look here, know what this is?" He picked up a figure made of thin rods of cast iron. It had elongated arms and legs and a small head with two pointed horns. The figure held a sharply pointed spear in one of its hands.

Ricky held it for a moment. He stared at the

long cast-iron penis between the figure's legs but didn't comment on it. "It looks fierce," he said.

"It's from Brazil," Pat said. "It's called Exú. He's the devil down there in their voodoo religion. A friend brought him up to me." He set the figure back down on the red satin cloth that covered the top of this table, this altar to Evil. "Know what these are?" Ricky shook his head. "Snake skulls from the Congo," he said proudly. "Each one was a living jungle snake and now their skulls are threaded together with these feathers and dried seeds between them. Real strong juju."

"Juju?"

"Medicine. Real strong medicine. And here, this statue, this is from Italy. It's real old. Go ahead, hold it. It won't bite."

Ricky examined it. It was about five inches tall, carved from old wood, in the shape of a woman. The face was ugly, deliberately ugly, Pat said. "And this?" Ricky didn't know whether to laugh or not as he pointed to a clump of hair that was glued between the figure's legs.

"That's pussy hair," Pat said. "Nun's pussy hair. That's what gives it its power. Whoever made this had to cut some hair from a nun's pussy and paste it right there. If not, it wouldn't work."

Ricky examined it more closely, letting his fingers feel the mound of coarse hair. "I've never seen nun's pussy hairs before," he said in awe.

"Not many people have." Pat laughed. "Not unless you're a priest." He laughed again as he took back the image and placed it on the altar.

Ricky let his gaze wander over the other items

on the altar. Pat had lit the six black candles that sat in each tip of the star that had been embroidered into the cloth. Their light shone across the small wooden boxes filled with herbs, odd-colored powders, and strangely shaped stones. There were coins and chunks of crystal. There was a deck of bizarre playing cards and bunches of dried flowers. There was a box of dried insects and a jar that looked like animal eyes pickled in brine. Pat assured him that's exactly what they were.

"I been studying this stuff for years," he said. "There's a lot to it. There's a lot people don't know. There is truth in Satanism because Satan is *true*." Ricky nodded wisely. "He makes Jesus and all those Christian saints look like the real losers they are," Pat went on. "He doesn't promise his faithful pie in the sky someday when they die. He promises them power on earth and power over the ignorant and the stupid. Satan knows how to handle wimps—he destroys them. He knows how to help those who love him—he destroys their enemies. You want something and you believe in Satan, he'll get it for you even if it means he has to knock down walls and split heads. I saw all that when I was in 'Nam, man. I know what I'm talkin' about." He shook his head with the weight of all this wisdom. "You got a joint on you, man? Got some of that good stuff with you?"

Ricky reached into the side pocket of his denim jacket and handed the thin cigarette to the older man. "Jamaican," he said.

"All right!" Pat smiled. The teenage boy watched as the white-haired veteran bent low over the table and lit the cigarette from one of the burning black candles. He inhaled deeply, held it, then exhaled loudly. "Really fine," he agreed. "You know I have all this stuff here, man, all this voodoo treasure, but this thing right here, this special amulet, is still my favorite." He tugged on the leather cord that hung around his neck and brought the brass medallion with the pentagram up out of his shirt. "This been with me since the 'Nam." Ricky reached his hand upward. Pat stepped backward. "No, man. I can't let you touch it. I can't let anybody touch it. It's too sacred, man, it's filled with too much power. Too much *knowledge* in here for the uninitiated to mess with."

Ricky looked hurt for a few seconds. "I ain't no amateur, man," he said. "I been in this Satan shit for a long time now."

"Sure you have, but *I'm* the one what's been places and seen things." Pat blew more smoke across his altar. "I'm the one that's got the knowledge. All you've done is read a few books."

"Well," Ricky protested, "living in this shithole, where am I supposed to get any knowledge?"

"From me, man, from *me.*" Pat put his hand on Ricky's shoulder. "You need to know something, I'll help you. You got a question, you ask old Pat. The yogis say you can't go looking for your guru, he must come to you. Well, I've come to you. Here I am."

Ricky considered this for a few moments. "And why should you do this for me, man? What's in it for you?"

"A little grass, a little weed, some acid from time

145

to time. You got the stuff I want and I got what you want. Fair exchange. Right?"

"If it'll help me get closer to my main man, Satan, then sure, it's a deal. But when I need you, you'd better be there. If not, you get your supply cut off. I mean it."

"No problem, man. I'll be here for you. I ain't goin' anywhere."

"And someday," Ricky added, "that brass thing around your neck will be mine. Right? Someday you'll give it to me?"

Pat shook his head and the long white hair tumbled around his shoulders. "No, man. That's not part of the deal. This was made for *me*. It's got *my* vibes on it. Nobody else can wear it. Nobody else can even touch it."

"Not even for a lot of really good stuff?"

Pat shook his head. "No way. Not even for all the good stuff in the whole fuckin' world."

"I thought you might be down here." Debbie slipped into the gazebo, joining Ricky and a few other kids who were smoking in the dark. A couple of the boys said "Hi" and Ricky smiled when he saw her. "I didn't have anything to do," she said.

"You want some?" Ricky held out a marijuana cigarette. Debbie shook her head. "Come on, try it once."

"No." She shook her head again. "I don't want to get addicted."

"Addicted?" one of the boys laughed. "What's that?"

"She means she doesn't want to grow a dick," another boy said quickly.

"You guys shut up!" Ricky shouted. "Here"—he motioned to a vacant place on the wooden bench next to him—"come sit here."

Debbie sat in the darkness, her eyes catching the glow of the tips of the cigarettes. She glanced out over the water and saw the flickering of the boat lights bobbing in the harbor. She looked toward the town and saw the few store signs that were lit at this hour. She wore a thin jacket and she pulled it closer around her shoulders. It was getting chilly and there had been a news report that there might be frost in the air. "Aren't you cold?" she said to Ricky. "With just that T-shirt on?"

"Nah. I got a jacket on too," he said.

"But it doesn't have any sleeves in it," she replied. "It's October already. You should take care of yourself."

"I don't need a mama." He grinned at her.

She sighed. "I'm sorry."

"That's okay. I'm doin' fine. I ain't cold. Believe me."

"Old Rick's got the fire of Satan in him, Debbie. He *can't* get cold." The blond boy laughed and the other boys laughed with him.

"Shut the fuck up, Gary," Ricky almost barked.

"But you do," Gary insisted. "You told me you did. You weren't shittin' me, were you?"

"Come on, Gary." Ricky didn't want to argue.

"I'm gonna get that fire in me too," Gary continued, his voice and his mind high from the dope. "I got me a book all about Satan. I read it a lot." He patted the back pocket of his blue jeans. "Take it with me all the time. Got spells in it and things to do to make people your slaves. Got everything in it." He patted his treasure again.

"Gary," Ricky said, trying to keep his voice even, "shut the fuck up. You don't know what you're talking about."

"Sure I do! Why don't I, man? You think you're the only one that can know these things? You got some kind of fuckin' patent on Satan?"

"Damn right I do," Ricky said loudly. "You don't know what you're talkin' about, so keep your mouth shut."

"Ricky thinks he knows it all. Everything. Well, anybody can learn it too." Gary was standing now, holding his small volume of Satanic lore. He waved it under Ricky's nose. "You're my buddy, Rick, but Satan is my *man*."

"Fucker!" Ricky jumped up, grabbed the book, and tossed it over the railing, onto the dark grass outside the gazebo.

"Hey!" Gary shouted. "That's my book!"

"Then go get it, man!" Ricky lifted Gary by the collar on his jacket and by the belt in his jeans and tossed him over the gazebo railing too. "Get your fuckin' book now, man."

Debbie had screamed when she saw what was happening and she started out to help Gary. "Never mind that little creep," Ricky gripped her arm. "He's an asshole. Let's get out of here. He's ruined this place for me tonight."

The other boys left with them and they headed toward the spot in the woods where they knew

Ricky would build a fire, talk about Satan, and, hopefully, hand out some more free dope.

Gary lay on the grass for several minutes after that. He tried, with his fingers, to staunch the flow of blood from his nose. His head ached and his forehead was scratched from the pebbles it had scattered as he hit the grass. His thin arm stretched out frantically into the darkness around him. His book, man, he had to find his book.

And Jimmy Troiano, in his prison cell, had by this time X'd out three full months on his wall calendar.

"I wish you could, but you can't," Debbie said. "My folks will be here for the entire weekend. They always make a big thing out of Christmas. There's no way you can crash here for it."

Ricky shrugged. "I'll find another place. Don't worry about me."

"But I do worry," the girl sighed. "I care what happens to you."

"I get by."

"But, Ricky, it'll be Christmas. It's *cold* outside. Where will you stay? Where will you *sleep?* You know I'd let you if I could."

"I know, I know," he replied. "It's your old man and old lady. I know it isn't you."

"Could you go to Billy's? Would his folks let you stay there?"

"They do sometimes," Ricky replied. "They got company comin', that's all."

"Company that sleeps over?" she asked. He nodded. "Damn!" she said.

"I got the Lucassis'. I could stay there. They got a bed in their rec room. They probably will be going to the Bronx for the weekend with their daughter. They might let me stay alone in the house."

"How about the tree house over at Beverly's? That got any heat in it?" He shook his head. "Too bad," she said. He nodded. "Well, it's too cold to sleep in the lumberyard." He nodded again. "You know," she said slowly, "you could go home for the holidays, Ricky."

He took another drag on the cigarette and handed it to her. "No way," he said as he exhaled loudly. "That's the last fuckin' place I want to go. Anyway, kids' families been good to me. You been good to me." He kissed her on the lips as she passed the joint back to him. "Your people gone almost every night, that's been great. But I understand. This ain't your house, it's theirs and they'd be real pissed to come home and find a curly-headed guy in your bed."

"And reefer butts in the ashtrays," she laughed.

"They still don't suspect?" he asked.

She laughed again and shook her head. "They'd kill me if they knew I smoked these things! Smash me up and flush me down the toilet!" And there was another laugh.

"And what about the acid? What would they say if they found the hits of acid?"

"They won't. That's why I make you take them

with you when you go. They would really shit, then."

"What do you care?" he asked. "They don't pay any attention to what you do. All parents are like that," he continued. "They tell a kid what to do and they go off and drink and screw around and get high themselves. Then they see their kid doing the same thing and they go bananas!" He wagged his finger in her face and said in a mock adult voice, "I told you not to do that! I told you not to smoke that terrible stuff!" Then he looked away and shouted, still in character, "Honey, will you fix me a triple martini?" She laughed. "Shit," he said, "there isn't one parent that isn't a fuckin' hypocrite!"

Ricky's last Christmas and his last New Year's came and went and in mid-January he dragged himself, like a dying alley cat, back through his parents' front door.

They put him to bed, in his own room, and fussed over him. His cough and his coloring got worse and they put him in the car and drove him to the doctor. It was diagnosed as a severe bronchial infection.

They took him out to the Walt Whitman Mall and bought him some warm winter clothes. New blue jeans, a couple of wool shirts, and a winter jacket. He got new shoes (not thin tennis shoes) and several pairs of warm woolen socks. Then they took him back home and put him back in bed.

A warm bed, food, and medicine soon had him up and moving around. He agreed to go back to school, a special learning center for problem students in nearby Commack. He went for a few days, but it was mainly to buy drugs and get high. It didn't take long for him to be suspended from the school for cutting classes.

His father, himself after all a respected school-teacher, was furious with him and laid down the law.

It wasn't long before Ricky walked out of the house. Determined never to come back. Again.

"It was always tough on Ricky's parents when he was home," says an adult friend of the family. "They never knew what he would do, how he would look, what he would say. Dick and Lynn tried very hard to raise him right. It was just that there is a terrible generation gap now. I've got three kids of my own, and if I tried to raise them the way my parents raised me, they might end up like Ricky did. It's tough to be a parent today. There are no guidelines. Things change almost overnight. What was correct last year is old-fashioned this year.

"If I had ever brought home a boy and told my mother he was going to stay with me in my bedroom overnight, I would have been beaten with a baseball bat and I would have deserved it. Today, a mother almost has to look the other way when her daughter says she's sleeping with her boyfriend. One time my ten-year-old daughter didn't come to supper when I called her. When I insisted she get down to the kitchen, she yelled, 'Mom, I'm reading an article about masturbation!' Masturbation? I wouldn't have *dared* to speak that word in front of my mother! Lord, I didn't even know what it meant until I graduated from school and started working. And, as far as I know—and I sure as hell will never inquire—my mother probably doesn't even know *today* what that word means!

"No, you may want to blame Dick and Lynn for what happened to Ricky, but you really can't. They tried their best, the best they knew how. They were years apart. Not just in age but in attitude and the way all three of them looked at life. Who knows about drugs? What parents with teenage kids ever went through that when they, themselves, were kids? It's a whole different parents versus children ball game than it was in the sixties and seventies. If I found out now that I was pregnant, I'd get an abortion. I would. I wouldn't even think twice about it. Who needs that responsibility?"

CHAPTER TWELVE

"Pull up over there, by that garbage can on the corner." Ricky pointed as his friend Hammie steered the Volkswagen and parked it. "Now we sit and wait a few minutes," he said.

"How does he know we're here?" Hammie asked.

"He'll see the yellow ribbon. That's why I put it there." Ricky pointed to the strip of yellow cloth tied to the car's antenna.

Hammie began to sing "Tie a Yellow Ribbon Round the Old Oak Tree."

Ricky grinned. "Yeah, something like that."

"How'd you hear about this guy?" Hammie wanted to know.

"Jimmy told me about him. He's one of Troiano's contacts."

"But Jimmy's in jail," Hammie said. "When did you see Jimmy?"

"I didn't. A guy I know just got out of that same place where Jimmy is and he gave me a note from Jimmy. Jimmy had this guy's telephone number."

"I didn't know Jimmy could write," said Hammie.

"Jimmy's no dope," Ricky replied.

"And hell," Hammie continued, "I didn't know you could *read!*"

Ricky grinned and took a swipe at him. He and Hammie had become close only in the past month. Hammie's folks had moved to Hauppauge right after Christmas. Hammie's father was in microchips. Because Hauppauge was another of those Long Island communities with nothing in it for a kid to do, Hammie insisted and got his father to buy him a car. He had wanted a Ferrari (his father could easily have afforded one) but he settled for a Volkswagen. Hammie had been looking to buy dope and had heard how convenient it was in Northport. Once in Northport, he was told about Ricky Kasso. The two boys liked each other on sight. Hammie was his grandmother's nickname for him. It was short for Hamilton. He was clean-shaven, his jeans and T-shirts were neat and unpatched. He was going to high school and was in the upper half of his class. He respected his parents and obeyed all their rules. He was the exact opposite of Ricky. Opposites attract.

Hammie looked up and saw the street sign: Pugsley Avenue. They were in the Bronx. He had never been to the Bronx before, well certainly hadn't driven through it anyway. This didn't seem to be the best neighborhood in this mile-after-mile of shops and high rises, but it wasn't the worst either. It wasn't nearly as bad as that Berlin-after-the-war-looking Bronx neighborhood you saw every time you came into Manhattan from the north by train.

Ricky sat staring out the front window. Waiting.

"What else did Jimmy have to say in his note?" Hammie hadn't met Jimmy, but he felt he knew him from listening to Ricky and his group.

"He's doin' lots of weight lifting and stuff like that," Ricky said. "They got him on some reading program too. Reading books, I think. He says he's keeping his distance from most of the guys in there cause most of them are real bad."

"What about dope? He getting any?"

"Oh, sure." Ricky smiled. "Shit, man, that ain't no church where he's at. It's a prison. There's always dope in prison."

Hammie nodded. He was impressed that by knowing Ricky he was also knowing someone who was in prison. He had never known anyone who had gone to prison. "Eight months is a long time just for breaking parole," Hammie said quietly.

"Plus the dust, man," Ricky reminded him, "don't forget that bag of angel dust they found on him. That's what did it. That fuckin' dust."

Hammie looked at his friend. "How come you never been in prison?" he asked.

"Not me, man. No way. Like I told my old man, if I ever get sent to prison, I'll kill myself. I will. I won't put up with that shit. I don't have the patience Troiano has. No way. I am a freedom person, man. I got to have my freedom." He started to say something else when a middle-aged white man wearing a light topcoat over his suit, shirt, and tie walked over to the car. Even though it was mid-February, there was little snow on the sidewalks. Ricky rolled down the window. "I'm lost and need directions," he said to the man.

"What part of town you tryin' to get to?" asked the man.

"East of the moon," Ricky said. "I hear that's where the canaries sing."

The man leaned farther into the car, glancing at Hammie and the interior of the automobile. "How much are we talkin'?"

"Three hundred hits," replied the seventeen-year-old boy.

"That's three seventy-five," the man said.

"I got it." Ricky handed the man a white envelope with three hundred and seventy-five dollars in it. The man expertly ran his thumb across the tops of the bills, then nodded. He reached into an inner pocket and brought out his own white envelope and passed it to Ricky. Ricky immediately dropped it to the floor and kicked it back under the seat.

"You go," the man said loudly, "down three traffic lights and then you turn to the right. It's about five streets after that." He gestured broadly as he gave these strangers directions. Both boys shouted, "Thank you," then Hammie started the motor and the car drove away. The man continued down the street.

"What the hell was all that about singing canaries?" Hammie asked.

"The code. I had to give him the code, man. Without that code, I don't get the stuff."

"Well, how'd he know to have three hundred hits all ready like that? Suppose you had wanted to buy more?"

"You gotta buy it in threes. That's the way he packages it. So you buy three, six, nine hundred, whatever amount of hits you want. Three's the minimum."

"Where'd you get three hundred and seventy-five dollars?" Hammie asked. "Steal it?"

Ricky laughed. "I got my sources." He grinned. "Some kids pay me in advance. Another older guy loans me the money. He charges a helluva lot of interest, that fucker, but I always repay him. My credit's good. Come on," he said suddenly, impatient to get back to Northport, "move this thing. I got people waiting."

By midnight Ricky had unloaded all his hits of mescaline. He sold most of them from the gazebo by the harbor or from the front seat of Hammie's car as they parked across from the Midway. He saved some and took them to Kings Park, about twelve miles away. He'd made a few phone calls, his clients were waiting at the junior high school parking lot.

Ricky had paid the supplier in the Bronx a dollar and twenty-five cents for each tiny purple dot of the mescaline. He sold each dot—each hit—for three dollars each. He usually kept several hits for himself to munificently bestow on special friends for free, but when he sold all three hundred of the hits, he made a profit of five hundred and twenty-five dollars for an afternoon's work. Not bad for a seventeen-year-old high school dropout who'd rather not fry up Big Macs for three dollars and seventy-five cents per hour.

Ricky preferred to deal with his steady clientele in Northport and Kings Park. He didn't have to look around for his customers and he didn't have to worry about being in competition with the big boys in the bigger cities. Ricky wasn't the only one selling dope in those two towns. There were other dealers, older men, who sold to the mid-twenties-and-up crowd. And, of course, most of the adults who were on dope—marijuana, mescaline, heroin, angel dust, LSD, or cocaine—bought their supplies from dealers in New York City and carried them back to Long Island in very respectable-looking leather briefcases.

There wasn't much of a moon that night, and while it was warm for mid-March, Debbie had a heavy winter coat on. She complained to her mother that she was cold all the time. Her mother told her to turn up the thermostat and offered to take her to the doctor. Ricky had told her this cold feeling was natural. Angel dust and mescaline both had a way of making your teeth chatter when you came down from their high. Don't worry, he told her. When summer came she could sit in the sun with him and there'd be nothing to worry about. And, shit, she didn't need to go to a doctor! He might find out about the drugs she was taking and

159

then all hell would break loose! No, just wear sweaters and wait for the sun.

Ricky was using a garden shovel. He had stolen it that evening from an unlocked garage. There was a fortune lying under the soil and nobody knew about it but him. As he dug Debbie stood in the shadows watching while Gary stood close by with a burlap sack (stolen from the same garage) to carry Ricky's unearthed treasures.

"That's what this lady told me"—he talked as he dug—"five hundred dollars for a skull and two or three hundred for a clay pot if it's in good condition. She said I had to be careful not to break the pots when I dug. I guess they're pretty fragile. They been in here for so long."

"What's she want with a dumb old skull?" Debbie wanted to know. "I mean, yuck! The skull of a dead Indian! Gag! I wouldn't want to have one!"

"She sells 'em to creeps, probably," Gary said. He felt honored Ricky had included him in this new project. "Maybe to schools and museums and places like that."

"Yuck!" Debbie said again.

"Oh, they ain't so bad," Gary said knowingly. "A skull is just the bones inside your head. That's all. We all got skulls. I ain't afraid of no dead man's skull."

"Good for you," said Debbie. She came out of the shadows long enough to put the end of a lit marijuana cigarette between Ricky's lips. That way he didn't have to stop digging while he smoked. "Here, hon," she said.

"In my book about Satanism," Gary continued,

160

"there's a couple of spells where you take old bones and grind them up and use them in the rituals."

"Use them?" Ricky was interested.

"Yeah. In one, you throw the powder from the bones into the candle flame to make it smoke, and the other, you grind up the bones and put some of the powder in a glass of juice and make a person drink it."

"Yuck!" Debbie said louder now.

"I know some witches and people like that." Gary watched as Ricky dug deeper into the grave. "They have a skull on their altar and they put a burning candle on top of it and the candle burns down and drips along the face and sides of the skull."

"That sounds dumb," said Debbie.

"Well," Gary replied defensively, "that's what they do. Isn't that right, Rick? Don't some witches do that?"

"Yeah," he said. "I heard about that." He was perspiring now from the exertion of turning over earth that hadn't been touched in at least two hundred years. It was an Indian graveyard, almost filled when the first white settlers purchased the area. It is said that several religious but superstitious Puritans were going to unearth the bodies and claim the land when they all saw what could only be described as "a malevolent savage spirit" floating toward them. The good Christians built around the burial site and not on it, a tradition that remained through village history.

"Hey," Gary almost shouted. "It sounds like you

found something." Ricky sunk the shovel in again. The same clinking noise was heard. "Yeah, man. I'll bet you found a skull!"

"Turn the light on a minute," Ricky said. He had been digging in the dark, not wanting to call attention by having the flashlight on all the time. "Over this way," he said, and Gary moved the light. "Yeah," he said with satisfaction, "it's a bone."

"Oh my God," Debbie moaned dramatically.

Ricky got down on his knees and started scooping the earth out with his hands. The grave wasn't deep, he hadn't had to dig more than three feet down. Like a dog, he pawed after the bone that the light revealed. "I almost got it," he said softly. "Just a little bit more." His hands worked faster now and soon he straightened up, a long, brittle, dirt-caked bone in his hand.

Gary came closer with the flashlight. "That's not a skull," he said.

"I know it's not a skull, asshole," Ricky replied. "It's probably from a leg or an arm."

"Are there any worms on it?" Debbie didn't want to see it if there were.

"Nah," Gary said. "Worms ate the meat off years ago."

"Oh, yuck!" Debbie exclaimed. "You guys are revolting!"

"The skull must be farther up," Ricky said. "Maybe if I dig a couple of feet farther up, I'll find the skull. Sure as hell don't want any old shin bone." Debbie brought the cigarette up to his lips again, but she didn't look into the open grave.

Ricky exhaled the smoke and got back on his knees, pawing at the earth, his fingers discovering more of the skeleton. Gary held the light.

"Maybe there isn't any head," Gary suggested. "Maybe this one got decapitated by some white settler. Or maybe—"

They froze as they heard the car come to a stop. Then they heard a man's voice: "Hey, you in there! Stop what you're doing and stand perfectly still!"

"Shit!" said Ricky. "The fuckin' cops!"

"Freeze!" the voice outside in the darkness commanded.

"Run!" Ricky commanded.

The cop turned on his searchlight, catching Ricky square in the middle of it. Gary dropped the sack and the flashlight and ran deeper into the cemetery. Debbie fled behind some bushes and started crawling, not caring that her winter coat was getting covered with dirt and brambles. The cop, all alone in his squad car, came straight for Ricky. The boy, unsure for a moment what to do, turned away, and as he did he tripped over the shovel and fell sideways into the grave. Before he could struggle out of it, he felt the cop's heavy grip on his arm.

"Where are the others?" the policeman demanded.

"What others?" Ricky answered.

"The ones that were with you."

"Nobody with me," the boy replied.

"I heard others talking."

163

"Maybe you heard ghosts, man. This here's a graveyard, you know."

"Nobody needs a wise-ass," the officer said. "Come on, Mr. Kasso, let's go to the station."

"How you know my name?"

"Who doesn't know *you?*" the officer said.

"Really?" Ricky beamed. The cigarette had worked its effect. "That's pretty neat."

"Depends on your point of view, kid."

"I guess I'm famous around here."

The cop kept his grip as he steered Ricky into the patrol car. "Fame is fleeting, kid. Especially *your* kind of fame."

"Hey, look at you!" Ricky grinned. "A fuckin' philosopher!"

Ricky was booked, made to sign some forms, and then released. He was told he would have to appear before a judge on June 18. They asked him what his father's phone number was. Ricky told them not to waste their time calling him. So they didn't.

CHAPTER THIRTEEN

"Jimmy!"

"Ricky! How's it goin', man?"

"Cool, man," Ricky said, "real cool. And you?"

"Also real cool," Jimmy replied, shaking Ricky's outstretched hand.

"Feel good to be out, man?"

"Real good. Feels fine! Super-fine!" Jimmy laughed. "Hey, man, you look a little white around the gills. You feelin' okay?"

Ricky nodded. "Sure. I'm fine. Just a cough sometimes and the shakes, but hell, that's mostly from bad weed and too much pussy!" Ricky had just turned eighteen. It made him feel more of an adult than ever. "I been gettin' me some of that regular," he confided to Jimmy. "You don't know her. Name's Debbie. She's from here, from the Port."

"Good for you." Jimmy grinned.

"Hey, man," Ricky exclaimed. "What happened to your teeth? What happened to your fangs? Hey, Drac? What happened?"

"The jail dentist filed them down for me. Didn't hurt and didn't cost me anything. Shit, I had nothin' else to do when I was in the house. Might as well get something for free from those fuckers." He grinned again and Ricky was disappointed to see the dog teeth gone.

"Makes you look human," Ricky laughed.

"Not like a skull?" Jimmy punched his buddy on the arm.

Now it was Ricky's turn to grin. "You heard about that?"

"A guy in prison told me. Said you was into some kind of black magic where you were using old Indian skulls to call up the devil."

"Shit." Ricky spat on the ground in front of the Midway, their old stomping ground. "I don't need no dead Indian to make my contact with my main man. I just call him and he's *there!* You know that. Hell, man, there is a store in Greenwich Village that pays five hundred bucks for a skull. I just about had me one, too, if that fuckin' cop hadn't come along. That little fucker Gary was with me. And my girl. Shit, they almost got caught too. Cops still don't know they was there with me." He paused, waiting for Jimmy to understand that he didn't rat on his friends. "When did you get out?"

"Today. Around noon. They let me go just before lunch, those fuckers. I haven't had anything to eat yet."

"You wanna pizza?" Ricky asked. "I'm buyin'."

They spent most of the afternoon taking up table space and bringing each other up to date on what had been happening. Ricky told of making the drug contact in the Bronx, on Pugsley Avenue, and how he was averaging about five hundred dollars a week from the sale of the mescaline.

"What are you doin' with it all, man?" Jimmy wanted to know. "Puttin' it in the bank?"

Ricky shook his head. "Shit no. I wouldn't let those fuckers touch my cash. I open an account and the first thing they do is call my old man and tell him. No way. No"—he smiled—"I was going to save it for my trip to California."

"You still have that dream?"

Ricky nodded. "That's where it's at, man. It ain't here. You know that." Jimmy nodded. "But I don't know what happens, man. I make all that money and by the end of the week it's all pissed away. I don't know where it goes. A little for booze, a little for dope, some for parties at other kids' houses, and then, shit, it's gone. I don't know what happens to it. You know what I mean?"

Jimmy nodded. "Used to be the same when we had that apartment together on Cherry Street. You remember? We worked our tails off selling stuff and we never had any dough left over."

"We gonna do it again?" Ricky asked. "Take another place together?"

"No, man. I promised my folks I'd move back with them. They want me to. They came to visit

167

me lots of times when I was in prison and they had several sessions with the counselors there. I owe them. I gotta go back."

Ricky was disappointed. "Shit, man, you're eighteen years old. Gonna be nineteen in December. You don't have to do what your folks want. You're of age, man."

"I'm not doin' what *they* want," Jimmy said evenly, looking his friend directly in the eyes, "I'm doin' what *I* want. I had a long time to think in there. Dope and pussy ain't the only things in life."

"Well, I'm not going to change," Ricky said. "I'm always going to be the same. I like who I am and what I am." He looked at Jimmy. "That going to make a difference in our friendship? The fact that you're going to obey the rules and I'm not?" He glanced anxiously at Jimmy, then quickly back at the pizza on his plate. "I mean," he said, "I waited for you to get out and I figured we'd still be buddies."

Jimmy grinned. He wanted to reach out and put his hand on Ricky's, but he knew boys didn't touch each other like that. Not straight boys. "What the fuck's wrong with you, man," he said, and hit Ricky a light tap on the side of his head. "Who said anything about not being buddies anymore? I didn't hear anybody say that, and I'm the only one at this table with you. Ain't I?" He paused and Ricky nodded. "Just because I'm going to live with my folks doesn't mean I'm gonna keep off the streets. I'm still going to use dope. I ain't gonna lock myself up in some closet and only come out on Sunday in time for church."

"Church? You're gonna start going to church?"

Jimmy shrugged. "I promised my mom. She says it won't hurt. Ricky, those people *adopted* me. I mean they took me in when my own folks didn't want me. They saved my ass, man. They've been super-good to me."

"You've been a shit to them," Ricky said quickly. "More than once."

"I agree. I've been a *real* shit. They don't deserve the trouble I dumped on them. But we've had long talks about it. They came to prison and we talked. Shit, man, we had *long* talks. You ever sat down and had a long talk with your folks?" Ricky shook his head. "I didn't think so. You know maybe it would help."

Ricky took a small bite of the pizza. "Oh, fuck you," he said as he chewed. "You know my old man better than that. We don't have talks together, he talks *at* me. You know why I left home this last time? After I went home sick and had that infection in my lungs? You know why I left?" He swallowed and Jimmy shook his head. "Because he wanted me to cut my fuckin' hair. That's why. He laid down all these Gestapo rules and the final one was that I had to cut my hair because boys don't wear their hair long, girls do."

"And that's why you left?"

"Fuckin'-a, man. That's why."

"My hair's short," Jimmy said. "I had it cut once a month in prison."

"Oh, come on, Jimmy. You know what I mean. It was the principle of the thing. You know that."

"Yeah," Jimmy sighed, "I do. We gotta have principles. Especially kids like us. Older people gotta respect our principles."

"Jimmy!" Billy came bounding across the large living room, his hand outstretched. "I didn't know you were out, man! This is great! When you get out?"

"This morning," Jimmy said, his eyes going from face to face as they stopped the party to stare at him. "I didn't know you was having this thing, man, or I wouldn't have crashed it."

"Are you kidding?" Billy was genuinely pleased to see Jimmy. "It's just a few of the regulars. The guys bought a keg of beer and some of the girls made sandwiches and stopped at Colonel Sanders for a couple buckets. It ain't no *party* party. Nobody's birthday or anything."

"Your folks home?" Jimmy had never met Mr. and Mrs. Evans, but he heard they were strict with their son. Nice people, with lots of money, but strict.

Billy laughed. "Are you kidding?" He gestured at the boys and girls on the sofas together, at the boys drinking vodka and orange juice in the corner, at the tape deck that was blasting the walls with the sound of Motley Crue. "Do you think this room would look like this if they were home?" He grinned. "Lemme get you a beer. Nah, my folks are in Philadelphia. Some business friend's daughter is getting married. Lots of flowers and white satin and all that. They went overnight. They'll be back tomorrow. Want some chicken?"

Jimmy shook his head. "No, I been eatin' pizza all afternoon. With Kasso."

Billy frowned. "I don't see too much of Ricky anymore," he said. "He's got himself a girlfriend now, you know." Jimmy nodded. "And he's into dealing more than ever. He don't look good, neither."

"What do you mean?"

"No color to his face. And always coughing. He was sick while you were gone. His folks thought he had pneumonia."

Jimmy nodded. "I heard. Shit, man, he don't eat. He don't take care of his body. We had a large pizza this afternoon and I ate almost all of it. He just picked it up and played with it."

"You look good," Billy said. "You been workin' out?" Jimmy nodded and flexed his right arm and the muscle with the tattoo across it jumped to attention. "Fantastic!" Billy said. "I should be doing that. I should be working out but I don't have the time."

Jimmy grinned. "Where *I* was I had nothin' *but* time."

He felt the hand on his muscle before he heard her voice. "Can you do that again?" she purred.

He turned and then smiled. "Liz! How you doin'?"

"Just great," she said, and flashed him one of her sweetest Elizabeth Taylor imitation smiles. That's why the kids called her Liz. She even wore her dark hair exactly the way Elizabeth Taylor wore

171

hers. Though young, her bust was fully developed and always peeked halfway out of whatever blouse she was wearing. Some kids had Mohawk haircuts to emulate Mr. T. and other kids pumped iron to look like Sylvester Stallone. Elizabeth Taylor was Liz's role model. "You been away," she said softly. "We missed you. At least *I* did."

"Yeah"—Jimmy blushed—"I was on a vacation. I just got back."

"Got back or got *out?*" Her fingers caressed his upper right arm.

"Both," he said. "You look real fine. What have you been doin'?"

"What or *who?*" She grinned.

"Both." He returned the grin.

Before they could renew their friendship any further, some boys came and surrounded Jimmy. How great he was back. How great he looked. How was it in there, man? Was he in a cell all by himself? Were the guards really that mean? Did he ever think of busting out? What you do for sex in there, man? Soon almost the entire party was around him, smiling at him, occasionally touching him, eager to be seen with him. Jimmy basked in the warmth of it all. He was somebody again. He was out of prison and back in town. These kids from Northport had never known anyone who had been in prison. They had never been close to a real convict. They might drink beer and smoke dope, but that was as far as they could go in breaking through the protective cultural shell they had been born into. They were Northport. They were Long Island affluence. They would go on to be-

172

come doctors and lawyers and businessmen and members of the country club. But here was Jimmy Troiano in their midst. A real law breaker. A kid who had just come out of prison! Man, this guy was something special. They didn't want to *be* Jimmy Troiano, but they made points just being *next* to him!

As the party wore on Jimmy got high. It seemed to him there was always a full glass in his hand and always someone offering him marijuana. He danced a few times with Liz, watching and waiting for her boobs to come popping out of her blouse. They never did. He talked the pros and cons of Jamaican dope versus Mexican. He listened as kids complained about the high school system in Northport and how glad they were it was April and there was just a short time till summer vacation. He kissed several of the girls and was groped by a couple of them in return. His head reeled with the idea of being free again, of being high again, of being important again. He passed out in one of the bedrooms.

While he was out of it Liz and two of the girls, also high, started going through the things in Billy's mother's dresser. They tried on a couple of her Saks Fifth Avenue blouses and doused themselves with her Georgio and Chanel. Then Liz found a small box underneath the lingerie in the middle drawer. She opened it and took out a glistening two-carat diamond ring. "Look at this thing!" she whistled. "Look what I found."

"That's some stone!" one of the girls said.

"Must be worth plenty!" the other one exclaimed.

"Let's see if it fits," Liz said. "It does. Hey, look, it fits my finger perfectly."

"Real great," one girl said.

"Yeah," the other one said, then added, "You better put it back now."

"Why?" Liz asked, holding her hand up to the light from the dressing-table lamp. "It looks great on me."

"But it's not yours," one girl said.

"It belongs to Billy's mother," the other girl, still wearing the Saks blouse, reminded her.

"It belongs to me now," Liz said. "I found it."

"Billy's mother never lost it," a girl said. "She'll be pissed if she finds it missing."

"Well, she didn't take it with her"—Liz admired it again—"so she must not think very much of it. She's got lots of others."

"Put it back," said one of the girls.

"I never give back a diamond," Liz breathed heavily, doing her actress imitation. "My fingers were made for diamonds, dahling. Diamonds were made for *me.*"

It was shortly after noon the next day when Jimmy's mother opened the front door. There were two policemen on the round cement stoop they called their front porch.

"Your son home?" one of them asked. Mary Troiano nodded. "Can we speak with him?"

"He's still asleep," she said. "What's wrong?"

"We want to ask him about a ring."

174

"A ring that was stolen last night from a home here in Northport," the second policeman volunteered. "Your son was at a party there."

"He doesn't know anything about it, I'm sure," his mother said.

"Can we talk to him?"

Mary Troiano shut the door, leaving the officers outside. She went into Jimmy's bedroom and started shaking him until he became awake. Finally, when her voice penetrated his smoke- and alcohol-clouded brain, he stumbled out of bed and went to the front door, clutching a towel around his waist.

"Do you guys think I'm so stupid that I'd steal a ring the first day I get out of prison?" he demanded.

"You were there," a cop said. "Mrs. Evans's son gave your name as one of the kids that was there last night."

"Do you deny you were there?" the other cop asked.

"Shit no, I don't deny I was there. Sure I was there, but I didn't steal no damn ring. Why would I do a stupid thing like that?" he repeated.

"Can we search your bedroom?" One of the officers stepped closer to the door.

"You have a warrant?" Jimmy's mother asked. The man shook his head. "Then you can't search," she said flatly. The last few years of dealing with her son's problems had given her a hardness she never expected. "My Jimmy is on parole. He has no intention of getting into trouble again. He has changed."

"Uh-huh," said one of the cops. "You know what they say about leopards and spots."

"Very funny," Jimmy said. "What about the other kids? Did you ask them?"

One of the policemen shook his head. "No. We came here first."

"Well, you fuckers!" Jimmy shouted in disbelief. "You came straight for me!"

"You're the most likely suspect," one of the policemen said.

"So now anything that happens in Northport, you're going to come looking for Jimmy first?" Mary asked, a touch of sarcasm in her voice.

"Yes, ma'am. Your little boy is a doper and a thief and a liar. It's natural we'd be here first." Then to Jimmy: "We've got our eyes on you, you little creep, so don't think you can pull any more of your shit on us. Now we want that diamond ring and we want it now!"

"And we want a search warrant," Mary Troiano said loudly.

The officers turned and walked down the curved sidewalk to their parked car. Mary could see neighbors peering from behind curtains at the goings-on. "We'll be back with a warrant," one of them shouted. "You'd better be here."

"Why don't you say it louder?" Jimmy yelled. "I don't think the people on the next block heard you!"

Mary Troiano closed the door and looked at her son. "Jimmy," she said softly, "I'm only going to ask you once and I want your answer to be a truthful one, an answer based on everything we agreed

176

while you were in that prison." He nodded. "Did you steal that ring?"

"No, Mom. I didn't. And that's the truth."

"Do you know who did?"

He shook his head. "No, I don't. I got high at the party and passed out early. I didn't see anybody do anything."

"I believe you," she said. "I have to start believing you."

The officers never came back with their warrant. By the time it was half written a phone call had come in from Billy's mother. The ring had been returned. Liz's mother had gone into her bedroom and seen her daughter asleep with the ring still on her finger. After Northport's teenage superstar admitted how she got the diamond and returned it, Billy's mother didn't want to press charges. The police never apologized to Jimmy or his mother.

CHAPTER FOURTEEN

Jimmy wiped his grimy hands on the rag in the back pocket of his coveralls. He had filled the lady's gas tank, checked her oil, and cleaned her windshield. She had paid him and then flashed him a dazzling smile. "Hell," he said half aloud as she drove out of the station, "maybe this job's not so bad after all."

Jimmy had gotten a job at the Mobil gas station on Laurel Road on his own. Two days after the party at Billy's house, he had walked into the station and asked the manager if he needed any help. In affluent towns like Northport, teenagers don't like jobs that leave dirt under their fingernails. Hardware stores, lumberyards, gas stations, and other such unfashionable places always find it difficult to get local help. Jimmy didn't mind the dirt and the smell of the gasoline. He was doing something he wanted to do, he was showing his folks he had changed and he was outside. That was important. After all those months locked up, he wasn't ready to take an inside job. The pay was lousy, the hours meant working weekends, but it was a start. Like the McDonald's job had been, this job was a start. He was getting only three dollars and fifty-five cents an hour, but it *was* another start.

At the end of the afternoon he took off his coveralls, washed his hands in solvent and then with soap, and told the manager he was going for the day. "You satisfied with how I did?" he asked.

"Yeah, you did okay. For a new guy, I didn't have to show you too much. Tomorrow at nine. Right?"

"Right." Jimmy smiled. "See you then."

He walked home. It was just a few blocks. It was mid-April and the leaves had not yet come entirely out on the trees. Instead, there were little bumps of green that peppered the bare branches. Some maple trees had already started dropping their buds and they crunched under his feet as he walked. There were even occasional daffodils snuggled up to a few front porches and the forsythia bushes already had a yellowish glow around them, a kind of preview of coming attractions. Jimmy felt good about himself and his world. Maybe he'd give Liz a call. Maybe he'd start seeing her regularly. She wasn't so bad, he smiled, when she wasn't play-acting.

He went into the living room. His parents were there, waiting for him.

"We have something to talk to you about." His father was the first to speak.

"Oh, the job went fine," he said. "I didn't goof up. Not once."

"That's not what we want to talk about." His father wasn't smiling.

"I thought you'd be interested," Jimmy said. "My first day and all."

"Not really," his father said. "Not now."

"Not after this." His mother held out her hand. "I found this in your bedroom."

"Oh, shit!" Jimmy said.

"This is mescaline, isn't it?" His mother's voice was calm, but he knew there was anger directly beneath it.

Jimmy nodded. "You're a nurse," he said flatly, "you know what mescaline looks like."

"Where did you get it?" his mother asked.

"In the Bronx. Last night. Me and Ricky."

"What are you going to do?" his father asked. "Take all these hits yourself?"

Jimmy was surprised his father knew the little dots were called hits. He shook his head. "Maybe a few," he said.

"There are four hundred of these things here," his mother said. "What are you going to do with the rest of them?"

There was silence. Jimmy didn't reply. He looked from one to the other and then down at the floor.

"You're going to sell them, aren't you?" His

mother said it for him. "You and that awful Kasso kid. You're going back to being a pusher, aren't you?"

"Ricky and I bought 'em. What more can I tell you?"

"The truth," his father said. "You might start with the truth."

"And the fuckin' day was going so well," Jimmy said.

"You know we talked about this." His mother didn't take her eyes from his face. "We talked about this more than once. You made promises to us."

"I know," he mumbled.

"Now you've broken those promises." Jimmy didn't reply. "You've broken your promises to us, you've gone back on the streets, you're selling drugs again. Everything you said you wouldn't do."

Jimmy kept looking at the carpet, and when he spoke his voice was low. "I can make more money with those things in one day than I can at that garage for a whole month."

"So it's money," his father said. "Is that why you're doing this? For money?"

"Sure. Why else?" His voice was still low.

"Then you've made your decision," his mother said. "There was a choice between the promises to us and the money from the street. Obviously these purple dots are more important to you than we are. Here," she said, holding out the strips of mescaline, "take these. They belong to you."

He raised his head, looking at her in puzzlement. He reached out his hand and retrieved the four hundred hits. "Why are you giving these back to me?"

"Because you'll need the money they'll bring to live on. We're asking you to leave, Jimmy. Pack a bag with your things and then leave. We don't care where you go or what you do. Not anymore. We've tried. Your father and I have tried until we are sick with trying. We don't know what else to do. You're eighteen years old. You're not a child anymore. You're a young man and you have made your decision. All we can do is pray you get your life together. Somehow."

"Look," Jimmy started to explain, "take these back. I'll straighten it out with Ricky. I don't think these are important enough to break up the family. I mean, I need a chance to—"

"You've already had all the chances we can give you," his father said. "Pack a bag and then get out."

"You're serious, aren't you?" the boy said.

"Very," his father replied. "Get that bag packed. You don't live here anymore."

Jimmy turned and almost stumbled into his bedroom. There were tears in his eyes. He didn't know if there were tears in his folks' eyes or not. He wasn't able to look them in the face to see. He got the cloth duffel bag from the closet floor. It was the one his mother had bought him when he was working out at the Y. He tossed a couple of pairs of blue jeans into it, added several T-shirts, some socks, and a pair of tennis shoes. He closed the zipper and went back into the living room. Maybe when they saw him with the bag in his hand, they would break down and let him stay.

His folks were not there. They were in the car driving aimlessly—anywhere—so they would not see him leave. He looked around the living room, opened the front door, and closed it softly behind him. He knew, deep inside, that this time his leaving was for real. He never set foot in that house again.

Ricky collapsed and was rushed by ambulance to the Long Island Jewish-Hillside Medical Center. He had been staying in a storage room behind the My Fair Lady Beauty Salon on Main Street. The doctors called his parents and told them he had double pneumonia. Immediately, Dick and Lynn Kasso asked the psychiatric director to commit him. To give him a complete mental examination and then keep him in there until he was mentally fit to be released. They told the hospital staff about his drug dependency. They told them that the school board had certified him as emotionally handicapped. They told them that their son had tried to kill himself more than once. Please, the Kassos begged, don't release him. It's for his own good.

The psychiatry department, after the medical department had taken care of the pneumonia, spent long hours talking with Ricky. He admitted everything his parents said was true. He was especially worried about the grave-digging charge. If he was convicted and sent to jail, he said, he'd kill himself. There were no two ways about it. The doctors felt he was confused, disturbed, and needed help, but they didn't think he was hearing voices, was schizophrenic, or suffering from delusions. They didn't think Ricky was a threat to society, only to himself. They said he was just showing "antisocial behavior." Therefore, he couldn't legally be committed against his will.

As soon as he was released from the hospital, he was back on the streets of Northport.

"Hell," he told Jimmy, "those fuckers in that place don't know what they're doing. I been that route before, man. I know what kind of answers they want to hear and I give it to them. I been examined by the best, man, and there ain't no shrink that's gonna take away my freedom. They're all so stupid. They can play their games with me if they want, but I always win those games, cause that's what I am, man, I am a winner!"

There was another spontaneous keg and Colonel Sanders party on April 21, 1984. It was in the family room of a teenage girl whose folks, again, were out of town for the weekend. Parents in Northport were—then—either gullible or careless. Or both.

Ricky and Jimmy were there. So were Gary Lauwers and Liz. So were Debbie and Billy Evans. So were Hammie and about ten other kids. All were in high school, or at least of high school age.

The tape deck was on, naturally, almost jumping off the table as heavy-metal great Motley Crue sang about being young and on the street in a song called "Danger."

184

Debbie was sitting close to Ricky, holding his hand but not really feeling it. Reality had mattered less and less to her since she met Ricky. Ricky and mescaline, Ricky and angel dust, Ricky and sex—those were her new realities, those were the things she thought about. Constantly. At the beginning of the semester she had been in the top one third of her class. Now, in the report card that was to come out next month, she was close to the bottom of the class. She didn't study, she didn't care. Who needs that? She had dope and love.

Jimmy and Liz were "a thing" and yet they weren't. She would fall all over him, muss his hair, and press her boobs against him in public, yet in private she was cold and unresponsive. Out of the bedroom and back on the party floor, she would flirt with other guys just to make Jimmy jealous. At first, he got angry. Afterward, he was merely amused.

"We almost didn't make it here, man," Ricky said to the hostess. "Jim and I did some traveling this evening. Went to the Bronx. Made a purchase or two." He was already high. He had started getting high on the angel dust as soon as he had pulled away from the supplier at the curb. Jimmy took the wheel before they got onto the Long Island Expressway. "Trip was worth it," Ricky continued. "Got enough here to pass to everybody." He reached into his denim jacket pocket and took out a bunch of small yellow-paper packets. He handed one to Liz.

She read the printing on the packet. "Sudden Impact," she said. "Sounds like a title for a movie."

"That's what's inside." Ricky smiled. "A sudden impact. It starts slow, then wham, man! I mean wham!" He gave one to Billy and another one to Hammie. Gary reached for one. Ricky scowled, then handed him one. "Take it easy with that shit," he said to Gary. "You know how you get when you have good stuff."

Gary grinned. "I love the *good* stuff!"

"Uh-huh," Jimmy said, "but you can't handle it. You get all fucked out of shape."

"Not like Ricky does," Gary protested. "He gets high and goes to sleep."

"That's better than thinking you're a Hells Angel," Jimmy replied, "ready to stomp the fuckin' world."

"I don't act like that when I'm high," the thin blond boy protested. "I keep my cool."

"Oh, Gary," Liz spoke up, "you ain't learned yet to play with the big boys. You still go home to your mama."

"Sure I do," he said quickly. "That's where I live. At least I still have a mama. I still got some place to go. I don't have to sleep in the streets like some people do."

"You bitin' the hand that feeds you?" Ricky scowled at him. "I just gave you a packet of good stuff—*gave* you—and you talkin' bad about *me?*" Ricky struggled to get off the sofa, but his knees weren't cooperating with his feet. "You treat me with some respect, creep. I'm the one that looks out after you."

"Yeah," said Debbie proudly, "he's the Acid King."

186

"I don't need no king," Gary replied.

"You need a fist up your ass," Ricky said hoarsely. "If I wasn't the *king*, I'd do it personally, but kings don't bother with lowlife. They've got other things on their minds."

"Yeah," Debbie said to Gary, "kings are too important to fool with fuckers."

"My," said Liz, "is that the *queen* speaking?"

"You bet your ass," Ricky said, and reached out to tousle Debbie's hair.

There was a lull in the activities in the kitchen and bathroom while the kids mixed their packets of Sudden Impact with their marijuana and rolled the papers tightly. Angel dust, a white powder with the official name phencyclidine or 1-(1-phenylcyclohexyl) piperidine was developed in the late 1950s as an anesthetic. It was designed to send the surgical patient "out of the body," not only to eliminate all physical pain, but to make the patient feel "totally removed" from what was happening to his own body during surgery. The drug worked —but there was one slight problem. Patients complained and raved on the operating table. They were very often delusional and irrational when recovering from the effects. When doctors tried the tranquilizer on dogs and cats, the animals went berserk and many had to be put to death. Both humans and animals had bad trips. A University of Michigan survey found that one in ten high school seniors had tried the drug at some time.

Ricky had his dosages all figured out. Kids watched him in awe. He would take one packet, wait ten minutes, then take another. Then a shot of booze. A two-hour wait and then another packet. That night he followed his pattern, and when he fell asleep on the sofa Debbie was with him and also asleep.

The party went on without him. Kids were floating on their one packets, the beer and the music were ever flowing. Jimmy and Liz had gone into a bedroom and shut the door. They weren't missed. Angel dust creates individual worlds for each user. Vast realms of space can be compressed into a teacup. Galaxies can be impaled on the hand of a clock. Ricky and Debbie asleep, Jimmy and Liz making out, that was unimportant to the success of the party. The party was going on privately, in individual brain cells.

Gary had not smoked his packet. He had sniffed it, smiled, and commented on it, but he hadn't consumed it. He had put it in his pocket. For use later . . . or for sale later, whichever came first.

Gary sat on the floor, his back to the wall as he nursed a beer. He shifted his body in time with the music and watched what was happening. From his vantage point, the floor shot upward into bodies and faces, he thought the kids at this party looked ridiculous. They were trying to act like adults, trying to look like they were having fun. No one paid him any attention. Few kids did. He was the loner. The perpetual outsider. Even when he was *in* a group most kids didn't consider him *part* of the group. None of the girls at the party wanted to dance with him. It wasn't that he was ugly or stupid. He was a good-looking kid, slender, with deep-set blue eyes and longish sandy-blond hair. In school, he had taken home good grades. Not the best report card in the class, but not a dunce either. When he dropped out his parents were stunned. The best word to describe him would be "average." Gary Lauwers was an "average" American teenager.

Until he formed his attachment to Ricky and started taking drugs.

He tapped his foot to the music and let his eyes move slowly around the room, seeing the kids in those funny positions in chairs, in each other's laps, holding up the walls. His eyes traveled to Debbie, asleep against Ricky. They went up her blue jeans and over to her breasts. Nice breasts, he said to himself. Nice face too. Flushed from the booze and dope, but a nice face. Then he looked at Ricky, asleep against Debbie, his blue-jeaned legs, thin arms poking from his T-shirt and denim jacket. At his wrists were four studded leather bracelets. Ricky had affected those recently along with a wooden cross on his chest—Gary smiled, the cross was inverted—and a swastika earring in his left ear. His face, normally thin, was still sunken from the bout with pneumonia, and his hair, that mass of brown curls that everyone said was his best feature, was covered with a blue polka-dot bandanna. His eyes, the ones that could bore through steel, were closed.

Then Gary's eyes caught the speck of yellow peeking out of Ricky's jacket pocket. There was a slight bulge to the pocket. Gary knew Ricky had more packets of angel dust. He had watched him hand them out, then watched as he put the rest in his pocket.

Quickly, Gary took in the others around the room. They were all busy. Nobody was paying him any attention. He got to his feet, trying to be nonchalant about such a normal movement, yet inside his heart was pounding. He walked past Ricky, carefully, listening to his steady breathing, wanting to make damn sure the anesthetic was doing its job. Then he walked over to the beer keg, slowly drew himself another glass, and walked back to Ricky. "You wanna beer, Rick?" he said quietly. Of course, Ricky didn't answer. "I thought," said Gary deliberately a little louder in case anybody was paying attention, "you'd like a drink."

He sat on the sofa, perched on the edge, and extended his left hand toward Ricky. The sleeping Acid King didn't move. "Great beer, man," Gary said, and as he said it his right hand darted fast to Ricky's jacket, then his fingers pulled out several packets of Sudden Impact. Gary palmed them, slid from the sofa, stood up, and said, "Okay. Lemme know and I'll get you a beer when you're ready." Then his right hand went into his own blue-jean pocket, where the packets fell silently to the bottom like a snake depositing her eggs.

Gary's guardian angel must have shuddered and made the sign of the cross. The noiseless depositing of those yellow packets was to cause an explosion that would shake and forever alter the village of Northport, an explosion that would be televised around the world.

190

PART TWO

April to July 1984

CHAPTER ONE

"There's the little son of a bitch!" Ricky shouted, and ran across the parking lot at the foot of Main Street that bordered the waterfront. "Help me get that fucker!"

Gary had been heading toward the gazebo. He heard the shouting, stopped, turned, saw Ricky and the others running for him, and didn't know what to do. So he just stood his ground.

Ricky was the first to reach him. He grabbed him by the front of his denim jacket and started shaking him. "I want those hits, you little fucker!" he screamed. "I want them *now!*"

"I don't know what you're talking about, man," Gary managed to say.

"The packets you stole from me at the party last night. I want them, man. They belong to *me!*"

"I ain't got any hits, man," Gary protested.

"I seen you take them out of Ricky's pocket, man," Hammie said. "He was sleeping and you stole them."

"I didn't," Gary said, "I don't know what you're talking about." He struggled to get loose, but Ricky held tight.

"There were ten of them, man," Ricky was yelling. "Ten fuckin' packets! I want them!"

"I ain't got them," Gary insisted. "Honest!"

"Honest?" Ricky hauled off with his free hand and slapped Gary sharply across the face. "Look, you scumbag. You stole from me and I want my merchandise. I want it now! You hear me, fucker?" He slapped Gary again.

Gary crumbled and sank to his knees. Two adult couples, on their way to view the boats in the harbor, looked away. "I only got half of them, man," Gary said.

Hammie started searching Gary's jacket and Gary tried to twist away. Ricky's hand—a fist this time—came crashing into the boy's face. Gary fell to the ground and lay there quietly while Hammie searched him. In his back pocket, tucked between the pages of Gary's Satanic primer, Hammie found five of the yellow-paper packets. He handed them to Ricky.

"Where are the rest of them?" Ricky shouted.

"I smoked them, man."

"Shit!" Ricky spat on the ground, almost hitting Gary. "You didn't smoke them. You couldn't have smoked five packets and be walking your ass around town today. No way! Now you still got 'em and I want 'em!"

"I'll pay you for the rest," Gary whimpered. "I'll pay you. I promise."

"You owe me fifty bucks and I want it now!"

"I ain't got any money, man. Not on me."

Hammie nodded. His search hadn't turned up any money in Gary's jeans.

"You go home and you tell your mommie you need fifty bucks and then you get your skinny ass back here and you pay me!"

"I can't ask my folks for it!" Gary was almost crying.

"Well, you ask somebody's folks, you fucker, because I'd better see you back here with the cash. And fast!" Ricky swung his right foot back, preparing to kick Gary while he was down.

"No, don't!" Gary yelled. "I'll get the bread! I'll be right back."

"You'd better, you piece of turd!" Ricky let go and his foot caught Gary sharply in his ribs. The boy curled up, instantly, like paper aflame. "Get the fuck out of my sight!" Ricky commanded. He kicked again and Gary screamed and rolled away, trying to ward off another blow. Ricky's foot caught him in the small of his back.

"Ricky," Hammie said, "that's enough. You made your point."

Ricky stood over Gary, spread-eagled, and spat in his face. "Little fucker said he was my friend. A friend don't steal from a friend. Friends don't steal when other friends are asleep. Especially, friends don't steal dope from each other. And," he said loud enough for everyone in earshot to hear him, "nobody steals from the Acid King! Nobody!"

Hammie put his hand on Ricky's arm. "Come on," he said, "let the kid go. Let him go home and get the bread. Okay?"

Ricky grunted and stepped back. Gary just lay there looking up at him. "Well, shit eater! Move!" Ricky raised his foot again and Gary scrambled to his feet. He scurried toward Main Street, both running and limping, and the other boys watched until he had disappeared amid the cars and pedestrians.

"I don't care who," Ricky said to no one in particular, "nobody steals from the Acid King!"

CHAPTER TWO

They crowded into Hammie's Volkswagen:
Ricky, Jimmy, Billy, Hammie, of course, and
white-haired Pat Pagan. The trip had been Pat's
idea. He had been sober when he suggested it and
Ricky immediately thought it was a great idea.
April 30 was, Pat explained, *Walpurgisnacht*—the
night when witches roamed the world and Satan
celebrated with his chosen few.

Pat and Ricky had decided such an important
date deserved a special place to celebrate it. They
had one nearby: *that* house in Amityville.

The sun had gone down by the time Hammie
stopped at Pat's apartment while he went in and
got a grocery bag full of paraphernalia. They
stopped at a liquor store and bought a couple of

bottles of cheap wine (for the demons) and a couple of bottles of cheap vodka (for themselves). Ricky had marijuana, mescaline, and angel dust. Whatever anyone wanted, he'd hand it out that night for free.

They drove from Northport over to Huntington and then straight down 110 to the town of Amityville. It's only about a half-hour drive from expensively preserved Northport to the rather ramshackle town of Amityville.

Perhaps the biggest difference between the two coastal towns is their citizens. Northporters are almost invariably white, even the tan ones beside their swimming pools or on their boat decks. In Amityville the many dark skins have more to do with African slave ships than luxury yachts. The Long Island Expressway bisects the island from west to east and the socially conscious Islander divides his terrain by it. Everything to the south of it is not "quality." Everything to the north of it is. Northport, of course, is *north*.

Hammie knew how to get to the house. He had been there before. When his parents moved to Long Island one of the first "tourist" spots they wanted to see was the famous haunted house in Amityville. They had been disappointed by it. They stood in front of the cast-iron fence the new owners had put around it and tried to peer through the many bushes that had been planted to shield it. It had been repainted—yellow with red-trimmed shutters. Hammie and his folks stood there waiting for a face to appear at the upstairs curved window or a swarm of flies to swoop through the yard or at least a shutter to start banging in the windless afternoon. Nothing happened. Hammie's mother had remarked that the book was much more believable—whatever that meant.

Hammie pulled the Volkswagen up to the curb and parked in front of the house next door. It was suddenly very dark. "Now what?" he asked.

"Let's get out," said Pat, "and go over there." He pointed to the house directly across the narrow street. It was a corner lot with a wide lawn and the residence sitting some distance back. The four teenagers and the white-haired older man scurried from the parked car to the darkness of the lawn.

"There's a light on in the house." Jimmy pointed at the famous structure. "Somebody's home over there."

"Probably a ghost," Billy whispered, and stepped a little closer to Jimmy.

"Ghosts don't turn on lights," Ricky said. "What the fuck they need a light for?"

"Maybe to see if they have a spot on their sheet," Hammie giggled nervously.

"Very funny, you guys," Pat said. "Let's get set up." He took a red plastic sheet from the paper bag and smoothed it out on the ground. Even though it was dark and they were in shadows, the boys could see the black five-pointed star and the other symbols that had been grooved into the plastic. "This is my outside altar," he explained, "for the ground and places like that." Then he took five black candles, about ten inches high, and stuck them into the holes that had been cut into each point of the star. There was a sixth candle remaining. He didn't light them. Out of a blue box he took a strand of beads and placed them in the center of the talisman. Then came the necklace of skulls.

"Those are real snake skulls, man," Ricky said to the others. "Came from the jungles in Africa. Didn't they, Pat?"

The white-haired man nodded. Then he took out a hunk of rock crystal and put it next to the skulls. Then he added what looked like metal filings, and then a silver coin. "Give me one of those bottles of wine," he said, pointing to the bag from the liquor store. He took it and unscrewed the cap. He poured about half the wine around the outer edge of the red plastic and set the bottle in the center with the other objects.

"What d'ya do that for?" Jimmy asked. "That's good wine."

"It's a libation," the man said. "It's for Satan. I pour it into his earth, and when he tastes it he'll want more. Then he'll have to reach for the bottle in the middle of the altar." He grinned at them, but they could see he wasn't kidding. "Old Satan just doesn't come around for nothin'. He likes to get presents. He likes to get paid."

"He comes for nothin' for Ricky," Billy said. "Ricky says all he has to do is ask and Satan is right there."

Pat started to laugh, and Ricky turned angrily toward Billy. "Shut the fuck up, man!" Then to Pat, in a calmer voice: "That ain't exactly how it works, Billy, just—"

"Yeah, man," Pat said, still smiling, "I know."

Jimmy glanced nervously at the house behind

them. They were on someone else's property and the people were at home. There were lights downstairs and in one upstairs bedroom. "How long's this gonna take?" he asked.

"Not long," Pat said. "Rick, lemme have one of your *good* cigarettes." He stretched his hand and Ricky put a marijuana and angel-dust reefer in it. Billy gave him a light with his Bic. Pat inhaled, let the smoke fill him, then exhaled softly. "Man, that's smooth," he said. "Feels so fine."

"You other guys want one?" Ricky handed each kid a cigarette. Again, Billy lit them. In the darkness the white smoke couldn't be seen, but anyone driving by with an open window would have recognized the tart, minty scent. They all agreed it was real good weed. "Now what?" Ricky asked Pat.

The man knelt down by the plastic altar and ordered them to do the same. They did, forming a semicircle around the red mat. Pat took a bandanna out of his army-issue camouflage jacket and tied his hair back off his shoulders. "Don't want to catch fire," he said, even though no one asked. They thought it was part of the ritual. "Billy"— Pat stretched his hand again—"lemme have your lighter." Billy passed it to him. "Okay, you guys. I'm gonna begin now. Pay attention and don't make a lot of noise. You guys gotta concentrate on what I'm doin'." They nodded. Pat flicked the lighter, and when the flame appeared he reached across the altar and lit one candle. "O Satan," he intoned, "I light this candle in your honor. To call you and to tell you we have arrived and are waiting for you." Then the lighter was relit and a second candle flared awake. "O Satan, I light this candle for my soul. It's here exposed in the night, waiting for you to take it and do with it whatever you choose."

"Jesus!" Hammie shuddered.

Pat glared at him. "I light this third candle for the souls of the guys here with me tonight. They are young souls and eager souls and they are ready to be yours if you want them to be." Jimmy was about to protest, but he decided against saying anything out loud. He thought the whole thing was a crock. "The fourth candle," Pat said as it burst into life, "is for our desires. We love you, Satan. We will follow you, Satan, but we need things here on earth. We need things like money and food and that kind of stuff. Please, O Lord of Darkness, grant each of us our material wishes." He turned and looked at the faces that were illuminated by the burning candles. "Okay, you guys, each of you start thinking of some things you really want. I mean *really* want. Satan don't grant pissant favors, just the big things. Think about it, but don't say it out loud. It takes away some of the energy when you say it out loud. He can read your minds." The boys looked at him and then at each other. Billy shrugged. Hammie looked thoughtful, trying to figure out what he needed that his parents hadn't already given him. Jimmy was thinking money and a new car.

"California," Ricky said aloud. "That's what I want. I want to go to California, get the fuck out of here."

"I said don't say it aloud," Pat's voice rose quickly.

Jimmy grinned and nudged Ricky. "You ain't going to California, man. You just fucked it up." He laughed. Jimmy never believed Ricky would make it out there anyway. "You done shit on your own dream." And he laughed again.

Ricky glared at his friend. "Oh, fuck you, Troiano. Satan's my main man. He'll deliver California to me when it's time."

"I thought I told you guys to keep quiet," Pat said loudly. "Jesus Christ, can't you have any reverence for anything? I mean, this is a serious *religious* ceremony here! This ain't some scumbag dopers meeting."

"I'm sorry," Jimmy apologized.

"Yeah, man, me too," added Ricky.

Pat went back to his ritual. "O Satan, I light this fifth candle so that you can see your way to destroying all my enemies and the enemies of each guy here tonight. Kill them! Smash them! Grind them into graveyard dust! O Satan, hear my prayer. See my candle flame. Grant my favor." He glanced up at the faces hunched over the glowing altar. "Okay, now you guys think of who you want killed. See your enemy or enemies and see them lying dead somewhere."

"I ain't got any enemies," Billy protested. He didn't like the idea of wishing people dead. It went against his Christian upbringing.

"I don't either," said Hammie. "Couple of teachers I'd like to see take the next rocket to the moon, but none that I want to see dead."

203

Jimmy shook his head. "Nobody I want either. How about you, Ricky? You wanna kill off your old man?"

Ricky grimaced. "No, not really. I don't want him fuckin' up my life no more, but I don't want him dead. Who'd take care of my mother and my sisters? Nah, I guess I don't want to kill anybody either."

"How about Gary Lauwers?" Hammie asked. "He still hasn't paid you for those packets he stole."

"Oh, yeah." Ricky was starting to feel the effects of the dust in his cigarette. "I forgot about that little creep. Yeah"—he smiled—"yeah, that's a good idea. Satan can get rid of Gary Lauwers. Chop him up and put him in a hole. Be better for everybody. Period. The end."

"Shit, man," Billy said. "That's heavy stuff."

"Sure it is," Pat said. "This is serious business."

"Shit, man," Billy said again, and shook his head slowly. The dope was getting to his brain too.

Pat reached out for the last unlit candle. "O Satan, I light this sixth candle, this special final candle for you. For you personally! It is my offering to you along with everything on this altar. Let it guide you to us. Let you see our glow and let you come—in person—to where we await you. O great one, O King of Darkness and rightful heir to all creation, we await you. We need you. We love you!" He put his hand into a jacket pocket and took out some red powder. He put it in the palm of his hand and blew it into the candle flames. They rose up, sparkling and sputtering and smoking.

Their snapping, in the drug-filled minds around the altar, seemed as loud as fireworks exploding.

"Oh, wow!" Ricky said. "That's great!"

"Yeah," the others added almost in unison.

Pat blew another pinch of the powder into the flames. Again they rose and sputtered. Then he began to chant. He closed his eyes, put his hands together in prayer, and started mumbling in a low voice. None of the boys understood the words. It sounded like nothing they had ever heard before. They didn't care anyway. The sounds just mingled with the flames and the smoke and the darkness and the PCP wafting lazily through the hallways and staircases and empty rooms of their brains. It was all so cool, man. It was all so fine.

It was all so shattered when the policeman's foot kicked the altar and sent it buckling up and over onto the sidewalk.

"What the hell do you creeps think you're doing?" the officer asked loudly.

"My stuff!" Pat screamed. "You ruined my stuff!" He lunged for the policeman's legs but the man stepped back and Pat's arms locked around empty air. He landed, face-first, in the dirt. "That's my stuff out there," he wailed. "Why did you do that to my stuff?"

The other cop got out of the patrol car and joined the group. He sniffed the air and wasn't sure what he smelled—pot, candles, or incense. "You guys from around here?" he asked.

They shook their heads. "Northport," Billy said.

"Hauppauge," Hammie said.

"What are you doing here?" the cop asked. "Why aren't you kids home in bed?"

"It was a ritual," Pat whined, his face still buried in the lawn. "A ritual. It's part of our religion."

"This ain't Sunday," said the cop.

"You don't understand." Ricky felt he had to take charge of the group now that the angel dust and the shock of destruction had overtaken Pat. "We're here to worship Satan. Tonight is a special night."

"Oh, yeah?" the cop looked at the thin teenager. "I'm a Catholic myself. What's so special about tonight and why here in Amityville?"

"Because"—Ricky pointed across the street at the famous house—"Satan lives over there, man. In that place over there."

"No"—the second cop shook his head—"he doesn't live there. A private citizen and his family live there. And another family lives where you are trespassing now. You are on private property and I'll give you five minutes to collect your stuff and get your asses out of here."

"You don't fuck with us, man," said Ricky, still in command. "We don't go anywhere we don't want to go."

"You'll go to jail, kid, in about two seconds if I get any more of your lip." The cop took out a flashlight and shone it on Pat. "You," he said, "get off the ground and pick up your junk over there. Move!"

Another patrol car came by and pointed its headlights at the scene, making each player stand out in detailed relief, creating enormous sharp shadows across the lawn. The boys managed to get Pat over to the Volkswagen and prop him up in the backseat, the debris from the ceremony stacked hastily around him. Hammie got behind the wheel, and the others crowded in the best they could.

"Now you kids get out of here." The cop stuck his head in the window, then flashed his light on Pat. "And take that fool home and put him to bed."

"He's a 'Nam vet," Ricky said.

"Then let me change that to take that *pathetic* fool home and put him to bed."

"Don't hassle us, man," Ricky said. "We got Satan on our side. We got *powers.*"

"And I've got *this* on my side." The cop took out his billy club. "You want a taste of *my* powers, punk?"

"Satan will get you!" Pat suddenly shouted from the backseat. "Satan will avenge us!"

"Look, buddy," the first policeman said, "if you hadn't been in 'Nam, I'd bring you in on charges of contributing to the delinquency of minors. But I was in 'Nam. I know where you been and I know what you've been going through back here. Get yourself some help. Stop smoking that stuff. Get your act together. Maybe you still have some time."

"Satan is my lord!" Pat shouted, his eyes glazed over.

"Take him home," the cop said to Hammie. He shook his head. "Maybe he's still got some time."

A week or so had passed and Ricky still talked to people about the ritual in Amityville. He was proud of it, impressed by it, and pissed by the fact that the police had profaned it. He remembered the candles and the sputtering incense. He didn't, however, remember willing death to Gary Lauwers. When Jimmy reminded him of it he paused, shook his head, and then grinned. "Not a bad idea, man. That little fucker had better pay me and soon!"

Gary had not come around with the cash, even though Ricky had gone after him one afternoon and slapped him so hard Gary's nose bled. Gary swore he was going to get a job, he was going to borrow the money, he'd even steal it if necessary, but yes, Ricky would be paid. Gary had been arrested for theft once. Ricky reminded him how easily he could raise the cash. Some kids called Gary "Midnight Auto" because of his ability to open parked cars after dark and steal their radios and tape decks. Gary was also an adept shoplifter. In a store, wearing a baggy coat or sweater, his small thin arm would dart like a lizard's tongue and—snap!—the item would be whisked off the counter and under his clothes.

Gary could have paid Ricky the fifty dollars, but the longer he delayed repaying and the more kids that knew about it, the bigger and braver he would seem. No one defied Ricky. Gary was always being put down. Maybe this time kids would see that little Gary/David could get the best of mighty Ricky/Goliath.

Jimmy and Ricky met here, at Northport Junior High School. (Photo by Jim Peppler/*Newsday*)

The Midway.
(Photo by Jim Peppler/*Newsday*)

Main Street, Northport, New York. (Nik Kleinberg/NYT Pictures)

Gary Lauwers's body was found in this shallow grave in Aztakea Woods. (© *New York Post*)

Ricky Kasso enters the courtroom to be arraigned for murder. (Mary McLoughlin/© *New York Post*)

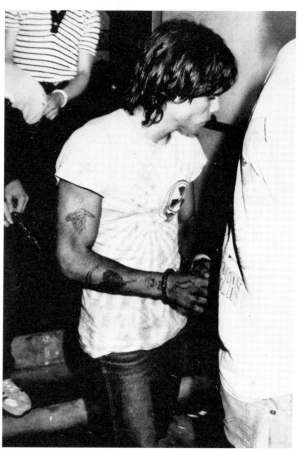

Jimmy Troiano at his arraignment.
(New York *Daily News* Photo)

Jimmy Troiano in jail. (Photo by George Ageroplos/*Newsday*)

The Gazebo at Cow Harbor Park, where Jimmy, Ricky, and Gary met the night of the murder.
(New York *Daily News* Photo)

Graffiti on boardwalk at Cow Harbor Park.
(New York *Daily News* Photo)

Troiano reenacted the night's events for the police.
(Photo by Ari Mintz/*Newsday*)

Albert Quinones, a witness for
the prosecution, being escorted
into court in Riverhead, Long
Island. (Michael P. Alexander/NYT
Pictures)

Gary Lauwers's funeral. His parents follow the coffin out of the church. (New York *Daily News* Photo)

* * *

Ricky led his ragged blue-jeaned pack across the streets of Northport. It was May, school was just about out, and the tourists were fluttering back into town, filling the stores and the dockside with their bright summer colors.

"Here," the clean-cut young man said, handing a brochure to Ricky. "You might like to read this."

Ricky and some of his followers were standing around Main Street, wondering what to do and where to go to do it. "What's this shit?" Ricky took the folded paper. "Can I smoke this?" He laughed and grinned. The others with him also laughed.

"It's about Christ and what He can do for you," the young man said. "I'm from the Northport Baptist Church. We're having a teenage membership drive. I thought you guys would be interested."

"Interested in what?" Ricky asked, confident all eyes were still on him.

"In coming to the church. In hearing what Christ can do when He enters your life."

"Christ?" Ricky's voice rose. "You're trying to sell me Christ?"

"I'm not trying to sell you anything," the clean-shaven young man said. "I just think you should read what Christ can do for you. How Christ can help you."

"Help me? Help *me?*" Ricky crumpled the tract and threw it back into the Baptist's face. "Christ can't help me! Don't you know who I am?" He raised his arms and shouted, "I am Satan! He is my main man! Satan is going to burn your precious Christ! Satan will destroy your God and take his

209

rightful place as ruler of this planet!" He advanced on the young missionary. "Do you hear me? Do you understand my words, punk?"

The young man hurried away down the street without even looking back.

"Ain't nobody gonna shove their fuckin' Jesus in my face, man," Ricky told his group. They nodded and some of them even smiled, but all of them— the oldest was about fourteen—were appalled that Ricky had become so violent so quickly and that Jesus's name had been spoken so in vain. It went against everything they had ever been taught in Sunday school.

Ricky and Jimmy, Ricky and Billy, Ricky and Hammie made more and more trips into the Bronx to buy marijuana, angel dust, and mescaline. The more Ricky bought, the more he took himself. He gave away much of it, but whatever cash he made went back to buying more dope. His living expenses were nil. He didn't have a car so there were no bank payments or tank fill-ups. He didn't need clothing—the jeans and the tennis shoes were worn day after day. So was the denim jacket. He could always borrow a clean T-shirt from a friend when the one he was wearing got so dirty it almost stood by itself. Rent was no problem either. With the coming of warmer weather, there were all sorts of places to sleep: the park, the gazebo, a lumberyard, a friend's back porch, a parked car, Aztakea Woods, a boat in the harbor, lots of places.

"When you do a lot of dope," Jimmy recalled, "you don't need a lot of sleep. If you start smoking it in the afternoon, you are wide awake all night. So you don't need a bed and a bathroom, you just need space, outside space to roam in. Many times when the weather got nice, Ricky would be awake all night and sleep during the day. The cops don't bother a kid who's asleep on a park bench during the day."

It was also that May when Pat Pagan staggered into the park by the harbor looking for Ricky. He found him, with several of his young camp followers, sitting on the steps of the white wooden Victorian bandstand. The Village of Northport has its own summer band. They give free concerts and people bring folding chairs and children and sandwiches and dogs and sit under the trees in the moonlight and listen to Souza. This afternoon the dopers were in command of the stand.

"Hey, man, how's it goin'?" Pat plopped himself down, heavily, beside Ricky. "How you been?"

"Okay, man," Ricky replied. "What's with you? Ain't seen you in a few days."

"Been sick, man. Real sick. Headaches and throwin' up and shit like that. Only today have I been able to get out of bed. Didn't think I'd make it over here. Been lookin' for you."

"Why?"

"I need some bread, man, I gotta have about ninety dollars. My landlord's yellin' that I ain't paid him this week. No food in the house either, man." He looked into Ricky's eyes. "Will you? Just till my government check gets here?"

"It ain't due for two weeks yet," Ricky said.

"I know, man, and I'll pay you in two weeks."

Ricky shook his head. "Naw, man, you'll piss that check away the minute you cash it. Won't be nothin' left to repay me with."

"Come on, man, I need the bread. I'll pay you. I promise."

"Just like Gary Lauwers promised me he'd pay me." Ricky spat between his teeth. "That little fucker."

"I ain't no Gary," Pat said. "Come on, man, I know you got it. Just for a couple of weeks." Pat shuddered and swallowed to keep down the bile that was rising in his throat. His head ached and his intestines were raw from the diarrhea that had seized his insides for the last several days. "I got this bug, man," he said weakly, "picked it up in 'Nam. It hits every once in awhile. I need the bread, man. Just loan it to me." Both his eyes and the tone in his voice were pleading.

"No, man," Ricky shook his head. He felt a sense of power now. Power over this man who was his teacher, who was his Satanic better. *Was.* Ricky decided, then and there, that he didn't need this white-haired fool any longer. He was out of it. Drugs and some gook bug had destroyed Pat's powers. Ricky was in charge now, now that the tables had turned and his "mentor" had come crawling to him.

"Ricky"—Pat was whimpering now—"I always been your buddy. I always showed you what you wanted to know. I was always there with you when you needed help. Okay now, man, I need

212

help. I'm comin' to you. What the fuck do you want me to do, get on my knees and beg?"

"No." Ricky shook his head. "I don't want you to do that. That ain't necessary. I won't loan you the money. I'll give you the money." Pat's eyes lit up. "I'll give you the bread in exchange."

"Exchange?" Pat's eyes narrowed. "In exchange for what?"

"That bronze thing around your neck. The thing you got in 'Nam. You sell me that thing and I'll give you the bread."

Pat tried to get up from the steps, but Ricky pulled him back down. "No way, man," said the vet, "this is my pride. This is what keeps me going." He put his hands to his chest, feeling the bronze medallion under his shirt. "Just loan me the bread," he said. "I can't sell this. No way."

"Then no way can I give you ninety bucks," Ricky said.

"I promise you. I'll repay you." The man was almost crying in his pain.

"Your promises aren't worth shit," the boy replied. "You want cash and I want that medallion. Even exchange. It's that simple." Ricky grinned at the kids who were taking this all in. None of them grinned back.

"No!" The white-haired man stood suddenly, somehow finding the strength to walk off the steps and start across the manicured park lawn. "Fuck you, Kasso!" he turned and shouted. "I don't need you. You need *me!* I don't need *you!*"

Ricky's long legs unfolded swiftly and he was beside the man in an instant. "I am Satan's man

213

around here!" he screamed. "I don't need nobody! I don't need you, you old fucker!"

Pat turned to run, but Ricky stuck out one of his feet and Pat fell over it, collapsing onto the ground. Ricky was on him, pushing him over onto his back. He slammed a fist into the man's jaw and then slammed another time as Pat tried to break the boy's grip.

"You been in 'Nam!" Ricky sneered. "Big fuckin' deal! You gonna be my teacher! Shit, man, I don't need no teacher! I graduated! I'm Satan now! You're a nobody! A has-been! I don't need you. Nobody needs you! You understand, you drunken old sucker? You understand?"

Pat tried to speak but could do no more than lie stunned on the ground.

"And since you aren't important anymore," Ricky continued, "you won't need *this* anymore either!" Ricky's hands tore at the buttons on Pat's shirt and exposed the Satanic bronze medal to the sunlight. "This is mine now," Ricky said loudly. "I won it. I deserve it!" Ricky grabbed the medal and with one swift movement lifted it up and over Pat's head. He jumped to his feet, the medal dangling from its leather cord. "Take a last look at it, you old fuck," Ricky yelled. "It's mine now! See?" He quickly slipped it over his head. The medallion hung in the center of his chest. "See that, old man? See that?"

Pat put his hands over his eyes and started sobbing. They were the tears of a strong man defeated. A man who knew when his end had come.

214

He tried to beg Ricky but the words were lost in a gush amid blood and vomit.

"Come on," Ricky motioned to the kids who sat motionless on the steps. "Let's get a change of scenery. This place sucks."

The band followed its leader. They walked far around the man who was crying on the lawn. None of them looked at him. It was almost indecent.

After some time had passed, Pat managed to sit up, then stand up, then finally stagger up Main Street to the police station. He reported that Ricky Kasso had beaten him up and has stolen his medallion. The police promised they would speak to Ricky about it. They never did.

Ricky's doped-up violence continued that same afternoon. He had just finished smoking a marijuana cigarette laced with angel dust and had just finished taking two hits of mescaline when he saw Gary Lauwers walking down the street. Main Street, the picturesque village thoroughfare with its antique shoppes and real estate agents and historical society. Ricky started to run for Gary. He was followed by Jimmy and a boy named Albert Quinones. Albert was a sometime friend of the Acid King, a beefy dark-haired youth who didn't talk too much.

"Hey, you son of a bitch!" Ricky grabbed Gary and slapped him across the face. "I want my fifty bucks, man! Now, man!"

"I ain't got it," Gary squealed. "I told you. When I get it, you'll get it."

They were standing in front of Trinity Church, a large white-painted wooden structure that sits inside the commercial area of Main Street. There is a parking lot on one side and a narrow space behind the church. "Take him around back," Ricky ordered. Jimmy and Albert steered Gary around back. Ricky grabbed the boy and slammed him up against the side of the building. "I want my bread, man, and I want it now."

Ricky pulled his hand back to hit Gary when Albert grabbed his arm. "Take off that ring, man," Albert said. "You could do real damage to his face with that thing."

Ricky looked at the cheap metal skull's-head ring he had been wearing for the past few days. He'd bought it in a head shop on one of his doping trips to the Bronx. Off came the ring, then down came the fist against Gary's face. Three times and with force. Ricky watched the boy crumple onto the ground. Then he put his scowling face next to Gary's bleeding one. "Look," he said, "this is the last time I'm gonna beat you up. If you don't pay me what you owe me, it'll be much worse the next time I catch you. I'm warning you. *Much* worse." Then Ricky turned and went back out onto the street. "Come on," he said to Jimmy and Albert. "I feel good. Let's go to Billy's place and have some of his old man's booze."

Gary sat with his back against the church building for a while, waiting for his head to stop thumping and his lip to stop bleeding. He felt for the knife he carried inside his denim jacket. It was still there. He had bought it to defend himself against

216

Ricky, but he hadn't had time to use it. "I'll be the one to get you, asshole," Gary said aloud. "I see you first, man, you're gonna get it."

"I told Gary more than once he should pay Ricky and stop all this shit," Jimmy recalls. "He told me he was going to but he never did. The stories in the newspapers all said that Gary had paid Ricky. They were wrong. Ricky never saw a dime of that bread Gary owed him. The reporters wrote that stuff because they were trying to make Gary out as some sort of goody-goody and me and Ricky as some kind of monsters from outer space. Everyone kept saying 'oh, poor Gary' this and 'oh, poor Gary' that, but the truth is, he was just another scumbag, another doper. He ran away from home several times and he was arrested several times and he beat little kids up. But nobody remembered any of that. They wanted to make him out to be some kind of angel. I didn't really know Gary that well, but what I saw, I didn't like. Ricky beat Gary up five different times. The fifth time was the last time."

CHAPTER THREE

David Condit remembers having both Ricky and Jimmy in his classes. He taught music in the Northport school system until he resigned in 1985. "I'm amazed that any kid survives around here," he says, "but they do. Kids are tough. They have to be. We live with this myth that we are part of New York City, part of the glamour and Broadway shows and all that. It's the Long Island syndrome and it's been carried down to every level. Northport is someplace close to heaven and then there's the rest of the world. Sunday night, at the dock, all those multimillion-dollar yachts and the people sitting in deck chairs so the less fortunate can stroll by and admire them.

"There's a push now to be the best school district in the country, to keep the SAT's way up. Then the kids who aren't the brightest get shoved aside. There are all kinds of educational programs going on that are well funded and so on but the local administrators don't know how to handle them.

"The kids here have been given this great gift. The gift is that they are part of Northport and all they have to do is live up to that obligation. To be the very best. What happens at fourteen or fifteen when a kid realizes he's *not* the best? What does he do? Lie? Commit suicide? Drop out? Move away? Take dope? When you believe you're a loser, you *are* a loser, especially if your own peers are telling you that. They may not say it in words, but they are saying it in their actions in the way they relate —or don't relate—to you. You're sitting in a classroom with thirty other people and the teacher never calls on you, you get the message pretty quickly.

"You sit in Skipper's Restaurant on Main Street, with a window onto the park, and you can see them selling drugs right across the street. Talented kids from Northport get to go to college and then they drop out. They were catered to in Northport, catered to by a system striving for excellence, but when they get to the university they are just one of the crowd and they can't handle it.

"You take kids like Kasso and Troiano and ignore their emotions long enough and they're going to resent it and react to it, especially at an age when they are reaching out for love and understanding. No matter how tough an attitude they may have, they want love. If their family life is less than desirable, it just adds to it. We deal with the intellect of kids and not their emotional development. We just don't give a shit."

Debbie's mother was sitting at her desk, writing out checks, when she paused and looked at her daughter, who was stretched out on the sofa watching television. "Today is June 3," the woman said.

"So?" Debbie replied.

"You should have a report card. School's almost out for the year. Isn't it?"

"Uh-huh."

"Well, where's your report card?"

"I don't know."

"You don't know?" Her mother's voice rose. "What do you mean you don't know? You always have a report card around this time." She stared at her daughter, unhappy with what she had been noticing these past few months, unhappy with the way the girl had been acting. "Are you going to answer me? I want to see your grades."

"I tore it up." Debbie didn't take her eyes from the flickering screen.

"Tore it up?" Her mother thought she was hearing things. "Why?"

"Because."

"Because is no answer, young lady. I want to see that card!"

"Why? You don't give a fuck about my grades. You don't care."

In an instant the woman was out of her chair

and over to the sofa. There was a loud cracking noise as her hand came down like a flash across Debbie's face. "How dare you use words like that with me!" the woman shouted. "How dare you! I'm your mother!"

"Fuck you." Debbie didn't look at the woman. She kept her gaze on the TV, even though her face was burning.

The woman raised her arm to strike her daughter again, then lowered it slowly. She sat on the sofa, beside her daughter, trying to appear calm, trying to appear as if she had the situation under control. "Debbie," she said evenly, "you've been acting very strange lately. You haven't been eating. You've lost weight. You walk around chilled to the bone all the time. You don't take care of yourself. Just look at your hair. You haven't even combed it this morning." She put her hand on the girl's shoulder. "What's wrong? Tell me."

The girl shrugged. "Nothin'. I'm okay."

"I think you should tell me," the woman insisted softly in her best decorator-salesroom tone. "What seems to be the trouble? Is it school?"

"Why do you care?" the girl answered. "What's the big deal all of a sudden? You never cared before."

"That's not true. I've always cared. You know that."

"I don't know nothin' like that," the girl said.

"Your father and I have always loved you. We've always cared."

"You've always been gone, that's what you've always been," Debbie responded. "You guys are

221

never here. You guys don't love me. You guys don't give a fuck what happens to me."

Now it was her mother's turn to feel she had been slapped across the face. She got off the sofa, slowly. She was shaken. "Tomorrow you and I will go to your school, young lady. I have an appointment in Trenton, but I'll cancel it. We'll go over to your school and I'll find out about your grades and what's causing this sudden new attitude of yours."

"It's not sudden," Debbie answered slowly. "It's been here for a long time. You just never noticed."

Debbie was not permitted out of the house for the rest of the day. She wanted to find Ricky and tell him her mother was going to talk to her teachers, but she was unable to get to him. Her mother tried not to show how distraught she was, but Debbie overheard her on the phone to her father, who was traveling somewhere west of Chicago, telling him that they had to get to the bottom of this. This new attitude was certainly not like the old Debbie. The girl grimaced. The *old* Debbie was dead.

It didn't take long, the next day, Monday, to get Debbie's grades from the school's dean of girls. Debbie had gone from being an almost perfect A student at the close of last semester to being almost a failure at the end of this one. There were two F's and nothing above a D. Once her mother had recovered from the shock, the dean sent Debbie from the room so she could be alone with the mother. The school had been concerned about her daughter, the school official said, and more than one of her teachers were worried that the girl was headed downhill. There was one report in the counselor's confidential file that stated the girl had been seen in the company of one Richard "Ricky" Kasso. She had been seen more than once, as a matter of fact. Did Debbie's mother know who Ricky Kasso was? The woman shook her head.

"Ricky Kasso is a drug dealer," the dean said flatly. "He's nineteen years old, a dropout, and he sells drugs to children." The dean went on to describe Ricky physically and then emotionally, according to the school's Committee on the Handicapped. Debbie was keeping company with a young man who had been labeled "emotionally handicapped" and who had been in and out of correctional institutions and psychiatric wards at his parents' request. The dean said she knew his parents personally and they had tried everything they could to get their son off drugs, but everything they could had not been enough.

Debbie's mother tried to adjust to this information and at the same time extricate herself and her husband from any hint of parental neglect. They had given Debbie everything. Why would she choose such a companion? Surely the school was mistaken. Surely the school didn't suspect Debbie of being on drugs too?

It had nothing to do with "suspecting." A couple of teachers and several students had observed Debbie taking drugs. Smoking at the gazebo in the park. Drinking and smoking at private parties, and it was rumored—just rumored, mind you—that

223

Debbie had almost been arrested with Ricky Kasso for digging up a grave at the Indian cemetery.

The scene, once Debbie and her mother got back home, was anything but peaceful. The woman accused. The daughter denied. Was she on drugs? "No!" Who was this Kasso person? "Just a guy." Did she know he was pushing drugs? "Yes." Did she buy drugs from him? "No." Why did the school think she was also taking drugs? "I don't know." People saw her and reported her activities to school officials, what about that? "All lies." What was her relationship with this Kasso person? "Just friends." Where did this pusher live? "I don't know." Had he ever been inside this house? Debbie shrugged. Had he ever been inside this house? "Couple of times." Couple of times? "Yeah."

"Where was I when this happened?" The woman was shouting loudly now. "Where was your father?"

"Who the fuck knows?" the girl screamed back. "How the fuck am I supposed to remember where you two were? You're never here, *that* I know!"

Her mother dropped her voice, trying to remain calm. "That word. I should slap you again for using that word, but I won't. I understand. Children today use that word all the time. It's like saying 'hell' or 'damn' when I was your age. You use it for shock effect. It means nothing to you."

"That's what you think." Debbie felt she had to defend her generation. "We know what it means and we know how to do it too."

Her mother laughed, nervously. "There. See? You're using it for shock value again." She paused,

224

looking at her daughter's teenage face. "It *is* just for shock, isn't it?"

"What do you want me to say?" The girl had a half-grin, her mother was almost on the ropes. One more punch and the girl would win the fight. "You want me to say Ricky and I fuck?"

Her mother's nervous laugh came again. "I don't want you to *say* anything. I just want the truth."

"Okay. The truth is that Ricky and I are lovers. We fuck. He comes over here when you and Father are out doing your professional thing and he stays all night. He loves me and I love him. He's a great guy and he needs me. I need him!"

Her mother leaned against the wall, emotionally exhausted from this battle with her daughter. It was the worst one they had ever gone through. "You don't *need* this young man," the woman said slowly. "You're too young to know what you need."

"I know I need somebody to hold me," the girl yelled. "I need somebody to talk to. I need somebody to be there . . . just *be* there."

"We try," her mother replied weakly, "your father and I, we try."

"Shit you do!" said Debbie. "Gimme a break, will you? The only thing you try for is more money."

"It costs money to run this house," her mother protested, "and to pay the bills."

"It doesn't cost any money to run *me*." Debbie pointed at herself. "Is that why I'm ignored? Because I'm here and I'm *free?*"

Three days later two men got out of a parked car

and walked toward Ricky as he was about to enter the gazebo. "You Ricky Kasso?" one of them asked.

Ricky looked them both up and down. "Yeah," he said.

One of the men flashed a badge. "We're here to give you some advice. Stay away from Debbie. You're bad news. Her parents have asked us to give you this message. You know what 'stay away' means?"

"Look, man, you can't tell me what to do."

"We're not telling you what to do," the other detective said, "just giving you a little advice. Debbie's parents don't want you hanging around their daughter. If necessary, they'll get a restraining order out on you."

"And if necessary . . ." The other detective hit his own palm with his fist.

"You don't scare me," Ricky said.

"We're not here to scare or threaten. Just to deliver a message. You are bad news and the girl's parents want you to stay away."

"And if I don't?"

"Accidents happen," one of the men said.

The next morning Debbie was driven to her maternal grandparents' home in upstate New York. All her summer clothes had been packed in suitcases. Her schoolbooks were in a picnic hamper. She would need them up there when the tutor arrived. She was to bring her grades back up to the old level, and when September came she was to be enrolled in an upstate New York girls' school. The tutor would make sure she studied and Grandma would make sure she kept off drugs. The servants were instructed to sound the alarm at the first sign of any unexpected visitors, especially a thin young man with brown curly hair.

Jimmy Troiano saw a door ajar and entered noiselessly into the car-repair garage. No need to break a window this time. The checkbook lay in the center of the workbench. Beside it was a wallet with all types of plastic identification. Just waiting for him. There was also one of those grass trimmers, a weed eater, just sitting there doing nothing. Jimmy decided to steal that as well—one of his buddies did lawns and gardens. He forged the signature on a check for forty dollars and cashed it in a convenience store. It had all been too easy. Then the police nabbed him. He was booked, lectured, and told his hearing would come up in five weeks.

Jimmy refers to it as "that stupid burglary."

CHAPTER FOUR

In the beginning there was some doubt about the date, but it was decided that it had to be June 16, 1984. That was the last night anyone saw Gary Lauwers alive.

It was a hot and muggy night in downtown Northport. One of those oppressive New York spring nights that warn of the way things will be in the summer. There wasn't a leaf stirring on the trees in the harbor park. The yachts sat lifelessly in the dark on the warm dirty water. Only a few noises drifted down from Main Street even though it was Saturday night. Skipper's and some of the better restaurants were SRO, but they were air-conditioned, so the windows were closed and the sounds didn't escape.

School had been out for two full weeks and already the kids were restless, looking for things to do. That was always a problem in Northport—nothing for kids to do. There were several of them sitting on the benches in the gazebo. Ricky and Jimmy were there. Gary Lauwers and Albert Quinones and Billy Evans were there. So were a half dozen others. A few kids were surprised to see Gary there. They knew about his feud with Ricky and they knew Gary still hadn't paid Ricky. Gary had told everyone that the debt had been paid, but it hadn't. Gary must have started believing his own story because he mingled easily that night in Ricky's company. Ricky even gave Gary a free hit of mescaline that night. One kid remembers Ricky putting his arm around Gary's shoulders as he laughed and joked with him. Only Ricky and Jimmy knew it was all an act. Ricky intended to beat Gary to a pulp that night.

"It was all set up," Jimmy recalls. "Ricky was still pissed off at Gary, still angry that he hadn't been paid. Ricky had a certain dignity to maintain. After all, he *was* the Acid King. He was the town's main supplier. How did that look when a punk like Gary could steal from the King and get away with it? At that point, with Ricky, it had become more the principle of the thing rather than the actual fifty bucks Gary owed him. You know what I mean?"

"What's happening tonight?" Billy asked. "Everybody going to Randy's birthday party? Gonna be lots of beer."

Most of the kids murmured and nodded. They

229

were going to the party. It was the only thing happening that night.

"We ain't," Ricky said. "Me and Jimmy weren't invited. Shit, man"—and he spat on the ground—"we wouldn't go if we *were* invited. We don't hang around with kids that don't wanna hang around with us. We got other things to do." He spoke scornfully, from his position as Acid King, yet everyone inside the gazebo knew Randy's parents had specifically *excluded* Ricky and Jimmy from the invitation list. The parents refused to have the foul-mouth dopers in their home.

"What are you gonna do tonight, Rick?" the girl asked.

He shrugged. "Do a little dope. Do a little music. Maybe go up to the woods and trip out. I don't know. Depends." He closed his eyes after he spoke, a clear sign he had already done a little dope. "Maybe get laid." He smiled.

"You're just jealous you weren't invited to Randy's party," Gary said.

Ricky fought down an urge to scream at the boy. "Me? Jealous? Of some dumb party with a cake and candles? Hell no, man. I got my own life and got my own ideas about what a party should be and it sure as hell ain't like the one Randy's having tonight. You invited?" He looked at Gary. "You goin'?"

"Yeah. I was invited."

"You goin', I asked you."

"I thought I might stop by for a while," the boy replied. "Check out the action."

"Oh." Ricky seemed disappointed. "I thought

maybe you'd like to go with me and Jimmy and maybe Albert here, go up to the woods. Do some dope. Play some music."

A warm flush of pride surged through Gary's body. Ricky actually wanted him along tonight! "Well"—Gary beamed—"I suppose I could go with you, man. Randy's party's probably going to be a fuckin' bore anyway."

"Right, buddy," Ricky said. "We'll go up there and have ourselves a ball."

The girl looked at Ricky. "What's all this buddy shit with you and Gary?" she asked. "Last week you were beating him up. This week he's your best friend."

Ricky took another hit of mescaline, swallowed it, and then smiled. "A man in my position gotta let bygones be bygones," he said. "Life's too short to always be fightin'."

"Right," Gary agreed with a huge smile on his face, "me and Ricky's friends again. We're buddies again. Ain't nothin' gonna come between us again, right, Rick?"

"Right." Ricky grinned. "Gary's my man again. He and I are cool together."

The girl tamped out her cigarette and put the rest of it in her blue-jeans pocket. She got up and walked toward the entrance of the gazebo. "I think you're both full of shit," she said flatly. Then to the others: "Look, if you guys are going to Randy's party, let's go. It's already started." Kids got up from their perches on benches and railings and mumbled their good-byes. "See you around, man," and "Take it easy" and "Catch you tomorrow"

231

filled the night air. Ricky and Jimmy, Albert and Gary watched them drift over the grass, across the parking lot, and head up the slight hill toward the lights of Main Street on that sultry Saturday night.

"Shit!" said Ricky as he spat on the ground. "A fuckin' birthday party!"

The four teenage boys sat in the darkness for a while letting the mescaline and marijuana and angel dust creep across their brains, unlocking tiny doors of perception and blocking tiny hallways of reason.

Finally Ricky stood up, his thin body as straight as the wooden poles that held up the gazebo. "Let's go," he said.

Jimmy stumbled over something, then reached down and picked it up. "Hey, man," he said, "Billy forgot his tape deck. Just went off and left it."

"Take it with you," Ricky said. "We'll use it when we get to the woods."

The four started out of the gazebo and through the parking lot. They crossed Woodbine Avenue, a narrow street that runs at the end of Main. The park is on one side of it. Several shops, stores, and restaurants are on the other.

"Hey, man," Gary said suddenly. "Know what I feel like? I feel like a doughnut and some orange juice."

"Yeah," Jimmy said. "Sounds good."

They stopped at a store and Ricky bought a half-gallon container of orange juice and a dozen jelly doughnuts. They kept walking down the street, munching on the doughnuts and washing them down with the orange juice. To all appearances, they were just four kids wandering around on a muggy Saturday night.

They got to the next corner, a dead-end little street with the magnificent misnomer of Fifth Avenue and turned left, away from the harbor. They trudged up the hill, crossing School Street, and continued until the "avenue" stopped. In front of them was Aztakea Woods. Dark and overgrown and silent.

Ricky knew the way. He had made the trip to "his spot" so many times he was able to do it in the dark. He didn't need a flashlight. This was his turf, this was his pathless route to the throne room of the Acid King.

The others followed Ricky, pushing a bush aside, stepping around a boulder, or ducking low to miss a tree branch.

"Jeez, it's dark up here," Albert said. "Ricky, I don't know how you manage to find this place. I sure as hell couldn't—"

"Shhh!" Ricky suddenly stopped, listening. "You hear that?" he said after a moment.

"Yeah," Jimmy said. "Yeah. What is it?"

The four youths stood there, in the complete darkness, straining to identify the noise in the trees above them. It was a rustling and scratching sound, and it came first from one location and then another.

"Must be a squirrel," Gary volunteered.

"Doesn't sound like a squirrel," Jimmy said.

The rustling and scratching came again. It grew louder, as if something heavy was shaking tree limbs over them.

"Shit," said Gary, "what the fuck *is* that?"

Ricky had the answer. "That's Satan, man. That's Satan up there and he is giving me a sign. He says everything is gonna be all right, everything's gonna be cool."

"Satan up a tree?" Jimmy almost laughed.

"He can be anywhere, man," Ricky replied. "Now he's up there, right over us. He's telling us it's okay."

"What's okay?" Gary asked in a hushed voice.

"Everything, man." Ricky grinned, but none of them could see it. "Everything is gonna be fuckin'-a." He continued through the underbrush. The others followed, silently, hoping that really wasn't the devil up there over their heads.

Ricky pushed through two large bramble bushes and entered into his cleared area. He had been there earlier that day and had piled some brush up for a fire. The twigs and branches had been damp from yesterday's rain and he hoped they would be dry in time.

While Albert tried to get the brush pile burning, Ricky ducked into the thicket and came back with a glass mayonnaise jar. He kept it buried up there for just such special occasions. He pulled out a strip of mescaline dots. He didn't ask if anyone wanted one, he just handed them out. The three kids with him mumbled their thanks and swallowed the hits. Ricky took one for himself. Jimmy had stopped counting the number of hits his friend had taken that evening. He got to six and stopped. He figures he had at least six himself, so possibly Ricky had eight or nine.

Albert found the page of a newspaper tangled in the bushes and it was dry enough for him to set it afire. He pushed it into the pile of branches and fanned the weak flames as they attempted to dry the wood before they consumed it.

Gary sat on the ground near the fire and turned on Billy's tape recorder. Instantly the sound of Black Sabbath's Ozzy Osbourne churned the air around them. He was doing his number "Bark at the Moon":

> "Screams break the silence,
> Waking from the dead of night.
> Vengeance is boiling,
> He's returned to kill the light.
> Then when he's found who he's look-
> ing for,
> Listen in awe,
> And you'll hear him bark at the
> moon."

Jimmy sat down beside Gary. "I really dig that song," he said. Gary nodded. "Ozzy is next to God." Again Gary agreed. "That fire ain't shit, man." Jimmy changed the subject. "Damn wood must still be damp."

"Lemme try," Gary said. He quickly untied his sneakers and then pulled off his socks. "This'll help." He smiled and tossed his socks onto the bonfire. The cotton socks sat on the branches for a moment, then began to smolder before they quickly burst into flames and were consumed. "That helped," Gary said.

"Not a helluva lot." Ricky sat down next to Gary. So it was Jimmy on one side and Ricky on the other. Albert sat farther back, away from the fire and bombed out of his mind on mescaline.

"What else we got to make the fire catch?" Gary asked.

"You got a jacket," Ricky said.

"This?" Gary ran his hands down the front of his blue denim jacket.

"Yeah." Ricky reached over and started peeling the jacket away from Gary's body. "It ought to burn good."

"Wait a minute," the boy protested. "I don't want to burn up my jacket!"

"We just need a little bit of it," Jimmy said. "Maybe just the sleeves. Maybe just the sleeves will do it."

Gary hunched his shoulders, protecting his jacket. "I don't know," he said. "My mother bought me this. . . ."

"Just the sleeves," Ricky said soothingly. "He don't even have to take off the jacket. Jim, only cut off the sleeves." Ricky reached into his blue jeans and pulled out a folded pocket knife. "Here. Use this."

Jimmy opened the knife. The shiny blade glinted dazzlingly in the firelight.

"Jeez," Albert said from his solitary spot, "that's a beauty, Rick."

"I bought it at the Midway. Today. Guaranteed for life."

"Whose life?" Jimmy grinned.

"Anybody's," Ricky replied evenly.

"Bark at the moon,
Hey, yeah, bark at the
moon."

Jimmy slipped the blade into the fabric, not touching Gary, and quickly hacked off each of the sleeves. Gary, in his own mescaline haze, watched mournfully.

"You toss 'em in," Jimmy said, and passed the sleeves back to Gary. "They're your sleeves, man."

Gary looked down at his mutilated jacket and then at the two hunks of cloth Jimmy had given him. "Sure," he said aloud, "what the fuck? Feed the flames, man. Lemme feed the flames." He tossed the material, it landed on the branches, began smoking, then transferred the fire to the drying wood and leaves. There was a crackling sound and the branches underneath started to burn. "See," Gary said proudly to Ricky, "I did it. We got a bonfire now."

Albert began to sway with the taped music. "You see that?" he pointed into the blackness. "You see how that tree bends?" They turned and looked in the direction he was pointing, but they couldn't make out any bending tree. "Yeah"—Albert smiled —"there it goes again. It starts out normal like, then it starts bending and it goes all the way over until its top touches the ground and then it comes slowly back up again. Yeah, man. There it goes again. It starts okay and then it slowly . . . real slowly . . . gettin' slower now, man . . . and there it is. Fuckin' top is touching the ground." His hand made the motion he said the tree was

237

making and he watched carefully—eyes glazed—as the tree righted itself again. "Jeez, man. I never seen anything like that before. It starts at the top . . ." His voice trailed off, his arm made the motion, his doper's eyes sent the image to his doped-up brain.

> "Bark at the moon,
> Hey, yeah, bark at the
> moon."

Ricky kicked out at the fire. "Still not doing shit, man," he said. "What else we got to put in there?"

Jimmy shrugged. "Got nothin', man."

"You can't use my tree, man," Albert spoke up. "It's green. Won't burn."

"I don't want your fuckin' tree," Ricky said. "Must be somethin' here that will burn. Somethin' dry." He reached out and let his hand tousle Gary's blond hair. Gary smiled in appreciation at the gesture of affection. "Your hair's dry," Ricky said. "Why don't you throw some of your hair on the fire?"

Gary instinctively put his hand to his head. "My hair?" he said blankly.

"Yeah." Ricky grinned. "It's dry. It oughta burn real good."

Gary shook his head. "No, man. Find somethin' else."

"No need to, man." Ricky was still grinning his doper's high grin. "No need to find nothin'. Your hair will do real fine."

Gary started to get to his feet. Ricky jumped up

238

and pushed him back down to a sitting position. "Jimmy," Ricky commanded, "take my knife and cut off some of this fine dry hair."

Jimmy got to his feet and came for Gary, knife blade searching in the humid air. Gary started squirming in Ricky's grasp, but Ricky held him firmly. Jimmy grabbed the end of a lock of Gary's hair and stretched it. Then he started sawing at it. The lock parted quickly. Jimmy tossed it into the fire, where it sputtered and shriveled and stank. Then Jimmy chopped off another hunk of Gary's hair and it did a sizzling dance in the flames. Gary was howling now—somewhere between a cry and a protest. His biggest concern was what his mother would say when he got home.

"That's enough," Ricky said. "Lemme have the knife." Jimmy gave it to him. Ricky released Gary and the boy's hands went to his head, feeling out the places where the roughly cut ends were. "You don't look too bad," Ricky said. "Jimmy would make a good barber."

"There the tree goes again," Albert sang out softly. "It goes down and then it goes up, it goes down and then it goes up."

Ricky kept his position, standing directly in front of the seated Gary. The blond boy looked up at him. "What you thinkin', Ricky?" he asked.

"Nothin'," came the reply. "Why? What *you* thinkin'?"

"I'm thinkin' strange thoughts," Gary said. "I'm gettin' strange vibes."

"What kind of vibes, man?" Ricky asked softly, the knife still in his hand.

"I'm gettin' that you want to hurt me," Gary said.

"Hurt you?" Ricky's voice rose slightly. "I don't want to hurt you."

"You don't?" Gary didn't sound convinced.

"Shit no, man," Ricky said, slightly louder now. "I don't want to hurt you. I want to *kill* you!"

"Kill me?" Gary tried to get off the ground. Jimmy held him down. "You're shittin' me, aren't you, man?"

"Like hell I am, you little fucker! I'm going to kill you!"

"Why?" Gary's voice rose shrilly.

"Why? You know why, you asshole. You stole from me! You stole those hits and you never paid me back for them! You owe me fifty dollars for a helluva long time and you fart around and never pay me!"

"Look, the other tree is doin' it now," Albert sang out softly.

"I've waited longer than I should have for that bread," Ricky shouted.

Gary started to whimper. What was happening to him had penetrated through the chemicals. "I said I'd get the money, man, I said I'd get it!"

"Shit on what you said!" Ricky yelled.

"Look at those trees," said Albert.

> "Bark at the moon,
> Hey, yeah, bark at the
> moon."

240

"Let him go, Jimmy," Ricky ordered. "Let him stand up like a man."

Jimmy stepped back, taking his hands off Gary's thin shoulders. The boy struggled to his feet. "Ricky, I thought you and me were buddies, man." Gary's hands were on Ricky's chest, his fingers clutching at the leather thong that held Pat Pagan's brass medallion. "I thought that we—"

Ricky's knee went up, quickly and savagely, hitting Gary in the groin. He screamed and fell back on the ground. "Piece of shit!" Ricky yelled. He hauled off and kicked Gary in the ribs. Again Gary howled. "Teach you to mess with me, you scumbag!" Ricky's foot smashed into Gary's rib cage.

"Yeah," Jimmy shouted, "you don't mess with him!" And his booted foot smashed into Gary's side. "You owe him, shithead," Jimmy yelled. "You owe him!"

"Now they got cats," Albert said in amazement. "There's a bunch of fuckin' cats climbin' those trees. God, never saw so many cats."

Then the impossible happened. The improbable. The unexpected. The bizarre.

Ricky raised the long blade over his head and sent it plunging into Gary's soft warm teenage flesh. "You're a fucker!" he screamed.

Gary stared at the knife handle sticking out of his body in disbelieving shock. There was no pain. The blood hadn't started to run yet. It was as if it was happening to somebody else.

Ricky withdrew the blade, swung again, and plunged the blade again.

241

This time Gary felt it. His was an unearthly howl of pain and astonishment.

"Say you love Satan!" Ricky yelled. "Go on." The knife slashed warm flesh for the third time. "Say it! Say you love Satan!"

"No!" Gary screamed in pain. "No!"

"Say it, you bastard!" Ricky demanded. "I'm gonna keep it up until you do! Say you love Satan!"

"No!" Gary yelled, and tried to roll away from the unerring blade. "I love my mother! I don't love Satan! I love my mother!"

"Satan!" Ricky hollered, and the knife blade found its mark again. "I won't stop until you say you love Satan!"

"My mother," Gary cried, "I love my mother!"

"Ricky," Jimmy said in a normal voice. "I think you did enough. You're killing him."

"He's gotta say he loves Satan!" Ricky plunged the knife once more, but it deflected off a bone and went flying into the air.

There is great debate about what actually happened at this point. Jimmy admits to retrieving the knife and handing it back to Ricky so he could finish the job. The prosecution claimed Jimmy then held Gary down so Ricky could do a better job. The defense claimed Jimmy just stood and watched. Jimmy claims that by the time he picked up the knife and handed it back to Ricky, Gary was dead.

They managed to get Albert on his feet and he took one of Gary's legs while Ricky and Jimmy took the other. They dragged the young body away from the bonfire and into the darkness. There was a clump of bushes some thirty yards into the woods. The three, all reeling from the combination of adrenaline and mescaline, started shoving the body under the bushes.

Suddenly, horribly, Gary sat up. He bent straight up from the waist into a sitting position.

All three boys screamed.

Ricky, knife still in his hand, began to babble and in a terrible frenzy started stabbing Gary's face. The knife blade plunged into the eye sockets, bringing the eyeballs to the surface. He slashed crazily at them, severing their cords and letting them stream down the smooth young cheeks. He slashed at the nose and the mouth, wildly plunging the blade over and over again until the body was flat on the ground once more and his terrible fright had passed.

When Ricky and Jimmy came back to where the fire still burned, they could hear the sound of Albert crashing blindly through the undergrowth below, stumbling over logs and rocks in the dark, sobbing loudly as he ran toward home, trying to erase the terrifying reality he had just witnessed.

Ricky and Jimmy stood by the fire, looking at each other. Overhead a crow cawed, then circled lazily. Even though the sky was pitch black, both boys could make out the bird's form as it flew and squawked above them.

"Satan's with us," Ricky said. "That crow is a sign. Satan approves of what we have done in his name." He squinted into the dark, trying to get a better view of his main man's feathered ambassador. "He approves, man," he said, and he reached out a hand to touch Jimmy, to steady himself. Jimmy pulled back. He could see that hand in the light of the fire. It was covered in blood, blood that still dripped from its fingers and from the blood-caked knife it still gripped tightly.

"You better get yourself cleaned up," Jimmy said. "You can't let people see you like that."

"I did it, man." Ricky grinned. "I made my first sacrifice, my first sacrifice for Satan."

The tape had come to the end, reversed itself, and was playing over:

> "Hey, yeah, bark at the moon.
> They cursed and buried him along with shame,
> And thought his timeless soul had gone, gone.
> In empty burning hell, unholy one,
> But he's returned to prove them wrong,
> So wrong,
> Ooh, yeah, baby."

The phone rang in the Northport Police Station. It was about 2:30 A.M.

"I want to report a disturbance," a woman's voice said.

"What kind of a disturbance, ma'am?" the officer asked.

"There has been screaming and there is a fire and they're playing loud music. It woke me and my husband up."

"Where is this?" asked the cop.

"We live on Woodhull Place. The noise is above us, in the woods."

"Aztakea Woods?"

"Yes, sir."

"Sorry, ma'am, but that's private property up there."

"So what? It's two-thirty in the morning! We can't sleep!"

"Private property, ma'am. Can't go up there without a warrant."

"But it woke us up."

"Probably just a bunch of kids, ma'am. They'll get tired after awhile. They'll stop soon."

"But we heard screaming."

"You know how kids are, ma'am."

"But suppose something's happened up there?"

"Private property, ma'am."

"But . . ."

"Go back to sleep, ma'am."

CHAPTER FIVE

Mescaline, also known as B-3, 4, 5-Trimethoxyphenethylamine, occurs naturally in the flowering heads of the peyote cactus. The cactus can be found in Mexico and the southwestern United States and has a long and lurid history of use and abuse.

Peyote buttons have figured largely in many Indian religious ceremonies. Even today the Native American Church, which has members from several tribes, continues to use peyote as a sacrament. Users and experts alike have said that a mescaline experience may result in new insights or cause intense fear and anxiety. Or neither. Or both. Outside this church, federal law prohibits the possession of the drug.

And a particularly potent drug it is. Structurally, the mescaline molecule is related to two hormones secreted by the adrenal glands—adrenaline and noradrenaline. A 350-*microgram* capsule of mescaline will launch a user on a twelve-hour trip complete with intense hallucinations. Whether the journey is good, or bad, or ghastly depends largely on the mood and personality of the person taking the drug and the setting in which the drug is taken. Or, as the authors of *Psychedelic Drugs Reconsidered* put it, "Giggly euphoria, irritability, fear, depression, boundless love and joy pass in swift succession. There may also be intense emotions without any apparent object, or several conflicting emotions at once."

Ricky went to Albert's house, where he washed his hands and threw away his blood-spattered T-shirt. Albert gave him one of his. His blue jeans, caked with dirt and torn before the murder, didn't seem to show the few drops of blood that had landed on them. Albert was starting to come down from his high, and somewhere from the back of his mind this tape of Gary sitting up and the knife blade destroying his face kept repeating. Over and over again. He urged Ricky to change and then leave—to go away—to take the memory with him. Ricky shrugged, grinned, and walked over to the home of a fourteen-year-old girlfriend and slept in her family room. In the morning she gave him some orange juice and sent him on his way before her parents awoke.

The sun had only just come up as he wandered

247

back down to the harbor. He was still high, both from the mescaline and from the euphoria of the killing. He was proud of what he had done. He was proud it had gone so well, almost effortlessly. He had proven his loyalty to Satan. He had proven his manhood. Killing Gary was the supreme rush of his short life. Gary deserved it. Gary had broken the rules. Gary had defied the Acid King. The norm. Gary had stolen and he didn't pay. He had to pay. And he did. It was over. The ledger was clean. Gary no longer owed him fifty bucks. Gary had paid his debt by dying.

Ricky reached into his blue jeans looking for another hit of mescaline. It was too early to come down off the high. His fingers touched something cold and sticky. He pulled it out and looked at it. It was the pocket knife. It was caked in dried blood, sticky where the blade folded back into the handle. His fingerprints were etched in the drying gore. That wouldn't do, he told himself. He liked the knife, it was a new knife, but shit, man, it wouldn't do at all to have this knife hanging around. He sailed the knife out across the murky harbor waters. It plopped noisily, made a splatter, and sank.

He sat for a while staring at nothing, his mind a blank. Then he picked at a gob of dried blood on his tennis shoe. It left a noncommittal shadow on the dirty canvas. He heard the church bells. It seemed to him as if every damned church in town was ringing its bell trying to drown out the bell of every other church. The bells were sharp and booming and annoying. There should be a law, he had said more than once, to keep those damned bells silent on Sunday mornings. He was a Satanist. He didn't ring bells and annoy Christians.

When the bells stopped he knew the various services had begun. A preacher couldn't talk above the clanging of his own bell. Several of the village churches were straight up Main Street, straight up from where he was sitting down at the harbor. The sounds of bells and hymns and prayers to Jesus flooded the street and poured downhill, emptying around him into the water. To Ricky it seemed like the sounds had turned to liquid, each sound with its own color, and the colors ran around him, over the stone retaining wall and into the muddy water of the yacht basin. He wondered why the boat owners didn't protest. The few that were already out there that morning must see those colors coming at them, must be aware that their white hulls were being stained blue and green and orange by the pious Christian sounds. Yet none of the owners seemed upset. When he got to California and got *his* boat, he'd make damn sure it wasn't moored near a church.

The bells rang again. That meant the church services were over and people would be going home. His parents would be going home. He had to talk with his father. He had to call him and make sure everything was set for tomorrow. He sat and smoked a marijuana cigarette, and when it was all gone he got up and walked to the pay phone near the boat ramp.

His father answered. "Is that you, Rick?"

Ricky tried to speak. His tongue was suddenly

249

thick, his entire body shook. "Yeah," he managed to reply. "Yeah."

"You okay?" the man asked. He waited but there was no answer. "Rick? What's the matter?"

Ricky hung up the phone without saying anything else. His hands were shaking so he could barely find and then light up another cigarette. He wobbled over to the gazebo, almost fell onto a bench, and silently asked the chemicals in the cigarette to steady his nerves. He hated calling his folks. He hated having to bring them back into his life. But tomorrow was important. God, how he hated facing tomorrow.

After about a half hour he managed to muster enough strength to walk back to the pay phone and dial his parents. Again his father answered. "Dad? Dad?" His voice was weak and his words were slurred. "You won't forget about tomorrow?"

"I said I'll go with you," his father answered. "I told you that."

"We gotta be at the court by ten. The judge wants us there by ten. You know that. You promised you'd take me."

"I know I did. I'll meet you at nine in front of the Midway. Right?"

"Yeah, Dad. At nine in front of the Midway is cool." He paused. "They can't put me in jail for that, can they, Dad?" Ricky had tears in his eyes. Tears in those piercing eyes were a rarity. "You promised you wouldn't let them put me in jail."

"Rick, I'll do what I can. It's up to the judge."

"There's no big deal about some old Indian bones." His words were slurred. His father found

250

it difficult to understand him. "I mean the fuckin' guy's been there for years and years. Hasn't he, Dad? Haven't those bones been there a long time?" His father agreed that they had. "Long time. Real long time. People live long times, don't they, Dad? Don't some people live long times? Butterflies, Dad. Butterflies don't live hardly any time at all. I heard, Dad, that butterflies live only for one day. Did you know that, Dad? Just for one day? Imagine, just for a day. That's sad, isn't it?" His father didn't answer. "I think it is. I think it's real sad."

"Rick," his father interrupted, "you want to come home for dinner? Your mother's about got dinner on the table. You want me to pick you up somewhere? Come and have Sunday dinner with us and your sisters?"

"I wonder if they know, Dad," he said. "I mean, here they are going through all that caterpillar shit and then that cocoon shit. All tied up and asleep for months and then they come out and they look so pretty and they start flying in the sun and then they die. Do you think they know, Dad? Do you think while they're flying in the sun and their colors are sparkling like a handful of diamonds that they *know* they only have one day? Just one day to live? Isn't that sad, Dad? Isn't life sad?" Ricky hung up the phone and walked back to the gazebo. He didn't know if the tears in his eyes were for the butterflies or the fact that he had to face a judge tomorrow on the grave-digging charge. He hated judges. They had complete power over his body. They could throw his young ass in jail and never let him out. They were like James Bond. They had

251

a license to kill. They could kill him tomorrow.
They could send him to jail and keep him there
forever. It would be like killing him, taking away
his freedom day by day. Tomorrow wasn't going
to be easy. He'd much rather kill another Gary
Lauwers than stand before a judge.

Ricky showed up at home about 7:30 the next
morning. His mother was shocked at his appearance. His hands and face were dirty, his hair wild
and uncombed, with bits of leaves and earth in it.
His mother pulled back in disgust—her son's body
stank. He said he had tried to sleep behind the
Midway but that the ground had been hard and a
couple of stray dogs had wakened him once he finally managed to get to sleep. He didn't tell them
he couldn't sleep because of the impending court
hearing. He didn't want them to know how concerned he was about it. The first rule of an Acid
King: Never let anybody, especially your old man
and old lady, know what's happening in your
head.

Tales circulated afterward that the Kassos were
so disgusted that they refused to let him inside
their home to take a shower. They were afraid he
would dirty the bathroom. Actually, Ricky didn't
want to shower. He didn't feel it was necessary.
He ran his fingers through his matted curls and
considered himself cleaned up enough to face the
judge.

The hearing lasted only a few minutes. The
judge had other things to do. The filthy teenager in
front of him had been charged with violating the

state's public health law for digging up a grave. Because Ricky had not stolen a skull or a hand, no grave-robbing charges could be levied. So the judge assigned the boy to counsel with legal aid and ordered the case to be continued. Ricky was so relieved, he could taste it.

After the hearing his father drove him to the Midway. That's where Ricky said he wanted to go. Some of Ricky's cronies, the kids who made Dick Kasso so angry, watched as Ricky and his father had one final argument. Emboldened by the ease with which he had swept through the dreaded hearing, Ricky went all out this time. When it was all over and his father was angrily driving away, Ricky sauntered over to his friends.

"I can't believe my old man. I asked for a fuckin' quarter for a bagel and he gives me shit about it," he told them. "He told me to come on home and get cleaned up and he'll give me a bagel. They got a whole refrigerator full of bagels he says. I don't need that shit, man. All I wanted was a quarter."

"Man, parents always think that you gotta take their bullshit if they're giving you money," said Jimmy.

"All I asked for was a fuckin' quarter," Ricky shouted. "It's not like it was going to break him."

While they were talking Dick Kasso's red Corvette pulled up in front of the Midway and man and boy faced each other once again. The youngsters standing by the building couldn't hear what Dick Kasso said, but the anger in both voices carried clearly. And when Ricky shouted, "Don't

253

worry, you won't ever have to see me again," they all knew just how serious this fight had become.

And his father never saw him again.

The next day Ricky and Jimmy were at Billy's house. They were downstairs in the rec room. They had smoked some dope, drunk some booze, and were listening to rock music.

Ricky was stretched out on the sofa. "I don't know what's wrong with me, man," he said. "I ain't been gettin' my z's lately. I get real tired and then I think I'm fallin' asleep but I don't sleep. I just keep wakin' up. You know what I mean?" They both agreed they knew what he meant. "I'm gettin' drowsy now, right here on your sofa, man. Maybe I'll take a hit and see if that helps." He took a strip of mescaline dots from his jacket pocket and popped one into his mouth.

"You look beat, man," Billy said.

"Yeah, I am. Don't know what it is."

"You ain't gettin' that pneumonia thing again, are you?" Billy was concerned.

Ricky shook his head. "No, it ain't in my lungs this time. It's in my head, man. Don't know what it is. It's in my head." He closed his eyes, and while the other two drifted off with the music, Ricky drifted off into sleep. Billy poured himself another shot of bourbon, Jimmy drank a beer. The two boys talked about girls and dope and parents and television and how they would run the world.

"You got any dope on you, man?" Billy asked. Jimmy shook his head. Billy frowned. "Would be nice to have something right now," he said. He listened to a few more minutes of music and then got up off the floor and went over to the sofa. Ricky was sleeping soundly. Jimmy watched as Billy put his hand into Ricky's jacket and brought out the strip of mescaline dots. "I'm gonna borrow one of these," he said. "You want one?"

In a flash Jimmy was off the floor and over beside Billy. He grabbed the hits and then took a swing at Billy. His fist connected and Billy staggered back against the wall. "You stupid son of a bitch!" Jimmy screamed at him. "Don't *ever* do that. Don't ever steal from him!"

Billy rubbed his jaw. "Jesus Christ, man. You didn't have to do that."

"Oh, yes I did," Jimmy said as he stuffed the mescaline back into Ricky's pocket. "You asshole! Ricky killed Gary Lauwers for that. He killed Gary for stealing from him."

Billy looked at Jimmy. He was sure he had misunderstood what he had just heard. "Ricky did what? You wanna run that by again?"

"I said, you asshole, that Ricky killed Gary for exactly what you just did."

"What? What the fuck are you sayin'?" Billy looked at Jimmy as if he had gone mad.

"I said Gary is dead and Ricky killed him. Don't you understand English?"

Billy didn't move. His eyes went from Jimmy over to the sleeping Ricky and back to Jimmy again. "You . . ." he said slowly, "you aren't kidding me, are you?"

"No," Jimmy replied. He went to the bar and poured himself a stiff shot. He hardly ever drank, but since Saturday night there was a taste in his mouth that he couldn't exorcise. "We were up in Aztakea while you guys were at the birthday party. Me, Ricky, Albert, and Gary. We built a fire and Gary started mouthing off to Ricky. They got into an argument. Ricky pulled his knife and aced Gary." He drained the booze while Billy stared. "We hid his body under some bushes. We gotta go back and bury him." Jimmy poured himself another large shot. It was difficult because his hand was shaking. "That's why I hit you, man. He killed Gary because Gary stole from him. I didn't want the same thing to happen to you."

Billy pried himself away from the wall and urged his legs to take him as far as the nearest bar stool. He sat on it, clutching at the bar as if the entire room were rocking. "You're really serious, aren't you?" Jimmy drank and nodded. "Oh, my God, Jim," he said. "That's terrible!" He paused. "That's *murder!* Ricky *murdered* Gary! Do you know what that means?" Again Jimmy nodded. "Ricky is a murderer! And you . . . you were *there.* That makes you an accomplice. Shit, man, you're guilty too!"

"I'm not guilty of anything," Jimmy replied flatly. "I've been giving it a lot of thought. Ricky did it all. I just watched. I'm clean."

Billy was still stunned. Stunned and appalled. "You were there, man. You are guilty as hell."

"Albert was there too," Jimmy said quickly, "don't forget that. Albert helped pull the body into the bushes."

Billy sat there, staring at Ricky-the-Murderer

sleeping peacefully on his parents' sofa. "Oh, shit, man, this is terrible. Who else knows about this? Gary's folks know?"

"Course not," Jimmy replied. "Nobody knows. You're the first."

"I won't tell anybody, man. I don't want to get involved. What are you gonna do? I mean about the body. They're gonna start lookin' for Gary, and when he doesn't come home they're gonna be suspicious. What are you gonna do?"

"Gary's run away from home lots of times," Jimmy said calmly. "His folks won't miss him for a while. By that time we'll have him buried. Maybe take him out in a boat and throw him in the Sound. I don't know yet. Ricky don't wanna talk about it yet. Ain't gonna be much trouble."

"Oh, shit, man. Don't you believe it. There's gonna be a *lot* of trouble. You guys are gonna be in a helluva lot of trouble!"

Ricky awoke with a start and began yelling at the top of his lungs, "Jesus Christ, no! No, man, no!"

Tommy, one of Ricky's junior high hangers-on, vaulted from his bed and over to the twin bed on the other side of the room. He grabbed Ricky and started shaking him. "Shut up!" he whispered loudly. "Shut up, goddamn it!"

Ricky opened his eyes. For a second they were tilted up inside his head. He managed to focus on Tommy. Then he began gasping for breath.

"Be quiet, man!" Tommy whispered loudly. "Jesus! Don't wake up my folks!"

"It was awful, man," Ricky panted. "There was this face and it was coming at me. It was all bloody and shit and it was coming down on top of me and I couldn't breathe! It was terrible, man."

"Look, Rick, I can't have my folks coming in here. They don't know you stayed over." Tommy remembered letting Ricky climb in his bedroom window around 3:00 A.M. "You gotta be quiet if you're gonna stay here."

"Yeah, man." Ricky filled his lungs with air and then sighed. "Sorry. It was a bad dream." He fell back against the pillow. "I don't wanna get you in trouble."

Tommy sat on the edge of the bed waiting to hear his parents come down the hallway. They had an air conditioner in their room and when it was on they couldn't hear any outside noise. Tommy was glad it was a warm night. "You know, Rick," he said, "they showed us a movie at school about drugs and nightmares and stuff. Maybe you've been overdoing it. Maybe you should slow down for a while."

"Yeah," Ricky agreed. "Maybe."

"They got what they call a rehab house. It's for kids to get unbent. Get off drugs for a while." Tommy was concerned about Ricky's obvious decline. "I ain't sayin' you're *sick*, man, don't get me wrong. Just that maybe a little time out for a while might do you good."

"Yeah." Ricky stared into the darkness of the room. He didn't want to close his eyes, didn't want that face to come back down upon him. "Yeah," he replied softly, "maybe you're right. Maybe that's

258

what I need. Thanks, man." He reached out to touch Tommy but the boy had returned to his own bed. Ricky was alone. Again. And if he closed his eyes, probably that terrible face would be there. Again. Tonight wasn't the first time. Every time he managed to doze off that face was there. Following him. Staring at him. Pushing down on him. Yeah, maybe he was burning himself out. Too much too fast. He'd look into that rehab-house thing. First thing in the morning. Maybe he'd go back and see Tom Fazio at The Place. Tom was still counseling kids there. Yeah, that's what he would do. First thing in the morning. But he had to get through tonight. Oh, God, man, he still had to get through tonight.

CHAPTER SIX

"Where's Gary?"

"What?" Ricky looked sharply at the boy asking the question. "What do you mean?"

"I mean I ain't seen him for a few days. We were supposed to go to the movies last night and I waited but he didn't show up. I called his house and his mom said she hadn't heard from him."

"Did she sound upset?" Ricky kept watching the boy.

"Nah. A little angry maybe. Gary's done this before, you know. Leavin' home and being gone for a few days and his folks not knowing where in the hell he's at."

Ricky spat on the ground. "Shit, he don't know where he's at *most* of the time."

"Oh, Gary's not so bad," said the kid. "A little juvenile sometimes, but he and me always hit it off pretty well."

"Yeah, I guess so," Ricky admitted. "Gary's not so bad."

"He still owe you that bread? For the stuff he stole?"

"Nah. He paid me. He don't owe me nothin'. Gary paid me in full."

"Where's Gary?"
Ricky and a few boys were over at Dunkin' Donuts, munching and drinking orange juice and just hangin' around. "Why?" Ricky asked. "You miss him?"

"Yeah," said the boy. "I haven't seen him around lately. I was talkin' with Glen and he said Gary was helpin' him fix his car. He hasn't seen him either. Gary left some of his tools and stuff over at Glen's. Glen's got some money for him, for helpin' him, but Gary ain't been by to collect it."

"Strange," said Ricky.

"Yeah," said the kid, "real strange. It doesn't feel right. You know what I mean?"

"Where's Gary?" Tyler, a thin blond boy who had barely turned fifteen remembers. "It seems everybody was asking that. Gary was one of those kids you didn't pay any attention to but when he wasn't around, you missed him. You know what I mean? One day I was in the round house at the end of the dock and Ricky was there, all alone and smoking some weed. I asked him where Gary was and he says to me, 'What do you mean?' and I says, 'I mean, where is Gary? I haven't seen him for a week.' Well, Ricky just kind of smiles at me and he doesn't say anything. Then I said, 'I talked with Gary's mom and she is really upset. This is the longest Gary's stayed away without at least contacting her. She told me some guy called her and told her that Gary was dead and that he had been sacrificed to Satan.' Well, Ricky just smiled at me when I said that and right away I suspected that he had called Mrs. Lauwers, but I didn't ask him. So he said to me, 'It's true. Gary is dead. I killed him.' Well of course I didn't believe him. Nobody who kills somebody is gonna come right out and admit it in a normal conversation. Of course I know that Ricky wasn't *normal* in the sense of the word. So I said to him, 'Come on, man. You're full of shit. You didn't do nothin' to Gary.' And he says to me, 'You wanna see? You wanna see Gary's body?' I said, 'Sure, man,' because I didn't believe him. You know what I mean?

"So Ricky takes me up to that spot in the woods. That place where he always used to go to get high and play music and things and, you know, you could smell it from about a half a block away. It smelled like fifty guys had all taken a crap and left it cooking in the sun. I didn't really want to go any farther, but Ricky was leadin' the way.

"We got past the clearing and then went into the bushes. The stink got stronger. 'Here,' Ricky said to me. 'You wanna see Gary? Here he is!'

"Man, he started to brush away the leaves and there was Gary's face! I mean it was disgusting!

There were no eyes and the nose had been sliced off and the lips were gone and there were these fat white maggots crawling in and out of Gary's face and I just wanted to puke, man. I mean I didn't know whether to shit or go blind. It was so *bad!* I hadn't really expected it, you know what I mean? I was sure Ricky was bullshitting me but no, there was Gary, black and puffed up and real dead.

"I turned around and started back down the hill. I didn't want to see any more. My stomach wouldn't let me see any more. And when I was about halfway to the street I started to throw up, and I stood there, leaning against a tree, and I threw up stuff I had eaten a week before, man. I mean I expected to see my shoes and socks come out of my mouth. It was the worst thing I ever saw in my life. I still have nightmares about it.

"Did I tell my parents? Are you crazy? Ricky had killed once, who was going to say he wouldn't kill again? No, I told a couple of my buddies, but they didn't believe me. Who would believe it? Who would believe that Gary Lauwers was lying up there, rotting in the woods?"

"Where's Gary?"

After ten days Gary's mother and sister began calling his school friends and anyone else they could think of who might tell them where he had gone. They became truly concerned. Yet, they never reported him missing to the Northport police.

* * *

On Sunday afternoon, June 24, Ricky took three kids into the woods and scraped away the leaves to show them Gary's body. By that time the maggots had done their work well.

On Monday, June 25, Ricky and Jimmy and Billy drew up plans to burn down Aztakea woods. If they poured gasoline on Gary's body and then scattered gasoline for several yards around his body, they could cremate it and no one would ever find it. They discussed how much gasoline it would take, whether or not the wind was a factor, and if the undergrowth would burn because it was so green. They planned to do it that night. It rained. They said to hell with it.

On Tuesday evening Jimmy waited in front of the Midway for Liz. The two kids were going to a movie that night. Never mind that Jimmy had participated in a murder and that the body was rotting where anyone might stumble across it. The important thing that night was a date with Liz. He looked at his watch. Liz was late, as usual.

That's when Laurie showed up. She said hello to Jimmy and told him that Liz had invited her to go to the movies with them. Jimmy wasn't too happy about this. He had hoped to be alone with Liz. Jimmy remembers Laurie had just come from "a heavy drug scene and she was still high."

"There were several kids there I didn't recognize," she said. "Lots of Mary Jane and mesc. Shit, man, the party must have started about a day ago, at least. What day is this?"

"It's Tuesday," Jimmy said, hoping she would remember she had another engagement for that day.

"Tuesday? Oh, wow! Yeah, the party started Sunday afternoon! So this is Tuesday? Wow! It was a really great party, man. Everybody was there."

"I wasn't," said Jimmy, "and neither was Ricky or Billy."

"No, that's right. You guys weren't there, were you? You know who else wasn't there?" She shook her head trying to remember. "Gary Lauwers wasn't there. Somebody said something about him not being there, but I forget what they said. You know, free dope and booze and Gary's *gotta* be there!" She shook her head. "Oh, yeah, now I remember. Somebody said that Gary was dead. Somebody said they knew a kid who had gone somewhere and seen Gary's body. It was all horrible and stuff. Most of us didn't know whether to believe this guy or not, but I personally did hear that Gary's folks are starting to go bananas about him not coming home. But dead? I can't believe that."

"Believe it," said Jimmy. "It's true."

"How do you know?" She laughed. "Did you do it?"

"No," he said quickly, "Ricky did. I was there. I watched."

"Oh, cut out the shit." She grimaced. "You think I believe that shit?"

"I tell you it's true. Gary is dead and Ricky did

265

it." Suddenly the entire story came tumbling out of Jimmy's mouth. He had been bottling it inside, holding it back for fear of letting anyone know he had been involved. He knew Ricky had taken some kids to see the body. He didn't know how many, maybe fifteen or eighteen or so, but he hadn't been back, he hadn't seen the body and he hadn't told anyone he had been involved in it. As far as he knew, Ricky hadn't implicated him or Albert in it. Ricky had bragged that he had done it all himself. That's fine. If Ricky wanted all the credit, he could have it. But Jimmy had to get it up and out of his system and he told Laurie the chain of events, bit by bit, as it happened in the woods. He ended up by saying Ricky killed Gary in self-defense.

"Oh, yuck!" Laurie said loudly. "I'm not going to hang around with *you* anymore! You're a creep and so is your creepy friend Ricky Kasso! Oh, wow, how disgusting!"

At that moment Liz appeared. The two girls embraced and then Liz kissed Jimmy lightly on the lips. "Ready for the film?" Liz asked them.

"Sure," Laurie said. "I hear it's real good. Lots of music and stuff in it."

The film the three kids sat through that night was *Desperately Seeking Susan*.

The police should have been desperately seeking Gary.

"I want you to ask your friend Russell," Ricky said to Jimmy. "Ask him to come over here with his car and a shovel."

"For what?" Jimmy looked at him. "Russell's got

nothing to do with this thing. Besides, he lives in Kings Park."

"He's a friend, isn't he?" Ricky asked, and Jimmy nodded. "You met him in prison and you can trust him. Right?" Jimmy said, "Right." "Then he's the kind of guy we need. He won't go bat shit on us and spill everything to the cops."

"I'll call him," Jimmy said, "but I ain't going with you guys. I don't want to see that thing up there. Not now."

"That *thing*, as you call him, used to be your friend Gary." Ricky frowned. "You're getting really chicken shit about this whole deal."

"What deal? This ain't no deal, man. This is murder and I got all the right in the world to be cool about not getting involved."

"You're already involved, buddy boy."

"I know," Jimmy replied, "but that doesn't mean I have to like it."

Russell drove over to Northport in his old Chevy. He had a shovel in the backseat. He picked Ricky up in front of the Midway. Jimmy was there, too, but Jimmy didn't get into the car. He just waved good-bye.

As they climbed the hill into the woods Russell said to Ricky, "I think it would be nice to know what I'm supposed to do up here, man."

"We got a little problem," Ricky replied. "It needs taking care of. That's why I asked you to bring the shovel."

"You got buried treasure up here? Something you don't want other people to see?"

"Somethin' like that, yeah. Somethin' like that."

They got to the bushes and Russell was sniffing the air. "What the fuck's that stink? What you do, man? Kill a skunk?"

Ricky bent down and quickly pushed away the leaves that covered Gary's decomposed and maggot-filled face. "Look at this, man," he said proudly.

"Jesus Christ!" Russell quickly turned away. "Who is that?"

"A friend," Ricky replied. "I killed him."

Russell looked again at the corpse. "Like shit, you did," he said.

"Like shit, I didn't," Ricky boasted. "He had it coming. He owed me, man."

Russell had looked away again. "Christ, I don't know what he owed you to make him turn out like this."

"He owed me for some hits he stole and he owed me for my honor. It was more for my honor, man, than anything else."

Russell shuddered. The sight of the body had started to get through to him. "Whatever you want to do," he said, "let's get it the fuck over with."

Ricky took the shovel and began to dig about ten feet from where the body had been lying. The soil was hard and crisscrossed with roots and tendrils. It wasn't easy going. He worked for about half an hour, in complete silence, while Russell smoked a joint and tried to get his mind off what lay in front of him. Finally, there was a shallow trench about four feet long and two feet deep. Ricky figured that was deep enough, especially if they covered it with dirt and leaves. In a couple of years, Gary would be part of the landscape. Who would know?

They each took a leg—Russell was afraid one of the decaying legs might just come off—and dragged the body over to the new site. They pushed Gary into the hole. He fell on his side, his hands turned under, his knees rigidly set now in a fetal position.

"What's that?" Russell pointed to something shiny that had become embedded in Gary's side. He reached down and picked up the round brass object. "Look at this," he said.

Ricky recoiled in horror. It was the first time he had shown any emotion that afternoon. "Oh, shit, man!" he shuddered.

"What is it?"

"A medal, man. It's mine. I got it off some old guy." He shuddered. "Put it back."

"You don't want it?" Russell held it out to him.

"No, man! For Christ sake, not *now!* Satan has reclaimed it! I don't want to see that thing."

Russell shrugged and tossed the medallion, still on its leather thong, atop the body. Ricky grabbed the shovel and made sure that the first load of dirt covered the medallion.

And if Ricky hadn't been through enough that day, he heard later on, down at the Midway, that his ex-girlfriend Debbie, the one he had loved, the one he had turned onto drugs, the one who had been sent upstate to school, was dead.

"O.D.'d, man," a girl said. "She got some bad stuff and didn't come down off it. I got a letter from a girlfriend who lives up there in that ritzy town. She said Debbie was a real mess, smokin' dope, boozin', and screwin' everything in pants. Her folks should never have made her go live with her grandmother," the girl said.

"Yeah," Ricky said, and tears started slowly rising under his eyelids. "Yeah. It was their fault. If anyone is to blame, it's her folks." He turned and walked quickly away before the girl could see he was crying. He didn't know where he was going, only that he had to get somewhere, somewhere where he would be by himself.

Finally, he couldn't hold it any longer. There was a garage in somebody's backyard with lots of bushes around it. He ran for the bushes, pushed his way into them, and sank to the ground.

"Oh, Debbie!" he moaned aloud. "Not you too! Jesus Christ, baby, not you too!" He put his grimy hands to his face and the tears ran down his fingers and pinged onto his blue jeans. "You were all I had left, baby. We were gonna make it together. You promised. Baby, why did you do it? Why, baby? How could you leave me alone like this? Jesus Christ, baby, *how?*"

CHAPTER SEVEN

All the kids called her "Gram." She had been somebody's mother at one time, but that had been years ago. Her children were grown and gone from Northport, seeking better jobs, better places to live. Gram had never been part of the commuter crowd. Her husband had been a clammer, a digger of clams. He never earned enough to open a savings account. The one-bedroom apartment she lived in was paid for by Section 8 Housing and Welfare checks. Most kids liked Gram. She was sort of a street person. Never a bag lady, and always around when a kid needed something.

Gram prided herself on being a psychic.

That Saturday night there were about half a dozen kids at her place. They brought some beer and Ricky had both booze and dope. The booze was for Gram. She could go through a fifth a day if she had it.

She arranged the kids around the living room, some on the sofa, some on chairs, others sitting on the floor. It was a kind of circle. She sat at a card table, her gray hair neatly combed up off her neck because of the heat. She wore a gray cotton dress with short sleeves that bunched the flab of her upper arms. Her hands shuffled and then laid out a pattern of ordinary playing cards. Next to the undealt cards was her whiskey and water.

"The aspects are good," she told the dark-haired girl who was getting the reading. "There seems to be no opposition at the moment. Did you say you were a Leo?" The girl nodded. "That figures. Leos have been having it rough lately, but you are about to come into your own very soon. Just don't give up. With a little more persistence on your part, you can get that advertising job and move to the city. I see it all happening where there is a three. Now that could be three days, three weeks, or three months from now. More likely, three months." She glanced at the girl. "Okay?" The girl nodded. Gram took a swig from the glass, bunched the cards back together, and started shuffling them. "Okay, who's next? Jimmy? You wanna be next?" Gram never charged for her readings. The booze and the company were all she really wanted. She liked kids and she gathered them around her. "Loneliness is far worse than poverty" was a favorite expression of hers.

Jimmy nodded. "Sure. You can do me next."

The woman's chubby fingers spread out the cards. She studied them silently for a minute or so. "You are going to travel," she said. "I don't think it's going to be very far away, but it is going to be away from Northport."

"That's good," said Jimmy, and the others laughed.

"I'm getting something about a stop along the way. Like in your travels, you come to a spot and can't seem to change it for a while, can't seem to move out of it for a while. You know what I mean?" Jimmy nodded. "And I see two people, two adults, a man and a woman, coming back into your life. *Back* is the word I'm getting here. It's almost as if these people had been part of your life but they went out of it but now they're on their way back."

"Is it my parents?"

She shook her head. "No, I'm not picking up on parents at all. These are two people who are very close to you, almost like parents but aren't, if you know what I mean."

"Well," Jimmy volunteered, "my parents aren't really my parents. I was adopted."

"Oh, then that's it." She smiled. "Yes. That's who these two are. They are your adopted parents. You don't live with them?" He shook his head. "Oh. Well . . . funny I don't see you living with these people again but they will *be* with you again, maybe in a nurturing sort of way, even though not actually living with you. Do you understand what I mean?"

"No," Jimmy said, "not really. My folks and I

had a real fight. They don't want me around anymore, not even if I was painted gold." He grinned and the others smiled.

"Well, I don't know what it's gonna be," she said as she picked up the cards and shuffled them, signaling his reading was over, "but you are going to come to a stop in your life and these adopted parents are going to be there when you need them."

"Great," said Jimmy, "if true."

Gram shook her head. "Maybe not so great. You've got a lot of shit to get through yet before that happens. Things are going to get rougher before they get better. Hold on and don't get discouraged. It'll all get better in the end." She looked around the room. "Ricky? You next?"

He shifted his position on the floor, back against the wall. He had smoked three marijuana and angel-dust cigarettes before coming to her place, and that plus his continued exhaustion made him feel like things were happening around him but too far away to touch. "Yeah, sure, Gram. Tell my future."

The woman spread the cards, studied them, and scowled. Then she picked them up again, hurriedly. "Let me lay them again," she said to no one in particular. Again, she placed them in a pattern atop the card table. Again, the studied scowl. Finally, she said, "I'm not sure exactly what this means. I'm getting something with fire. Now don't give me that Satan shit of yours," she added quickly, "I mean a *real* fire. Something that has been set and blazes high, like a bonfire almost."

"Yeah, man. I know what you're talkin' about."

"Good, because I don't. Now there is a broken clock coming into my head. The clock is broken . . . time is broken . . . it's like something happened . . . in the past . . . that was broken suddenly . . . or ended suddenly. Yes, that's it. Something that *was* and now is no more. Something that existed for a time and doesn't exist now." She looked at him, sharply. "Do you know what I'm talking about?"

"I do," said Jimmy. Ricky glared at him.

Gram closed her eyes. She was no longer getting her information from the cards but from some inner consciousness. "There's the clock again, but there is a lot of dark liquid coming out of it. It's like when it broke it spilled this dark fluid and the fluid is running down and soaking into the ground. And there's that fire again. The clock and the fire and the liquid are all in the same place. You do, Jimmy? You know what this means?"

He shot a glance at Ricky. "Yes, ma'am."

She took a deep breath. "I don't like this feeling I get from this thing . . . this broken thing that seems to bleed this liquid . . . bleed . . . yes, yes, it could be blood . . . it could be blood that I'm seeing. Something or . . . somebody"—she opened her eyes, glanced quickly at Ricky, and shut them again—"or somebody with blood on him . . . cut down . . . yes *cut* . . . down before his time. . . ."

"Yeah," Ricky said from his position way down the corridor, "I know all that. That's in the past. I need to know the future. My future. Fuck the past,

Gram. You see California anywhere? When do you see me going out to the West Coast?"

She was frowning. Jimmy thought her hand was trembling, and he wondered if she knew more than she was admitting. "Let's see the next card," she said. "Let's see what the next card says about your future." She turned over the card atop the pile. "King of Clubs," she said. "Authority. A man with authority." She reached for another card. "King of Spades! More authority. Jack of Spades. Still another authority figure. Looks like you're surrounded with authority figures, Ricky. Not too good, could be the police." She laughed. "Okay then, this last card. Let's see it." She picked up the next card and turned it face up atop all the others in the pile. She stared at it and then at Ricky. Her face paled. "It's nothing," she said quickly. "Doesn't mean a thing."

Jimmy rose from his seat on the sofa and saw the card. "It's the Ace of Spades." He whistled. "Shit, Ricky. That card means bad luck."

A girl spoke up: "I think it means more than that. I think it means death."

"Yeah," Jimmy added quickly, "just like in the movies. Ricky, you got the fuckin' death card!"

Sunday afternoon, July 1. The phone rang in the Northport Police Department. It was a girl's voice.

"I know where Gary Lauwers is."

"Who?" the officer on duty said.

"Gary Lauwers."

"Who is he?"

276

"He's the kid that's been missing. I know where he is."

"I don't know about anybody with that name who's missing," the officer replied.

"He's dead," the girl said.

"Who's dead?"

"Gary Lauwers. They killed him. He's in the woods somewhere. Up there, in Aztakea."

"Miss, will you give me your name, please?"

"Gary is up there. I don't know exactly where. You'll have to look. Jimmy Troiano told me. He was there and so was Albert Quinones. He said Ricky Kasso did it."

"Wait just a minute—"

"I thought you police ought to know. You can tell Gary's folks. They've been looking for him."

"Miss, I need your name. Miss, who gave you this information? Miss—" But the phone line went dead.

Laurie sat in her bedroom looking at the now silent phone. Well, she had done it. It had taken a lot of courage, but it had been on her mind ever since she and Liz and Jimmy had gone to the movies that night. She had kept the secret for four full days. She couldn't keep it any longer. Gary had been her friend. It was the least she could do for him.

A few hours later an attorney, representing Laurie and her family, telephoned the police. He wanted to confirm what she had reported. . . . Did the attorney have any more information? Just that the body was somewhere in Aztakea Woods and that Jimmy, Ricky, and Albert had killed

277

Gary. Were others involved as well? The attorney didn't know, Laurie wasn't sure. There could have been some other kids there. Maybe another half dozen or so.

The police began their search that afternoon.

They had been lucky. The old Black guy driving the pickup truck with the load of used furniture was going all the way to Paterson, New Jersey. They had been trying to hitch a ride for only a few minutes when he stopped and told them to get in the back. Ricky sat in an overstuffed chair and rode backward, watching the exhaled smoke from his cigarette compress into a jet stream as the truck sped forward. Jimmy curled atop a mattress and held on to an inverted table leg.

At last they were on their way. Out of Northport for good. This truck ride was the first step in their pilgrimage to California.

The plan was to go up to Greenwich, New York, where the Kassos were spending the summer. Ricky would pretend to make peace with his folks, and then borrow enough money for bus tickets to Los Angeles. They'd borrow a little extra, too, a guy's gotta eat when he hits L.A.

On the other side of Hackensack, they got off the truck, thanked the old man, and waited for about two hours for someone else to give them a ride north, on busy Highway 17. A college kid on his way to visit his girl gave them a lift next. Jimmy sat in front talking with the kid and Ricky was in back. The kid's sport jacket was draped over the front seat. He gave them a ride as far as Newburgh, in New York State. It was almost midnight when they got out of his car and thanked him for the lift. They laughed and wondered how long it would take the kid to find out that Ricky had stolen two hundred dollars from the wallet in his sport coat.

They had a cup of coffee and a hamburger and a trucker said he'd take them as far as Saratoga. He was heading straight up 87 but he couldn't detour over to Greenwich. It was no problem, man. Saratoga would be just fine.

They got into Saratoga about 3:00 A.M. It had been a long day. They had money in their pockets, but the idea of checking into a motel never occurred to them. They had both become street people, people who live nowhere and sleep anywhere. They found a dry spot under an overpass and stretched out on the strip of grass that bordered the concrete. They lit a cigarette laced with angel dust and lay in the darkness looking at the stars and listening to the occasional car or truck that passed over their heads.

"You know, I don't think I wanna see my folks," Ricky said. "I been thinkin'. All it'll do is cause a hassle. My old man will yell and my old lady will try and talk some sense into me and in the end it'll be another fuckin' fight."

"So what do you wanna do?" Jimmy couldn't see him, he listened to the voice in the darkness.

"We got some extra money from that kid. Let's buy a junker and spend the rest on dope. I know a supplier in Cambridge. That's just on the other side of where my folks have their place. We can

279

buy some dope from him and sell it along the way to California. It'll give us some ready cash."

"Good idea," said Jimmy. "A car and some dope and away we go."

"Yeah, man. First thing when we wake up, I'm gonna see an old buddy of mine here in Saratoga named Tony. He's cool. He's got wheels and he can take us to the supplier and to a used-car lot in Cambridge. Tony knows cars, he'll get us a good deal."

They did visit Tony Mallory that morning, and when Tony innocently asked Ricky what he had been up to, Ricky told him all about the murder. When Tony, eighteen, was questioned by a reporter for *Newsday*, he admitted, "He said that kid (Gary Lauwers) for a long time had been ripping off people, and it was time someone did something about it. As he was talking to me, he told me that if he ever got caught for what he did, he wouldn't spend the rest of his life in jail. He said he would kill himself."

In Cambridge the three of them decided on a battered 1971 maroon Pontiac sedan. The dealer wanted only fifty dollars for it. Ricky thought it was beautiful. Jimmy wasn't too sure.

"It ought to get us at least as far as Chicago," Ricky said.

"Then what?" Jimmy asked.

"Then we'll get another car. That's simple."

"On what?" Tony asked.

"On the money from the hits we're gonna sell." Ricky had it all figured out.

"I don't know, man," Jimmy said. "We're takin'

a chance. Wouldn't it be easier to sell the stuff in Northport and then head out for California? I mean, at least in Northport we know how to find our customers. In Chicago what are we gonna do? Put an ad in the paper?"

"Don't worry," said Ricky. "I know what I'm doin'."

Tony drove away shaking his head. Ricky sat behind the wheel of his new prize and raced the motor a few times. It coughed and spat out oil and smoke. "Like a kitten," he said as he patted the dashboard, "runs like a fuckin' kitten." Then he drove to his supplier and spent one hundred and fifty dollars for mescaline while Jimmy waited in the car.

Ricky headed for Albany, New York's state capital. The air conditioner didn't work, so they had the windows rolled down. The radio *did* work, however, and they soon found an FM station that played heavy-metal music. The old Pontiac chugged right along. Very few people took notice of the two scruffy and uncombed teenagers behind the wheel, but those who had their car windows down couldn't help but notice the loud music.

CHAPTER EIGHT

In Northport the police were combing the woods for Gary's body. Rain had hindered the search, but now the Suffolk County police were in on it too. They brought in their trained dogs.

Ricky and Jimmy passed through Albany, marveling at the new downtown center's towers of glass. Then they continued southwest. The plan was to take 88 down to Binghamton, then take 81 south to the Pennsylvania Turnpike. From there it would be Route 80 straight across the country, straight across to freedom.

At Binghamton they hung around a truckers' cafe, having a few beers and trying to strike up a conversation that would lead to the sale of some of their dope. Both boys thought they should have a little more cash in their pockets before they hit the interstate. Finally, one of the waitresses came over to them.

"Look, kids," she said softly. "You better get the hell out of here. The manager's called the cops. He knows you're trying to push some stuff in his place and he don't like it. Pay for your beers and get out fast. Pushin' dope don't go well around these parts."

Ricky and Jimmy got back into the Pontiac and churned gravel getting onto the highway. They drove for several miles, constantly checking the rearview mirror. If the cops had really been called, they weren't trying very hard to catch them.

Ricky drove in silence. It was starting to get dark and only one headlight worked. "You know," he said, "I don't think we'd better continue any farther tonight. Why don't I just pull off the road and we sleep it out until morning?"

"Fine," Jimmy agreed. "I've been thinkin', too, Rick. We almost got our asses busted back there, trying to find a customer for our stuff. That was dangerous. I don't know whether it's such a good idea to try and sell the stuff as we go along. You know what I mean?"

Ricky nodded. "I know. I been thinkin' the same. What do you say we turn back and hit Northport again? We can unload the stuff on the kids we know, then we can split. It'll delay us for another day, but hell, man, what's a day? I been tryin' to get to California for years. One more day won't matter."

"Good idea," Jimmy agreed. "We'll sell the stuff, maybe borrow some bread from a couple buddies, and then split. It's better that way. Safer, too."

"Yeah, man," Ricky agreed, "and right now, we gotta be *real* safe."

The police didn't find the body that day. It had started to rain as darkness descended and the dogs had been unable to pick up any scent. Even though tomorrow was a holiday—the Fourth of July—they agreed to start searching early.

Independence Day was in the middle of the week, so there weren't as many tourists in the Village of Northport as on some other years. Still, the harbor at the foot of Main Street was full of small craft and flags flew and motors sputtered. Most of the shops were closed. The air was still muggy from the previous day's rain, but the sky was blue and a slim breeze off the water convinced some hardy souls to keep their air conditioners turned off.

And up in Aztakea Woods the dogs came to a barking, sniffing, pawing halt.

"It was pretty disgusting," said a policeman who was there. "There had been an attempt at covering the body, but the rains had washed much of the earth away. I glanced at what was once the face and couldn't look any longer. I'll always remember the terrible stench and the maggots. They put it in a morgue bag and carried it away for an autopsy. Photographs of the grave were taken and the site where the body had lain before the kids decided to bury him. That place was all black. The grass and leaves that had been under the corpse were black. You know how a dead cat will make a mark if it lays too long on your lawn? Well, that's what happened with Gary."

Now the police had two difficult tasks ahead of them: to notify the Lauwers family so they could identify their son and to bring in Kasso, Troiano, and Albert Quinones. Those were the three Laurie had said were there when Gary was murdered. The cops had a file on both Jimmy and Ricky. Albert was unknown to them. He wouldn't be for long.

The maroon Pontiac came off the Long Island Expressway and turned north, toward the Sound. Ricky was at the wheel. "I sure thought we'd never see this place again," he said as the town of Huntington came into view.

"It won't be for long," Jimmy said. "We sell the stuff and split."

"You gonna try and call your folks?" Ricky asked.

"Christ, no! Are you kidding?"

"Maybe you could raise some extra bread, man."

"No. There's other ways to get bread. I'll drop my folks a postcard from Beverly Hills."

"With a picture of our *mansion* in Beverly Hills!" Ricky laughed aloud. "An overhead view, with the palm trees and the swimming pool in the backyard!" And the laugh came again.

They turned off Fort Salonga Road, left onto Woodbine Avenue. They were back in Northport.

Jimmy yelled and Ricky slammed on the brakes. A black cat stood stock-still in the center of the road, staring at them. Ricky blew the horn and shouted. The cat examined the car, trying to decide whether to lick its paw or get out of the way. The cat made its decision and darted back across the road.

"I don't know, man," Jimmy said as Ricky turned the ignition key in the stalled car. "That was a black cat. Black cats mean bad luck."

"Not for me they don't, man." Ricky laughed. "A black cat is Satan's favorite animal. Mine, too. Seein' that black cat means only one thing—lots of luck for both of us."

The police couldn't find Ricky or Jimmy, but Albert was at home. They put him into a squad car and drove him to the Suffolk County station in Yaphank. Albert claims he was physically beaten by the police. The police deny it, and Jimmy says, "He told everybody that just to get sympathy. He told all about us with his own free will. Maybe if it looked like he was gettin' the shit beat out of him, the other kids wouldn't call him a rat. But he is a rat. He ratted on me and Ricky."

Albert later told a reporter, "The detectives were beating the shit out of me. See, I don't trust them, man, I don't trust no one anymore. They picked me up at two, and they were beating the shit out of me for like two and a half hours, in Yaphank. They brought me up to this room, and they started questioning me and shit, and they were beating the shit out of me. They didn't tell

286

me they were going for Ricky and Jim. I don't
know what to think. My head's screwed up ever
since that night—and it's still screwed up, man."
Albert was all of sixteen years old at the time.

Ricky parked the old Pontiac in the lot near the
gazebo. There was a great deal of foot traffic
around the harbor docks that afternoon—tourists,
local citizens, and kids looking to get high. They
managed to sell their mescaline in less than an
hour.

The police admit they took special precautions
to make sure word of finding the body and the
search for Ricky and Jimmy didn't get out. Albert
was put under special surveillance and warned not
to tell anyone except his parents about the case.
Troiano and Kasso were street people with no
known addresses, but their friends formed a net-
work just beneath the surface of village life, a net-
work that could tip off the alleged young murderers and give them time to disappear.

"We made extraordinary efforts to keep the investigation into the homicide as secret as possible,"
Northport Police Chief Robert Howard told *The
Observer*. "We even changed the frequency we used
on our radio calls to remain undetected." Every
man on the force was shaken by the fact that so
many kids knew about Gary lying up there in the
woods but nobody told them. Two full weeks had
gone by before Laurie's phone call. "I'm concerned that they were talking about it and that we
didn't find out about the murder until July 1. Why

couldn't anyone place an anonymous phone call earlier to us, or even the press? I just thank God someone finally did."

The sun, some smoke, the successful sale of all their dope, the fact that they were finally going to leave Northport, added up to a terrific high. It had been a great day. They had seen old friends and bullshitted old tales. They had shaken hands, pinched a couple of female rear ends, and said their good-byes. Yes, it was true. They were off for California. Sure, they'd let kids know where they were out there. Somebody back home would get a postcard. Sure, they'd have a real nice place out there, with lots of room for friends to crash when they showed up. It's been real great, man. It'll be better out there. Much better, man.

Ricky slowed down the Pontiac. They were on Bluff Point Road, already heading the wrong way if they were going to get to California. "Do I look as bad as I think I do?" he asked Jimmy. "I mean, do I look like a bum, or what?"

"You look like an or what," Jimmy said. "The catsup from that last hot dog is all over your face."

"Free food tastes good." Ricky smiled. "I'm glad Sherri always has a Fourth of July cookout. She's neat."

"Yeah," Jimmy agreed. "Her old man didn't take too kindly to us, though. You see the way he looked at you when you speared that hamburger off the grill with your bare fingers?"

"Yeah"—Ricky grinned at the memory of it—"and when he asked me if I was afraid I'd get burned, I said that mescaline makes my fingers numb. I don't feel pain."

"Dumb fucker believed you." Jimmy laughed. "Sherri's brother's a dork, you know? He told me he only smokes weed from Haiti. He pronounced it 'Hay-tie,' the asshole. I told him weed from Haiti is marinated in monkey piss before it gets sent here. He didn't know whether to believe me or not. Stupid fucker's gonna go into junior high this year and pretends he knows all about weed." He glanced again at Ricky. "Yeah, man, you do look like shit. I think we better wash ourselves off. I can still smell the charcoal lighter Sherri's dad drowned those poor coals in."

"How about over there?" Ricky parked the car and pointed to a low flat building directly across the road. A white sign emblazoned with a blue flag and a red star announced the place was the "Northport Yacht Club." Underneath was the added information "Members Only."

"The Yacht Club?" Jimmy shook his head. "I never been in that place. I don't think it's a good idea."

"Come on." Ricky started getting out of the car. His legs wobbled slightly from the many drugs he had taken during the day. "I know how to get to the showers. It's easy. I've done it before."

Jimmy started across the road with him, then glanced back to see that the car was safely parked. Its front bumper was almost touching a sign that read "No Parking Anytime." Then just a few feet farther was a second sign, about three feet square with heavy black letters: "No Parking on Any

Street in Entire Area. PD." Jimmy grinned and followed Ricky. "Car looks safe enough there, all right."

With all the elegance that the Village of Northport shows to the world, one would assume its Yacht Club would be elegant as well. One can't assume in Northport. The club is a cheaply constructed square with a parking lot in front. The first thing a visitor sees as he rounds the side and glances at the waterfront is the men's locker room and then the women's. There is a snack bar for hamburgers, hot dogs, and soft drinks, and a cement balcony that looks down on an Olympic-size pool. A wrought-iron fence keeps people from falling from the balcony into the pool. There are a few round redwood tables with matching chairs on this balcony, but the tabletops have been scarred with people carving initials, hearts, dates, and telephone numbers into them. There is a ramp that leads down to a beach strewn with rocks and pebbles but no sand. Then there's a wooden dock that stretches out into the water. If a member gets there early, he can tie his boat to the dock. If not, there is a kid in a noisy outboard who'll take the owner to his boat parked farther out. On the upper floor is an unexciting restaurant and bar. Membership, providing you are recommended by two other members, costs five hundred dollars. It's another five hundred dollars if you want to keep your boat there. Jews can be members, so can Blacks. No Blacks want to, however.

Ricky and Jimmy stripped off their soiled clothes and took showers, luxuriating in the club's warm water and free soap. Then they dried themselves with the free towels that were piled on a bench. They got dressed and went out to sit on the balcony and watch the moon ride over the water. Upstairs there was music and voices.

"You wanna go up for a drink?" Ricky asked.

"Nah," Jimmy said. "I'm still full from all that stuff at Sherri's."

They sat for another hour or so, enjoying a marijuana cigarette and watching its smoke float over the railing and down over the illuminated swimming pool.

"When we get to California," Ricky said, "we'll join a place like this."

"Yeah, but only better. Okay? This place would suck in L.A."

They sat for a little while longer, dreaming their California dream aloud. At no time was Gary's name ever mentioned.

Finally, they decided it was time to go back to the car, drive around, and find a place to sleep for the night. The maroon Pontiac was right where they left it.

Ricky got behind the wheel. "Well, for Christ sake!" he said loudly. "When did you do that?"

"What?"

"Break the fuckin' ignition key? Look at the damned thing! It broke off. It's broke in two."

Jimmy flicked his cigarette lighter and examined the key. Ricky was right. The key had been broken in half. "Is the rest in the ignition?" he asked.

"No," Ricky said, examining the ignition with the still-lit lighter.

"Well, how the hell did it break off?" Jimmy demanded. "What did you do to it?"

"Me?" said Ricky. "I didn't do anything to it! Why the hell should I? Now what the fuck we gonna do? Can't move this pile of junk."

"Shit!" Jimmy said, and spat out the window into the darkness. "Gotta get a key made. Tomorrow. I know a guy in Kings Park that does that. He comes in a van and makes you a key when you don't have your own."

"Let's go call him," Ricky said.

"At this hour? He won't be in his office at this hour. Besides, it's a fuckin' holiday. Remember?" Jimmy spat again. "First thing tomorrow, I'll call him. He'll come over tomorrow. He can't do nothin' tonight."

"Guess we'll just sleep here tonight," Ricky said. "Sleep in the car."

"We've done worse."

Ricky got out and stretched across the backseat. Jimmy lay on his back in the front seat, his feet sticking out the window. Ricky lit up two cigarettes and passed one to Jimmy. The two friends stayed like that for a while, letting the marijuana and the angel dust cloud their brains even further.

"You remember that black cat?" Jimmy asked after a while.

"What black cat?" Ricky asked.

"The one that was in the road today when we came into Northport?"

"Oh. Yeah. What about it?"

"I told you it was unlucky. Now here we are with a fuckin' car that won't work."

"Black cat didn't have nothing to do with that key, man."

"Put a jinx on us," said Jimmy.

"Shit!" Ricky replied. "You're startin' to sound like me."

"I *told* you that cat was unlucky."

PART THREE

July 1984 to April 1985

CHAPTER ONE

"Officer?" the woman's voice was shrill over the phone.

"Yes, ma'am?" the policeman said.

"I want to report a vagrant's car. It's been there all night and it's still there this morning."

"What kind of a car, ma'am?"

"I don't know anything about cars," she said. "I'm not a used-car dealer! This is an old one with four doors. It's red and it's a mess and it doesn't belong where it is."

"Where is it, ma'am?"

"On Bluff Point Road, right across the street from the Yacht Club. There's somebody in it. I can see his feet sticking out the window."

"Feet, ma'am?"

"Yes. You *do* know what feet are, don't you, Officer? I live in Harbor Point. We don't pay all those taxes to have our road looking like a junkyard."

"Yes, ma'am." The cop knew that a lot of newly arrived and very important Northporters lived in that expensive development. Houses there cost from three hundred and fifty thousand to half a million dollars. "Yes, ma'am. I'm sorry, ma'am. Get someone on it right away."

Somewhere a black cat must have smiled.

Jimmy was the first to awaken when he heard the voice shout "Freeze!" and he looked at the pistol that was pointed at his face. "Don't move!" the voice demanded.

The uniformed officer pushed Jimmy's feet off the window ledge and yanked open the front door. "Out!" he said. Before Jimmy could sit up, he was grabbed by his ankles and pulled from the car. In a flash they had him up against the automobile, hands behind his back and legs spread.

"I didn't do nothin', man!" Jimmy protested. "What the hell's the matter with you guys?"

Another policeman threw open the rear door. "You!" His gun was pointed at a groggy and hung over Ricky. "Get out and don't try anything smart!"

"What?" Ricky stammered, trying to focus. It was only 7:30 A.M.

The policeman grabbed Ricky's legs and pulled. Ricky was out and standing near the car. Jimmy glanced at his friend and saw Ricky going for a knife he carried in his back pocket. The cops saw him, too, and they grabbed his arms and hand-cuffed them behind him. After giving him his rights, one of the cops waved the knife in Ricky's face.

"Is this the one you used?" he asked.

"What are you talkin' about?" Ricky found it difficult to form his words.

"When you killed that kid up in the woods? Is this the knife you stabbed him with?"

"I didn't kill nobody, man," Ricky said slowly. "What the fuck you talkin' about?"

"Look, Kasso, we know you did it. People told us."

"You know my name?" Ricky glanced around at the other officers there.

"That's pretty easy," a cop replied. "Your name and Troiano's name have been on everybody's mind for days."

"Mine, too?" Jimmy was surprised. "Why? I didn't do nothin'."

"Sure," replied the officer. "Both you scumbags are as innocent as puppies."

They grabbed the boys and hustled them into a squad car. Neither of them spoke. There was a great deal Jimmy wanted to tell Ricky, but he kept quiet. He was not about to give these damned cops anything at all. If they wanted something, they'd have to work for it.

Their stay at the Northport Village Police Station was brief. Just long enough for them to be booked, to have the other officers on duty stare at them, and then they were hustled into patrol cars of the Suffolk County police and driven to the station in Yaphank. Driven in separate but equal squad cars.

"When we got to the station and I saw Ricky," Jimmy recalls, "I was sure they had worked him over on the ride down there. He looked angry and one side of his face was red. Probably he had mouthed off to them and they hit him. It wouldn't have surprised me."

The two boys were not permitted to talk to each other, and both of them, out of ignorance or arrogance or naiveté, signed away their rights to see an attorney.

"They took me into a room and fingerprinted me first," Jimmy recalls. "They did it fast and the cop pressed down hard. They didn't talk much and I didn't offer. Then I went out of the room and Ricky went in. He looked at me and winked. I didn't do anything. Shit, man, I didn't know what to do. But when he came out of that room, there was ink on the crotch of his trousers. What I think happened is that once his fingers were smeared in that ink, one of the cops kneed him in the balls and his first reaction was to grab himself down there. That was why he had ink there. I can't think of any other reason. Then they began to play with us. You know, one against the other. The good-cop-and-the-bad-cop routine. Shit, I had seen that done a thousand times on TV. I wasn't about to fall for *that*."

The scenes in the locked rooms went back and forth. Outsiders were forbidden anywhere near the boys. The press had already picked up the scent and the telephones at the Fourth Precinct were ringing off the walls.

Jimmy says he held out for the longest time before admitting to even being at the bonfire that night in the woods. "I didn't know what they knew and I waited for them to tell me. They told me Albert had said I held down Gary while Ricky stabbed him. I said Albert was full of shit. They asked me if Albert had helped kill Gary. I said no. I said that Albert was whacked out of his mind on drugs and kept watchin' some tree that bent back and forth. They wanted to know who else was there. I told them nobody else was. Just me and Ricky and Albert. They said word on the street was that there was about fifteen other kids there and that we were having a Satanic ritual and that while Gary was being sacrificed, the kids were chanting and singing to the devil. I told them they were full of shit. I told them Ricky had had a fight with Gary over some bags of angel dust that Gary had stolen and never paid for. I said that Ricky had killed Gary in self-defense. They asked me what I was doin' while all this was goin' on. I said I was there, I was watchin', but I didn't kill Gary. They said I held him down. I told them they were full of crap. They said Albert told them one time when Ricky lost the knife, I picked it up and handed it back so Ricky could finish the job. I said, yeah, maybe I did do somethin' like that, but by the time I handed him the knife, Gary was already dead. I told them I was stoned on drugs. I didn't remember what had happened and what the sequence was. I was high and so was Ricky and so was Albert. They wanted to know if Gary was high. I told them, who the hell knows? Ask him, why don't ya? They wanted to know where the knife was. I said I didn't have a clue.

"Whose knife was it? they asked me. It was Ricky's, of course. He always carries a knife. They saw that when they arrested him. Where did Ricky get the knife? I said ask him. I mean, Jesus Christ, he's got all those answers, I don't. Then they started back again. What were the names of the other kids who were there? Tell them about the Satanic ritual that Gary was being sacrificed to. Who were the others in the cult? Was Ricky the high priest of the Satanic cult? Was I a priest in the cult? I told them there was no cult. That Ricky liked to pretend he and Satan were buddies, that Satan was his main man. Was there a temple somewhere? Was there an altar and a place where babies were sacrificed? You know, shit like that. Who were the adults involved? Finally, I told them I had said all I was going to say and I thought they were all full of shit."

The police put Jimmy alone in a room and he waited, looking at the painted walls and the wire screen over the window, waited and wondered what the cops' next trick would be. God, how he hated cops! Then the door opened and Ricky came in. Alone.

"Jesus, man," Jimmy said. "You look bad."

"They gave me a hard time," Ricky said. Jimmy didn't ask him about the ink on his crotch. "Albert gave them the whole story."

"Yeah, I know. Little fucker."

"The cops say you told them I killed Gary."

"Yeah, but in self-defense," Jimmy said.

"Yeah. Thanks, but I told them I killed him deliberately. I already admitted it."

"You admitted it?" Jimmy couldn't believe it. "Why, man?"

"Why not? They would have kept up on me until I did. You know that. Those fuckers are mean and they would have done anything after a while to get me to confess."

"Jesus, Ricky." Jimmy walked to the window and looked out. Green grass and leafy trees suddenly looked wonderful to him. "What did you say about me, man? Did you say I did it?"

Ricky shook his head. "I told them I did it and that you held Gary down."

"But that was only in the *beginning*," Jimmy exploded. "When he was still on the ground, before you started stabbing him. You know that!"

"Christ, man, I was all fucked up on dope," Ricky tried to explain. "I know you held him down sometime that night. I didn't remember exactly when. They asked me if you held him down and I said yes."

"Well, did you tell them you didn't remember exactly?" Jimmy was almost shouting at his friend. "Did you tell them you were high?"

Ricky nodded. "They know that. I told them I didn't remember all of it. I only remember pieces. They had what I said all typed out. They made me sign it." He put out his hand, touching Jimmy on the shoulder. "I don't know whether I fucked up or not, man. I made a statement and I copped out in it."

"Jesus!" was all Jimmy could think of to say.

"I'll get a lawyer and I'll tell them you didn't do it. I mean, they ain't gonna electrocute us without a lawyer and a trial and everything. You won't have any problems, man. I'll see to that. My old man knows some high-powered lawyers. When we get bailed out of here he'll take us to see some."

"Yeah," said Jimmy softly. "Sure."

The door opened. "Okay, Kasso," a cop motioned. "Let's go."

Ricky shrugged. "See ya," he said, and started from the room. Then he turned back. "You know what I did?" He was grinning. "After I signed the statement I turned it over and I wrote 'Gary Lauwer deserved everything that I gave him.' Neat, huh?" The door closed.

They let Jimmy stay in that room alone for almost a half hour—a calculated thirty minutes for him to think and reconsider. Then the door opened again. It wasn't Ricky, but two policemen.

"Okay, Jimmy," one of them said. "Tell the truth. We know you are more into this than you've said."

Even though Jimmy claims he was "still high" and "I was so whacked out from last night's dope that I didn't know what I was doing," he read the typed statement that afternoon and signed it.

In the days before the trial Ricky's signed statement was never given out. It was always "misplaced" or "out of the file" when anyone wanted to read it. However, Jimmy's *second* statement, the one in which he implicated himself, was published complete and unedited almost three months before the trial. Reading material for any and all prospective jurors.

I, James Vincent Troiano, do make the following statement. I have been told by Detectives Louis Rodriguez and Robert Amato of the Suffolk County Police Department's Homicide Squad that: 1. I have the right to remain silent. 2. Anything I say can and will be used against me in a court of law. 3. I have the right to talk to a lawyer right now and have him present before any questioning. 4. and that if I can't afford one and want a lawyer, one will be furnished for me before any more questioning. I understand all these rights they have explained to me. I do not wish to contact a lawyer. With all the rights in mind and what they explained to me, I do wish to talk to them and tell them the whole story without a lawyer.

I want to add that I have a court case on the calendar for July 11, 1984, on a burglary case at 1st District Court in Hauppauge and I was asked if I had a lawyer on that case and I told them that I did not.

On Thursday, July 5, 1984, during the morning hours, I was taken by detectives of the Homicide Squad to Yaphank where I was told that a guy I know as Gary Lauwers' body was found murdered in Northport. The detectives asked me a lot of questions and I told them some answers but not everything. Not that I wanted to lie to them but since they hadn't asked certain questions I didn't offer a lot of things. I made it look like I hadn't done too much during the killing of Gary, that Rick Kasso had done most of it. When I finished telling those detectives the first story, I left there with Rodriguez and Amato and headed for Northport Village. It was during this time that I realized that I should tell it all, that is, how the murder of Gary Lauwers went down. I knew that if I did this, I would end up feeling better.

I took Rodriguez and Amato into the woods to show them where the fight had started that night in June, the 16th, Saturday about 2:00 A.M.

Before we went there, me, Rick, Albert Quinones and Gary, had been at a Dunkin' Donuts and Albert had told me that Rick wanted to beat up Gary who had taken some angel dust from Rick. When we arrived at the woods known as "Aztakea Woods," Albert told me Ricky was going to kill Gary. I decided I didn't care because Gary should not have taken the dust belonging to Rick. In the woods, Rick started a fire and Gary gave him his socks and then the sleeves on Gary's jacket. I cut the sleeves off the jacket with either Rick's knife or my knife. Gary was on the ground saying he felt he was going to be beat up or something. I saw Gary and Rick start to fight. All of a sudden I heard Gary say, "I love you, Mom." When I looked, Gary was on his knees and Rick was stabbing him in the back. I was pretty high but I am sure it was around this time that I went to

Gary's side and as hard as I could, I kicked him in the rib area. I know I broke some ribs because I felt that side cave in. Gary managed to run from us and we chased him into the woods. Rick and I dragged him back and I believe during this time, we took turns cutting hair off Gary's head. I guess I cut about three pieces off. Rick was holding Gary as I did this and Rick told Gary to repeat "I love you, Satan" which Gary did even though he was really hurting. I knew that Gary had to be killed or he would rat us all out if he lived. While I held him, Rick also cut some hair off and stabbed him some more. I didn't see Albert Quinones do any of this, I guess he was just watching. I saw Ricky put Gary in a headlock and Gary was saying something like "Please don't kill me." Ricky stabbed him some more. Like I said, I was glad because Gary could not leave those woods alive. Ricky was saying some shit about Satan over Gary's body. He's into things about Satan and the devil. I saw Gary lift his head slightly and Ricky went buggy and started stabbing Gary in the face. I don't have any idea how many times but it was a lot. We, Ricky and me, dragged Gary into the woods and covered him with leaves and branches. Rick realized he had lost his Satanic star which was on a chain. We couldn't find it in the dark. About this time, the three of us left the woods and Gary and went to Albert's home where I showered. I left them and went to Kings Park. That night, I saw Ricky Kasso and he told me he threw the knife he killed Gary with into the harbor off the "New Park" dock in Northport. Today, Thursday, July 5, 1984, I was photographed pointing at several spots where this killing took place. I also pointed out and had my picture taken at the spot where Rick and I buried Gary Lauwers with a shovel this past Saturday, June 30th, at about 11:00 A.M. We found chunks of Gary's hair and I had my picture taken pointing at them.

I wish to add that I am eighteen years of age with a date of birth of December 10, 1965, in Schenectady, New York. I now live with my adopted parents, Mary and Vincent Troiano. I am currently unemployed and gone through the ninth grade in Northport Junior High. I have read this statement of four pages and I swear it is all true.

Jimmy now says that statement is "more or less true." The sequence of events has changed in his mind. He did not go to the woods to help bury the body. Also, he doesn't know why he admitted saying *"While I held him,* Ricky also cut some hair off and stabbed him some more." Not true, he claims.

"I was really high when the murder took place and still don't remember it exactly. Then the day the cops made me sign that statement, I was just coming down from another high that I'd been on with Ricky. Christ, man, it had been over two weeks from the murder to the arrest. I know lots of people who never take dope who can't remember exact details that long."

308

CHAPTER TWO

While Jimmy was writing his statement in Yaphank, another statement was being handed out in Northport. It would turn everything upside down.

Newsday reporters and others from New York City papers had heard that a boy had been killed, his mutilated body found, and two of his friends arrested. The media began screaming for the details—for the facts. The confusion started there and grew until Jimmy's trial was over.

Police Chief Robert Howard later explained the first snafu to his friend Mark McGuire, who was studying to be a journalist at New York's St. Bonaventure University. McGuire wrote up the confusion as his undergraduate thesis for his Bachelor of Arts degree.

When the Northport police and the Suffolk County police realized the press wanted in on the case, they agreed that a press statement should be issued. Chief Howard talked with Chief of Detectives John Gallagher—of Suffolk County—who said not to worry, the Suffolk office would write one and send it over to Northport. "After all," Howard maintains, "they have their own public relations department and people who specialize in that sort of thing." Chief Howard went home to get some sleep.

At the Suffolk Station, Chief of Detectives Gallagher pushed a button on the recorder and dictated the information the press was to receive:

Today, July 5, 1984, homicide detectives arrested one Richard Kasso who has no known address and by his own admission lives in the streets, but whose parents reside at 40 Seaview Avenue, Northport, N.Y.

Kasso was arrested on the charge of murder Second Degree in the stabbing death of one Garry Lauwers, age seventeen years of 15 West Scudder Place, Northport. Lauwers, unemployed, had been missing although not officially reported as such, since June 15, 1984.

Kasso, also seventeen years of age, is a member of a satanical cult and worships and partakes in rituals honoring the devil.

It is believed Lauwers stole ten bags of a narcotic commonly known as angel dust from the defendant, Kasso.

Kasso learned of the theft and sought revenge against Lauwers. The revenge turned out to be the death of Lauwers.

This came to the attention of the Suffolk County Police Department as a result from a call from the Northport Village Police Department. The Northport Village Police on Sunday, July, 1984, had received an anonymous phone call indicating that a body was buried in a wooded area commonly known as "Aztaki Woods" in the Northport area. The wooded area is known to the Northport Police Department who conducted a preliminary search and additionally made attempts to identify the anonymous caller. The searches on Sunday and Monday were unsuccessful. However, they felt that a continuing investigation should be made and Chief Robert Howard requested aid from the Suffolk County Police Department.

On Tuesday afternoon, homicide detectives and canine units from the Suffolk County Police Department responded to the wooded area described. Because of inclement weather and heavy rains no search was made.

Again, on Wednesday, July 4, 1984, at about 1:30 under the direction of Chief Howard the search was reinstituted. At about 2:00 P.M. a canine dog located a skeletal remains of a human body buried in a shallow grave in this wooded area in another direction than that that was searched by the Northport Village Police.

The remains were tentatively identified as the victim, Gary Lauwers, and indications revealed that he had been stabbed numerous times. The condition of the body indicated that it had been left in the woods for approximately two weeks and further, had been recently buried. The body was pronounced dead by the medical examiners office and removed to the morgue for further examination.

Homicide detectives and Northport Village Police officers, under the direction of Northport Village Police Chief Robert Howard conducted and persued an intense investigation.

Information uncovered, revealed that the defendent, Kasso, stabbed the victim numerous times and dragged his body, thinking he was dead, to the place where it was located. When Kasso began to leave the site, Lauwers sat up and according to Kasso, stated I love you mom. These are the last words uttered by the victim.

At this point, Kasso returned to where Lauwers sat and inflicted further stab wounds into the facial area, cutting out his eyes. Kasso further indicated that on this last stabbing of the victim he heard a crow cry out. This was an indication to him as a satin worshipper, that the devil had ordered him to kill Lauwers.

Investigation is continuing to determine if and how many accomplices were involved in this murder.

Additionally, detectives of the Suffolk County Police Department are presently searching for the murder weapon believed to be in the waters off the Northport Village dock area.

Gallagher reread his work, liked it, and gave it to his secretary. She phoned the Northport Station, got Officer Art Molin on the line, and he turned on *his* tape recorder and recorded the message. That tape went to Village Clerk Rita Salerno, who transcribed it, made spelling errors, made numerous copies, and handed it to the police, who started handing it out to the eager press.

Chief Howard returned to the station later that day and was extremely upset by the release. Gary's name, the name of the woods, and even Satan's name were mispelled, and those were the minor errors.

Of course Chief Howard did get *his* name mentioned three times, making it obvious to the press who was in charge. "There was no way I would have released that," the chief later told journalism student McGuire. "You are never supposed to give out the substance of an admission, confession, or any statement by a defendant."

William McKeown is the Suffolk County Police Department's "assistant to the commissioner for media relations." It's his job to write the press releases. "I make it a point," he said, "to stay away from the motives and admissions of a defendant. That might possibly taint a case. Something like that is best taken care of in court."

Only *after* Chief Detective Gallagher's secretary

had phoned in the copy of Northport did Mc-Keown see the release. McKeown grabbed his red pencil and edited Gallagher's copy drastically. He cut 299 words out of Gallagher's *Dragnet* prose and reduced his text from fifteen paragraphs to nine. He spelled Gary's name correctly. He said Ricky "is believed to be a member of a satanic cult that honors the devil." He didn't say Ricky *was*. Also, Gary "may have" stolen those ten bags of angel dust and that it's *alleged* Ricky stabbed Gary because of them. The "canine dog" was turned into "K-9." There was nothing about Ricky hearing a crow caw in Satanic approval. Nothing about Gary sitting up and saying "I love you, Mom" as his last words. Chief Howard was mentioned only twice.

The revised release was typed, proofread, and *never* phoned into Northport. The first, and more exotic, release continued to be handed out to the press. In fact, Chief Howard never knew there was a second version. "Although I thought the content was bizarre, there was no reason to doubt that the release they gave us was what they wanted put out," the chief said. "McKeown never called back and notified us of the error."

And not once, in either version, was Jimmy's name mentioned as an accomplice in Gary's murder.

The next day, July 6, is known as "Day One of the Story."

There on page one of *Newsday* were head shots

of Ricky and Jimmy and a close-up of the play area near the gazebo with the word "Satin" written on one of the wooden pilings. "Two Held in Ritual Killing of Teenager in Northport," the headline blared. On page three was a photograph of police divers searching for Ricky's knife in the harbor waters and a yearbook head-and-shoulders shot of a mild-looking blond, thin-lipped adolescent boy. It was Gary. The article, written by Jim O'Neill and Dennis Hevesi, started the whole Satanism press mess.

The first article reported that the police were calling Gary's murder a "sacrificial killing" by a "devil worshipping" group. They gave a couple of paragraphs about the boys, right out of the press release, then they quoted Detective Lieutenant Robert Dunn, who threw more fuel on the fire: "You've got a whole group of satanic worshippers. This was a sacrificial killing. They built a roaring fire in a field near the woods. They cut the sleeves out of his shirt and burned them and they took his socks off and burned them. I don't know what this is supposed to mean, but this is what they did. It's pure satanism. . . . Just before they killed him, they forced him to say 'I love Satan.' After he did say that, they did kill him."

So much for police accuracy or the presumption of innocence.

The reports stated that summonses had been issued for at least twelve youths who were witnesses to the crime. One article went on to report that Northport Chief Howard said "there have been rumors of a devil-worshiping cult in the commu-

315

nity for several years." Specifically, he mentioned finding the burned carcass of a baby goat in Cow Harbor Park in 1981. There were rumors at the time that it had been sacrificed to Satan.

Newsday reported that the victim's family had been notified of Gary's fate by the detectives. Despite the fact that their son had been missing since June 15, the Lauwers, according to Gallagher, told police they hadn't reported Gary missing because he had previously stayed away from home for periods of time—the longest period for four days. "Last night Mrs. Lauwers would say only, 'We're not sure it's him, but there's very little hope.'"

The *Newsday* report concluded with a human interest touch. "At 6:00 P.M., the Troianos received a phone call from their son. During the conversation, Mrs. Troiano said, 'I know you wouldn't do anything like that. . . . I love you, too. Maybe you should say a little prayer.'"

For the world, and especially the residents of Northport, this was the first time anyone had heard about the murder. It would certainly not be the last.

CHAPTER THREE

On July 6, Ricky and Jimmy were transferred to the security unit at Riverhead, Long Island.

Photographer Tony Jerome of *Newsday* was there covering the story. When Jimmy saw the camera he tried to turn his face away but he got caught in a three-quarter mug shot, eyes cast downward, chin and jaws tight, his long black hair hanging down to his shoulders. He wore a T-shirt with the symbol for atomic energy emblazoned on a grinning skull directly over his heart. In the photo his right arm is behind him but his left has come forward slightly, showing the handcuff on his left wrist. The arm came forward because he was being pulled by a steel-link chain that fastened behind his back and came around and across his left hip.

Photographer Jerome's shot of Ricky was completely different. Here was the defiance and arrogance of a king—the Acid King playing to the camera's lens. He stared straight into it, his mouth open as if to shout, to scream. His long hair—the hair his father had wanted to cut—curled around his shoulders and twisted in wide sharp ringlets framing his face. He was wearing a T-shirt with an AC/DC logo emblazoned on it in red and black.

But it was his *eyes*—wide, oval, piercing, mocking—that riveted everyone's attention. The reports of Satanic rituals and death grabbed readers everywhere, but it was those eyes that put Ricky Kasso on America's front pages and at the top of the six o'clock news.

The cops put the two boys in the bull pen and refused to let the clamoring press anywhere near.

"What are you going to do?" Jimmy asked Ricky. "Gonna call your folks? Gonna plead insanity or what? I need to know, man, then I'll do the same."

"I'm not going to do anything," Ricky said.

Jimmy remembers "a funny feeling" coming over him. He looked at Ricky, stared at him directly. "Level with me, man," he said. "Are you gonna kill yourself?"

Ricky shook his head. The soon-to-be-famous eyes widened in surprise. "Hell no, man. I wouldn't do that to you. No, I'm just going to hang around for a month."

Jimmy didn't believe him. "And then what?"

"Then," he replied, "then I'll hang myself."

The cell door opened and an officer entered. "Okay, Kasso. You're first. Let's go."

"First for what?" Ricky asked.

"The shrink wants to see you. Dackow's his name."

"I don't give a fuck what his name is," Ricky responded. "I ain't gonna tell him nothin'."

"Come on, tough guy," the cop said. "Move it."

Ricky grinned at Jimmy. "See you later, man."

"Yeah, man." Jimmy replied. "See you."

When it was Jimmy's turn to be interviewed by the jail psychologist, Ricky had been taken and put in a separate cell.

They never saw each other again.

Jimmy had started to come down from his high. Had begun to realize that he was in the biggest trouble he'd ever been in in his life. This was not just another arrest for burglary or pushing dope. This was a bust for murder. It was a murder he recalled *seeing* but did not recall *doing*. There was no doubt that Ricky had stabbed Gary. That *he* had held Gary down while Ricky stabbed him, there was *great* doubt. It was his word against the evidence. His word against his criminal record. His word against a community that was growing very angry over what had happened in Aztakea Woods.

Psychologist Dackow spent approximately five minutes with each boy. The time, the tests, they're all routine. Dackow thought Ricky was in good spirits but that Jimmy "was suicidal."

They took Ricky's shoelaces and belt from him and placed him in what they call a "segregation cell." They kept him separate from other prisoners because of "this Satan thing." Ricky was one of twenty prisoners under the watch of a single guard.

They removed Jimmy's shoelaces and belt as well—part of the usual prisoner admission procedure—and put him in a quasi-hospital atmosphere where there are only four prisoners to each guard. Jimmy—instead of Ricky—was under maximum security, maximum observation.

Reporters descended on tiny Northport, pushing their microphones and their notepads into the faces of anyone who would tell them about the terrible Satanic cult that had shattered the town. Television crews roamed picturesque Main Street sticking their lenses everywhere, recording reels of nothingness that would later be turned into "news."

"L.I. Cops Hunt Killer Cult" ballyhood the *New York Post*'s page-one headline. "Homicide Chief Blames Rock Videos." This ran alongside a picture of Ricky—the *Newsday* shot was better—in handcuffs and grim-faced. Those eyes still shot fire, however. Under the picture: "Suspected cult killer, Rickard Kasso, a drawing of Satan emblazoned on his AC/DC rock group sweatshirt, is brought handcuffed into court for arraignment on murder charges yesterday."

The *Post* noted that Jimmy "allegedly did not take part in the stabbing, but helped carry the victim into the woods and urged Kasso on, police said."

Long Island's main paper, *Newsday*, which had broken the story, still went after the cult and Satan angle but did stop long enough to listen to what Northporters told them:

"Law enforcement sources yesterday repeatedly referred to a 'Satanic cult,' which they said was composed of ten Northport youths, both male and female. But young people acquainted with Kasso and Troiano questioned whether the group was so structured."

Anonymous friends of Kasso told the reporters that while he bragged of devil worship, they did not believe a cult existed. The kids said "Kasso had painted the ceiling of the gazebo in Cow Harbor Park, on Northport Harbor, with the words 'Ricky, the Acid King.' Also painted on the ceiling is Lauwers's name, surrounded by the letter 'X' and the number '666.' The number 666 in the Bible's Book of Revelation is the mark of the anti-Christ."

The prisoners in Ricky's part of the jail were allowed to watch a little TV after the evening meal. Ricky sat there, with several others, as his face suddenly appeared on the news. He beamed in pleasure and looked to make sure the others knew that was *him* up there. Then the newscaster mispronounced his last name.

Ricky jumped to his feet, screaming at the officer in charge. "Goddamnit, they can't even say my name right!"

The officer told him to sit down and shut up.

"No, I won't. It's Kaaaaso. Like in asshole. It

ain't Kay-so! Shit." He shook his fist at the set. "Those dumb fuckers up there! A guy finally makes the grade and they fuck it up!"

"Look," said the officer, "do you want me to put you back in your cell?"

"Yeah, I do," Ricky replied. "This shitty society's all fucked up!"

At 12:30 A.M. the guard looked into Ricky's cell. He was asleep on the cot.

At 1:00 A.M. the guard looked again. Ricky was hanging from the cell door.

Sometime early on the morning of July 7, Ricky decided to keep the promise made to his parents and friends: "If they ever put me in jail, I'll kill myself."

Ricky had tied a bed sheet around his neck, had shinnied up the cell door and tied the end of the sheet to the bars above the door. Then he turned around, pushed his long legs as hard as he could against the bars, and swung out, then down. Down into death.

"Hey, Troiano, wake up!" A guard stood over Jimmy, shaking him.

Jimmy opened his eyes. God, how he hated to be awakened. "What's the trouble?" he asked. "What time is it?"

"It's 2:27 A.M.," the officer said. "I've got some news for you."

Jimmy stared at him, the overhead light hurting his eyes. "Well," he said, "what is it?"

"Your friend blew it."

322

"What? What are you talking about?" He still wasn't awake.

"Your friend, Kasso. He's dead."

Jimmy sat up on the bed. "Dead? What are you talkin' about, man?"

"I'm talking about dead"—Jimmy didn't know if the cop was enjoying being the bearer of this message or not—"gone . . . finished . . . kaput."

Jimmy brushed at his face with his hand, trying to eliminate the few cobwebs of sleep that kept him from being fully there. "How? How did it happen?"

"He hung himself. We found him in the cell."

With the message delivered, the officer abruptly left the cell, turning off the overhead light and leaving Jimmy in the darkness.

The boy lay back down on the bed, his head creasing the hard pillow. For a few seconds there was nothing there in the blackness of his mind. Not an image, not an emotion, not a thought. Then he felt the tears start welling up in his eyes. They brimmed across the bottom of his lids, then peaked and coursed down his teenage face. It was the first time he had cried since he had lost Lucia. Now he had lost another friend. Now Ricky was gone too.

He turned over quickly to hide his eyes in the pillow and to let the tears be absorbed by the cotton fabric. It wouldn't do to have anyone see him like this. He knew, in a matter of time, that the cops would be back, questioning him about Ricky and why Ricky did this thing to himself.

"I asked you," he said aloud, "I asked you the

last time I saw you if you were going to commit suicide and you said no. Shit, man, you said no and I believed you! Then you went and did it anyway! Jesus Christ, Rick, why did you do it? What about all that bullshit about big-shot attorneys and your father's contacts? You forget all about that, man? You forget about your promises to me? Don't you see where that puts *me*, man?"

He got up and went to the window. There were no stars. He wished he could see some stars and maybe see Ricky up there with them. There was nothing. Just black emptiness.

"We were buddies, man," he said in a soft whisper. "We were supposed to be in this together. I went along with you on it. I didn't try to cop out. But you did. You blew it, man. You blew me away with it too. You and me were going to California, remember? We were going to get out of here and go out West and start all over again. It was a promise. A promise we made to each other. How, man? How are you going to get to California now? Huh, Ricky? Tell me. How are you gonna get there *now?*"

The *Newsday* headline read, "Satanic Cult Murder Suspect Is Found Hanged in Jail Cell." *Newsday* continued, "Richard Kasso was found by a guard at 1:00 A.M. hanging by a bed sheet knotted over a bar at the top of his cell door in the Riverhead Jail."

Ricky, so adept over the years at telling the authorities what they wanted to hear, had conned the Suffolk police. "There was no indication he was

324

under any kind of stress, no signs of any suicidal tendencies and no psychological problems," Sheriff John P. Finnerty was quoted as saying. "Otherwise, we would have put him in an observation cell."

Jail psychologist Dackow also defended his error in judgment: "When I spoke to him around two o'clock, he was planning for his future." The psychologist admitted he had talked to Ricky for only five minutes. "He wanted to see the drug counselor, and was trying to figure out if that would help him in his case. There was no indication at that time that he was thinking of ending his life."

He described Ricky as "calm and cool," but when reporters questioned the wisdom of placing Jimmy under special guard and leaving Ricky on his own, the psychologist claimed that Jimmy was the opposite of Ricky, "remorseful and depressed." Jimmy had them worried. "We took tremendous precautions with him, because in the interview process we detected him as being suicidal."

Jimmy claims they never asked if he would kill himself and so they probably didn't ask Ricky either. Jimmy shrugs off the five-minute psychological interview as "routine bullshit."

"Wherever you went there was a reporter or a television camera," an attractive downtown salesclerk remembers. "Everyone was giving interviews. Everyone had opinions. If we didn't know the boys in question—and I certainly didn't—what did we think Northport was going to do about it all? I didn't know what Northport would do, but I knew what *I* would do. I'd mind my own business and stay out of it."

The Midway was visited by every reporter who hit town. They photographed the outside, turned their lights on the inside, and gave it a worse reputation than it already had. "Sigi" Baldwin is the son of the Midway owner, George Baldwin. Sigi is a couple of years older than Jimmy. When the *Post* reported that the murder weapon had been purchased at his dad's shop, he waxed indignant to his journalism buddy, Mark McGuire.

"Where did they get that information? After we got robbed in the spring, Kasso would never come by here. We banned him from the store earlier because he would hang out and never buy anything. And I know for a fact that Kasso did not buy the knife used to kill Lauwers here."

"Bullshit," says Jimmy. "We didn't have to go *in* the place. We did our business in *front* of the place. Ricky did buy the knife there. He told me so."

Larry Decker is a mild-mannered young man who owns Village Books on Main Street. It used to be a shop for astrological and other occult-type books. Ricky got his copy of *The Satanic Bible* there, but that was before Decker took over. "We bought the store a couple of years ago and decided to clean up the image and not sell books such as this. We wanted to change to best sellers. A number of kids, maybe twenty, came in and wanted to buy *The Satanic Bible* but we told them we no longer stocked that sort of thing."

After the body was discovered, someone smeared blood across his front door. Decker didn't think too much about it. On July 9, when Decker came to the shop, he was so preoccupied with the news people milling around up and down Main Street that he unlocked the door but forgot to turn around the "Open" sign on the door. The "Closed" side remained facing the street.

A camera crew from WTNH, Channel 8, in New Haven, Connecticut, stopped in front of his place. The news-gathering lady started reporting:

"The Village Book Store has been temporarily closed due to harassment by the Satanic cult!"

Decker ran out on the sidewalk, trying to correct her error. "It was a nightmare," he remembers. "After telling her we were open, and that we don't sell *The Satanic Bible* anymore, she turns around and accuses us of censorship because we didn't carry Satanic-oriented books anymore. It was a no-win situation."

The New York *Daily News* really irked the local townspeople with a story titled "Where Evil Dwells":

"In Northport? Friendly, charming, picturesque Northport?"

"Evil? There's no evil here."

"It's all a mistake."

"It's all because of a few kids who went bad."

"In Northport, we love our children."

"This could have happened anywhere. Why single out Northport?"

"We have the best school system in the state."

"Why don't they write about our churches?"

"And our Memorial Day parade?"

"That God-damned Jimmy Troiano!"

"Look what he's done to our town!"

"God-damned dirt bag!"

"God-damned drop out!"

"I hope he gets what he deserves!"

"He's ruined this town!"

"I hope they give him the chair!"

"He'd better not come back to Northport!"

"I'll take care of the son-of-a-bitch personally!"

"And after all we did for him, too."

The story needed a name. The newspapers couldn't just keep calling it a "cult" killing and "a Satanic rite." Someone finally remembered that several years before the murder there had been a gang of high school kids who called themselves the Knights of the Black Circle. They had gone around wearing identical jackets, were into marijuana, and listened to rock and roll. They also enjoyed frightening kids younger than themselves, but what older kid doesn't enjoy doing that?

So New York City's *Daily News* decided Ricky and Jimmy must have been members of the Knights of the Black Circle. After promising on the front page "Devil Cult Gang to Bare Details," they reported that the long-defunct Knights were alive and well and "a Satanic cult with about fifteen to twenty hard-core members and up to thirty others who view the cult's sacrificial rites." Jimmy swears he and Ricky were too young to join the Knights. "They were older kids," he says, "we were never part of it." Why didn't the *Daily News* check with him on this story? "Who knows? The cops weren't too keen on me talkin' with reporters."

The *New York Times* ran stories almost daily on the murder.

The story appeared in the Los Angeles *Times*.

It was on both AP and UP wire services.

The Times of London published it.

The *Daily Rand* of Johannesburg, South Africa, gave it half a page.

So did the *Sun* of Winnepeg, Manitoba, Canada.

So did *The Observer* of London.

The *Daily News* of New York wrote an editorial about it.

ABC's *20/20* began their television story about Satanism in America with Ricky's wide-eyed face.

The *National Enquirer* gave it the front cover plus ten photographs.

The story appeared in Spanish in most of the major Latin American papers.

It appeared in Portuguese in Rio de Janeiro's *O Globo*.

It was in most of the larger metropolitan dailies of Europe.

Dick and Lynn Kasso, who had learned of their son's arrest from the newspapers, heard of his death from the police. They came down from their

Greenwich summer home to Central Suffolk Hospital on July 9. Both refused to talk with reporters. A nurse later said Dick Kasso was profoundly shocked and almost unable to speak. "I tried to tell him I was sorry," she said, "but he could only nod and look away from me."

The Kassos identified their son's body. Ricky was taken to the Brueggemann Funeral Home in East Northport, where he was cremated. There were no members of his family there. There was no service. No one said anything over his body. He had neither a Christian nor a Satanic ceremony. The ashes sat unclaimed.

The seventeen-year-old Acid King was dead.

In sic transit gloria.

CHAPTER FOUR

On Tuesday, July 10, they held an inquest to see if Jimmy should be indicted for murder or not. It took place in the County Court in Riverhead. Jimmy sat impassively as six of his friends—five boys and a girl—told about what they knew.

Had they been there when the murder was committed? "No." Did they know about Gary lying up there in the woods? "Yes." Had they all seen the body? Three yes's and three no's. Did they believe Ricky Kasso killed Gary? Six yes's. Did they believe Jimmy Troiano helped kill Gary? Six shrugs and stammers among several muttered I don't know's. Did they know Kasso and Troiano were on drugs, that they dealt in drugs? Six definite yes's. If they knew about the murder, why didn't they tell their parents or the authorities? The five boys: "Didn't want to get involved, man," or "None of my business, man," or "I didn't want Ricky coming after me next." The one girl: "I did do something. I phoned the police." The judge smiled at her. Could they identify James V. Troiano? Where was he sitting in court? Six index fingers pointed to Jimmy. Jimmy smiled and gave each of them a slight wave.

"How does the defendant plead?" the judge asked. Jimmy, wearing blue jeans and a blue plaid shirt, glanced at his attorney, Eric Naiburg. Jimmy's fingers touched the crucifix his mother had given him, which was now hanging from his neck.

"How does my client plead?" Naiburg looked at the judge. "Innocent, of course."

They held Gary's funeral on the eleventh. High school kids packed the St. Philip Neri Church in downtown Northport. They wore clean shirts and blouses and freshly pressed blue jeans and chinos. They hung on to each other and sobbed and remembered and cherished their own personal recollections of Gary Lauwers. Most had gone to school with him. That he had dropped out and hadn't seen many of them for months wasn't important. That he had run with dirtbags and dopers, that he had been arrested for menacing one of their peers, that they had hardly ever spoken to him when they ran into him at a party or a beer bust was not important. *Their* Gary had been martyred. *Their* Gary had become famous. *They* wanted to be a part of *their* Gary's death. Mr. and Mrs. Lauwers, their son, Michael, and their daughter, Nicolle, sat in the front row, all four sobbing quietly during the ceremony.

The Reverend Thomas Colgan made no mention of how Gary died or of drugs or Satanic cults. "We have the opportunity of making this death right. Let us reason what has happened to ourselves. Let us understand we are not lost." In what was, obviously, an attempt to bring Gary's soul back into the fold, the minister said, "Gary was a believer. Everyone eventually comes to Christ. For some it may take ten minutes, for some it may take ten years." Had the murder not occurred, one wonders how long it would have taken Gary to exchange Satan for Jesus.

The casket, unadorned of flowers, was taken from the church by six teenage boys, all friends of Gary's and all wearing suits and ties. The family followed down the steps.

Michael, Gary's older brother by seven years, told a reporter, "My brother had his problems, like everyone else going through adolescence. But he was working through them. He had come through the worst."

What about Gary's use of hard drugs?

"I've studied psychology and sociology and health, and I can tell when someone's not there, when they're on drugs all the time. And Gary wasn't." Again, one wonders just how often Gary's family actually studied him.

While this was going on a large group of concerned citizens and young kids descended on Cow Harbor Park and the gazebo. Armed with sandpa-

per, bleach, paint remover, and soap, they attacked
the graffiti that Ricky and his friends had smeared
around the structure. They rubbed at "Ricky, the
Acid King" and "Satin Lives" and "666" and
"Ozzy is God" and "Fuck Everybody." They
scrubbed hard to get rid of the words, to get rid of
the memory, as if they could make Northport better by erasing the evidence.

The *Daily News*, alone among the many papers
covering the story, got to Gary Lauwers's family.
The boy's father had little to say other than "My
son was very fearful of this particular person," and
though "Gary was never on hard drugs," thought
Ricky had accused Gary of the theft "just to scare
other kids." Asked whether Gary was religious, he
replied, "He was fearful of death."

On Wednesday, July 11, while Gary's funeral
was being held, Jimmy was indicted for Gary's
murder.

On Thursday, July 12, Huntington's a *Long Islander* report indicated that drugs and heavy-metal
music were the villains here but things were getting better every day.

CHAPTER FIVE

As always happens when a notorious case is about to be tried, the public starts paying more attention to the lawyers than to the defendant. It was okay, in everyone's mind, to let Jimmy sit on his jail cot dangling his feet and waiting for news as to when "they" would either free or condemn him to death. The actual murder had not been done by his hands—everyone agreed to that—and now the trial that would determine the rest of his natural life was out of his hands as well.

Because of all the publicity the murder had generated, big legal guns were hauled in who were assured of making the case even more interesting to the press. Big guns who knew the value of winning a newsworthy trial.

In this corner, for the prosecution: Mr. William J. Keahon. Forty years old.

Bill Keahon (pronounced KEY-on) has been described as a street fighter. He looks like a boxer, compact build, broad shoulders, and a stance in the courtroom that intimidates as well as assures. He has a scar across his right cheek and chin. The souvenir of a street fight when he was twenty years old. Those who have worked with the sharp and savvy attorney recall the time he so upset a defendant that the man threw a water pitcher at him and then jumped him. Keahon swung at the man in self-defense and missed. He hit a sheriff's deputy, breaking his nose in two places.

He knows how to play a jury, knows how to stare down a witness, knows when to attack or when to be cool. *The New York Times* quoted him: "Some lawyers come across as erudite, as very sophisticated. I don't. I come across as a straight shooter. Having done so much as a kid, having experienced so much, having fought a little, I could understand when a kid got into trouble once. But only once."

In the other corner, for the defense: Mr. Eric W. Naiburg. Forty-three years old.

Eric Naiburg requested being assigned to Jimmy's case. He is athletically trim, with straight shoulders and narrow hips. One look and it's obvious, here is a man who lives well, dresses well, and takes care of himself. No witness would dare throw a water pitcher at him—it would cost too much to replace the suit. He was Assistant Suffolk County District Attorney before going into a very

336

lucrative private practice. *The New York Times* quoted the dark-haired defense attorney: "The most exciting type of case there is is a homicide." He compared being a criminal lawyer to playing at net in tennis. "You don't have to know the law that well, but you have to be quick."

The referee in the center of the ring: Judge John Copertino. Fifty-six years old.

John Copertino's father owned a fish store and the smell of it clung to the boy's clothing so badly that people moved away from him in the subway. His mother told him to learn a profession where he would be his own boss so people would respect him. He chose the law. He, too, was an Assistant Suffolk County District Attorney and was elected a District Court Judge for the county in 1969. He tried gambling and rackets cases in the early seventies and in 1977 was elected a Suffolk County Court Judge. When Jimmy's case came up before him, he had been reelected three times. While he reads the classics and doesn't go in for a lot of exercise, he manages to maintain the posture and agility from his two-year hitch as a special counter-intelligence agent in the United States Army. His black hair, even though it's receding, is a perfect frame for his round face and arching eyebrows. *The New York Times* quoted him: "This is the age of strident judicial criticism. We're judged by our visibility. The first ones that come under a magnifying glass are the judges. But the critics don't realize how much work it takes. The courtroom excites me. There's nothing more exciting than having a jury come in and render its verdict.

There's tension; it's a dramatic scene." The *Times* quoted another judge as saying, "He's courageous. He's willing to take the unpopular decision. He's fair."

To that Jimmy adds, "Uh-huh."

Almost immediately after taking up Jimmy's cause, Attorney Naiburg decided Jimmy's civil rights had been violated. The police officers who had questioned the boy upon his arrest should not have done so without Jimmy's lawyer present. "The cops should have inquired to see if he had an attorney at the time. I'm quite sure they went ahead with the interview without checking." As far as Naiburg could see, the only evidence the state had against Jimmy was the second statement he had signed for the police. Naiburg was sure the cops had made Jimmy issue a second statement because the first one didn't jibe with what Albert Quinones had said took place that night in the woods. Jimmy had not implicated himself in the first statement. In fact, police officers admitted, they had not even considered Jimmy as a *suspect* until he had "confessed" to helping Ricky in the second of the two statements. The New York State Court of Appeals had ruled that statements to police are inadmissible if an attorney representing a suspect in a pending case has not given permission for the suspect to talk. When Jimmy's statement was finally shown to Naiburg he saw that, indeed, Jimmy had waived the right to talk to an attorney.

The trial was set for November.

On September 8, in a move that Judge Copertino

called "unusual," Naiburg got custody of Jimmy for five hours and took him back to Northport to have him retrace his movements the night of the murder. At just a little after noon two white unmarked squad cars belonging to the Suffolk County Sheriff's Office pulled into Cow Harbor Park and stopped near the gazebo. Jimmy and Naiburg were in the backseat. The door opened and the two got out, Jimmy in blue jeans and a short-sleeved plaid shirt. He was wearing blue and white sneakers and there was a chain around his waist and wrists. He had to hold his hands one atop the other, down near his crotch. He was clean-shaven but they had let him keep his long hair. It hung thick in back, down around his collar. It was his second time back in Northport since the morning of the arrest.

"Hey, Jimmy?" someone shouted as he was led into the gazebo. "What are you lookin' for?"

He smiled slightly and called back, "I can't talk about it. I'm under a gag order." After a few minutes Jimmy and his lawyer got back into the car, Jimmy having difficulty bending his body into the backseat without using his hands.

Two Northport Village squad cars arrived and they led the way out of the park, made a quick right onto Main Street, and the procession went up Main and stopped in front of Trinity Episcopal Church. Naiburg got out of the car and entered the church. Jimmy sat and waited. When the dapper attorney—dark blue suit, loafers, and a pinstriped silk tie—returned, he refused to comment on what he wanted in the church. A local wag said

339

later, "He knows his client hasn't got a chance. Probably praying for Troiano's soul."

The procession turned around in front of the fire station and went back down Main Street, turned left on Woodbine, and then another left into Fifth Avenue. The street is a dead end. The cars stopped, and Jimmy and Naiburg got out. A Northport cop with a two-way radio and the Suffolk County sheriff also got out. They opened the door of the second unmarked white county car and a large police dog jumped down. Another uniformed man from the sheriff's office took its chain. The party left the street, moving into the bushes and up to the spot where Gary had been killed.

"It was right here," Jimmy said. "The bonfire was here." He looked around for signs of it, but there were none. Someone had cleaned up the site, sweeping away the burned branches and charred leaves. It had been only two months, but already the woods had started to reclaim the deceased Acid King's throne room.

He paced through the murder for his attorney. The officers and the dog kept to one side of the clearing. "Albert was sitting over there," Jimmy said. "On the ground. He only got up when we had to move the body." Jimmy looked thoughtful for a few moments. It was the first time he had been back there since his indictment. "Gary was sitting here and I was sitting here, beside him. Ricky came and sat there, on the other side of Gary. There was a tape deck, too, with some Ozzy Osbourne on it. It was on the ground, next to Gary."

"Where were you when Ricky started stabbing Gary?" Naiburg asked.

Jimmy frowned. "Here." He shook his head. "No, more like over here. I was high. It's difficult to remember. I was a few feet away from them. They had started arguing and I walked away. Then I heard the fight start and I stood about here and watched it. At least I *think* it was about here. I was high, man, I told you." Naiburg nodded. "Ricky started stabbing Gary and then I came back over to them and told Ricky he was killing the kid."

"Was that before or after you kicked Gary and broke his ribs?"

Jimmy looked at the lawyer. "After. I kicked Gary when the fight started. I moved away right after."

"Then what?"

"Then Gary was dead and Ricky asked me and Albert to help drag the body into the bushes."

"The knife," Naiburg said. "When did you go and get the knife and bring it back to Ricky?"

"Before," Jimmy said. "Before Ricky asked us to move the kid. Ricky stabbed him and the knife must have hit a bone or somethin' and bounced off. I went for it, about over here maybe, and handed it back to Ricky."

"You recall doing that?"

"Sure. I already told you. But Gary was already dead by that time."

"How do you know?"

Jimmy stopped. "Like I told you, I don't know

341

for sure. It was a gut reaction. I just felt, you know, *felt* the little bastard was dead."

Then, silently, doing Naiburg's bidding, Jimmy pointed to the place where Gary had been hidden after his death. "I don't know where they buried him, man." Jimmy shrugged. "Ricky said it was near here."

"It was over there." A Northport cop spoke up: "Just a few feet from where you're standing. That roped-off section."

Jimmy looked at the shallow grave with the police markers around it. "Yeah, that must be it."

"Is that all you have to say?" one of the cops asked.

"Yeah," Jimmy answered. "Can one of you guys give me a cigarette?"

The blockbuster hit Jimmy and his lawyer: Albert Quinones, who had not been charged in the murder, had agreed to testify for the prosecution.

"He agreed to *what?*" Jimmy almost yelled at his attorney.

"To testify against you. For his being excused as a suspect. He was the only witness and now they've got him."

"But he was *there!*" Jimmy had been looking out a window in the room lawyers and their clients were permitted to use. It was a change of scenery from the cell where he had been held all these months. "Albert was *there*. He helped carry Gary's body into the bushes. He let Ricky take a shower at his folks home afterward. He knew all about it. And now what's he gonna say?" The boy came

342

close to his lawyer's face. "What's he gonna say? That I'm guilty? That I held Gary down?"

"I don't know," Naiburg answered. "We'll have to wait and see and then play it by ear."

"What kind of a witness can he be, man? He was high that night. He was whacked out of his skull with mescaline. He saw trees bendin', man, and cats running up and down their trunks. That's a witness? That's a *reliable* witness?"

"Cool it," Naiburg said. "He's all the prosecution's got."

"And what do *we* got? Huh? We don't have *no* witness! All we got is me sayin' I didn't do it. Just my word all by itself. Nobody's gonna believe me, man. Shit, everybody in Northport wants to see me hangin' from a lamppost on Main Street as it is. Those people in that town have made up their minds, without any witnesses. They want my young ass dead, man. They don't care if I'm innocent or not. They just want me dead. Sweep Troiano into the garbage can! Get rid of him! Let's keep beautiful downtown Northport clean!"

The November trial date was postponed.

In January, Attorney Naiburg was again asking for a delay in the trial because the magazine *Rolling Stone* had published an article on the now-famous Northport Satanic murder, quoting from sources both named and unnamed. Free-lance writer David Breskin, titling his story "Kids in the Dark," had been to town, had turned on his tape recorder, and had interviewed all sorts of people

343

who said they had been friends of the three boys involved. It was a sympathetic story, and while neither Ricky nor Gary came off looking too good, Jimmy's part in the story was fairly presented. In fact, when he read the article, Jimmy commented: "This guy what did this article has got his information good."

What jangled Naiburg's legal chimes was that *Rolling Stone* printed comments supposed to be direct quotes from star-witness Albert Quinones that said the detectives "were beating the shit out of me . . . they picked me up at two and they were beating the shit out of me for like two and a half hours, in Yaphank." If that statement was true, then that must be how the police turned Albert into a state's witness. If true, then Albert had not come forward willingly. If true, then the State had no witnesses at all.

Naiburg told Judge Copertino, at a special hearing in January, that he wanted those tapes from *Rolling Stone* magazine. The magazine's attorney, Harriette Dorsen, argued that the New York State Civil Rights Law of 1981 protects reporters from having to reveal confidential sources. She cited the state constitution as well as the First Amendment of the Bill of Rights guaranteeing freedom of the press.

Prosecutor Keahon stood delightedly by. He wasn't going to get involved in Naiburg's battle with the magazine, but if Naiburg did get those tapes and notes, he told the judge, he wanted copies of them as well. Copertino later dismissed the whole thing as being unimportant to the case.

* * *

The trial was set for March 12, then changed to March 26. And, amazingly, that's when jury selection finally began.

In his cell, Jimmy gave a sigh of relief. It had been almost eight months since his arrest. Eight long and lonely months taken from his young life. Eight months that he would never get a chance to live the way he wanted to live them—no matter what the final verdict would be.

CHAPTER SIX

When they led Jimmy into the courtroom that fourth day of April, 1984, the seats in the gallery were full. His mother and father sat in the front row and he waved at them. Mary Troiano managed a smile, but Vincent Troiano sat stony-faced. There was nobody from the Lauwers family there. None of the Kassos showed up either. Instead, there were reporters from newspapers and magazines and television, plus artists who were already at work making sketches for publication or transmission. As usual, all cameras were banned from the room.

The jury was already in place. Eight men and four women. All of them residents of Suffolk County who had left jobs or occupations as accountants, dental technicians, television repairmen, and housewives in order to sit in judgment on one James Vincent Troiano, nineteen.

Jimmy sat behind the defendant's table. He was wearing a blue shirt—prison issue—gray dungarees and white sneakers. At his attorney's request, he had gone to the prison barber and his hair was now neatly trimmed up around his ears and across the back of his neck. Everyone in the room stared at him. If that bothered him, he didn't show it.

Prosecuting Attorney William Keahon rose from his counsel table and walked across the carpeted floor to where the jury waited. In this small wood-paneled courtroom, he didn't have to raise his voice. He talked for thirty-five minutes, softly, making it seem like he was conversing with each of them during an intimate dinner. The handsome young attorney said that Jimmy had admitted holding Mr. Lauwers while a friend repeatedly stabbed him. He added that Jimmy admitted helping to bury the body near the bonfire site. Telling the jurors what he hoped they already knew from the sensational press reports, he said that before Gary was killed—and Gary was only seventeen years old—Jimmy and his friend, Richard Kasso, forced him to pledge his love to Satan. Jimmy had also, he said, participated in several other hideous Satanic rituals before the actual killing took place.

"That young man there, sitting right there in this courtroom"—and he pointed at Jimmy—"he held him while Kasso stabbed him." Then he said that Jimmy helped Ricky drag the body into the woods and when Gary sat up, still alive and pleading for his mother, Jimmy—again the accusing finger—"held him while Kasso stabbed him in the face."

Eric Naiburg took only eight minutes to address the jury. Slim, dark-haired, and as sharply dressed as if he'd just come from a White House luncheon, the defense attorney agreed with the prosecutor, that this case was "a drug-induced revenge killing for the theft of drugs from Ricky Kasso." "There is no doubt that Jimmy Troiano was present when this killing took place, but there is great doubt that he was involved. I take issue," he said, looking at each juror as he spoke, "that James Troiano is in any way a participant in the murder of Gary Lauwers. Being there is not the same thing as being guilty. Please keep that in mind. Your job, ladies and gentlemen, is not easy. Only you, as the supreme arbiters of the facts, will determine what is real and what is not. Only you will determine what is truth and what is not . . . what should be believed and what should not. And most important of all, only you will determine whether the guilt of that young man has been proven beyond a reasonable doubt. Your task is not going to be an easy one. No one is going to leap to his feet from the last row of the courtroom, admit his guilt, and relieve you of your struggle of mind and conscience. Whatever decision you finally make, you will have to live with for the rest of your lives."

The first witness called was Laurie Walsh. The sixteen-year-old girl walked rather nervously to the stand. Her blond hair was neatly combed and she wore a dress with a frilly white bodice. It was the first time Jimmy had ever seen her in a skirt. Keahon asked what her relationship was with Jimmy and she replied simply, "A friend." Then he asked her about her drug experiences.

"Well, if you mean you want me to start at the beginning, I guess it would be when I was about fourteen years old. I was in junior high. In Northport. I started with marijuana and then it was mescaline and LSD and that sort of stuff."

"Did you take these things by yourself?"

"Oh, no. I was with my friends. I had lots of friends who took drugs."

"In junior high school?"

"Uh-huh."

"How many times over the last two years have you used drugs?"

"Oh, gosh, I don't know. Some things about every day, I guess."

"Let's confine ourselves just to LSD. How many times do you think you have taken LSD?"

She paused and thought for a moment. "Oh, probably about seventy-five times or so."

"Where did you get it?"

"From people." She shrugged. "People would be selling it around school or down in the park near the harbor. Sometimes I bought it from Jimmy."

This was the first time the gallery buzzed.

"From the defendant?" Keahon's voice rose. "Mr. Troiano sold hard drugs to you when you were a junior high student?"

"Yeah." She nodded. "A kid always knew he could get the good stuff from Jimmy and Ricky.

Nobody ever had a bum trip with their stuff that I ever heard about."

"Did you ever take drugs with Jimmy? I mean," Keahon explained, "did he ever *force* you to take his drugs?"

"You mean to get me hooked? Oh, no. Jimmy wouldn't do anything like that. Ricky Kasso would though. He would work on the little kids."

"Miss Walsh, Ricky Kasso is not on trial here."

"Oh. Yeah. Well, one time Jimmy and I went to a beach and we stretched out on the sand and watched the moon and had some dope together. That was nice. Another time, I was in the woods where he and Ricky used to hang out and he was high on LSD and he gave me a hit and asked why didn't the two of us fly out together."

Attorney Keahon asked her how drugs affected her studies and was told she was a "problem student" as far as her teachers were concerned. She claimed, at that moment, she was free of drugs. Her parents had worked "real hard" to get her off them. Her parents, sitting in the rear of the courtroom, nodded. "Drugs really hurt a kid," she added.

"Well, if they hurt you, why did you take them?"

"Well, it's neat because it puts you in another world. You feel like you're in another universe. Everything stays the same and yet everything changes. You know what I mean? I saw trees change color. I saw them go from being green to being purple. And clouds would change. I don't mean the way they normally do when you look at them, but you can look at a cloud when you're high and *make* it change into any shape you want. You can form them into dragons or cars or whatever shape you choose. It's neat."

"When did you first hear about Gary's murder?" Keahon changed the subject.

"Jimmy and I and a friend of ours was going to go to the movies. In Northport. He told me then. I asked him how Ricky was and he told me he was okay, just hanging out but that he had killed somebody. I asked who and he said it was Gary. Well, it made a lot of sense to me because I had been to a party that morning and kids there were saying that Gary was dead. Nobody said Ricky had killed him but they talked about him being dead. I didn't believe it until Jimmy told me. He asked me if I wanted to see the body but I said no. I mean, I really liked Gary, but dead people give me the creeps."

"What made you decide to tell the police?" Keahon asked.

"I called Gary's house that night and his mother answered the phone. I asked to speak to Gary and she said he hadn't been around for about two weeks. She said she was worried about him. Had I seen him? I said I hadn't. Did I know where he was? I told her I didn't know. I mean, hey, I wasn't about to tell his mother that he was lying dead somewhere."

"Why did you wait so long to call the police?" the prosecutor asked.

"It was only four days," she said indignantly. "Lots of other kids knew about it long before I did and they *never* told anyone. I called them because it

351

had started to eat away at me. I mean, the idea of Gary laying up there in those woods. All alone. And dead."

Jimmy's lawyer didn't spend a great deal of time with Laurie. He asked her if she was positive she had purchased drugs from Jimmy and positive he was the one to tell her about Gary being murdered. She said she was positive.

"When you are high on drugs," he asked, "if you saw a car, how would you know if it really was a car?"

She looked at him, puzzled. "What?"

"If you saw a car and you were high on LSD, how would you know if it really was a car?"

"I'd know," she stammered, "because, well, because I *saw* it."

"Yet, you told the court that you have seen trees turn from green to purple."

"Yes." She nodded.

"And your mind, full of LSD, can make clouds change form just by willing them?"

"Sure."

"So what you are telling us is that when you are high on drugs and you see something—you are a *witness* to something—you are never sure whether it is exactly what you are seeing or not?"

"I don't follow you." She glanced up at Judge Copertino and shrugged.

"What I am trying to get at," he said, "is that you can see something and its reality can change. Reality for most of us is constant, yet when you are on drugs, your reality changes."

"Yeah," she agreed, "but you don't see anything that isn't there."

Off the stand and on her way out of the courtroom, she smiled at Jimmy. He smiled in return.

Suffolk County Police Detective James Mc-Cready was the next witness for the prosecution. He explained how the body was found and what it looked like when it was dug from the shallow grave. There were photographs and they were handed to the jury. Most of the jury glanced at them hurriedly and passed them on. McCready said that next to the grave was a patch of blackened earth where the body had lain and decomposed. He said the police had also recovered the boy's jacket, minus the hacked-off sleeves, and that it had twenty-two knife holes in it.

"Twenty-two?" Keahon asked in mock astonishment.

"Yes, sir. Most of them in the area of the back and lower spine."

Keahon had him relate how word had gone out to bring in Ricky and Jimmy and how the pair had been found sleeping in the old Pontiac across from the Yacht Club. Then he related how the boys had been driven to the precinct station in Yaphank, been photographed and fingerprinted and their statements taken.

Keahon reminded McCready that Jimmy had made *two* statements. The second one, the more incriminating one. Did the defendant give Detective McCready both statements? No, sir, just the first one. Detective Louis Rodriguez had taken the

353

second statement. Did Attorney Naiburg have any questions?

He did. Before further questioning, however, he asked for permission to read both Jimmy's first statement and the second statement to the court, to introduce them as evidence. The judge agreed. The defense attorney read the first statement, then started on the second statement, raising his voice and staring at the jury at each place where the second—and more incriminating confession—differed from the first.

Naiburg wondered why it was necessary to get two statements from his client and he was told by McCready that he wasn't sure "Troiano had been telling him one hundred percent of the truth."

McCready admitted that Jimmy wasn't considered a suspect when the first statement was taken and that he was quite cooperative, giving the police the names of nine other kids who had either seen or known about the body in the woods.

"There seem to be some discrepancies here," Naiburg said, "especially where Jimmy says in statement one he had been told about Gary's murder while in Northport, yet in the second statement he says he didn't become aware of why he was being arrested until he got to the homicide division in Yaphank." McCready admitted that *was* a discrepancy, but he couldn't explain it. "And in the first statement," Naiburg continued, "Jimmy says Gary got up and ran into the woods *before* Kasso started stabbing him, while in the second statement he says Gary's run to escape occurred *after* the stabbing began."

354

McCready acknowledged that Jimmy was confused about when the running actually took place.

McCready then went on to detail how he took Jimmy into a room to talk with Ricky after the first statement had been signed.

"What time was that?" Naiburg wanted to know.

McCready thought it was about 11:45. After that Ricky dictated a statement and signed it.

"What time was *that?*"

McCready thought it was about 12:50.

"So Jimmy was the first one to make a statement and Ricky Kasso was second?"

"Yes, sir."

"But then, afterward, Jimmy signed a second statement? A statement where he admitted he held down Gary Lauwers while Ricky stabbed him. Is that the sequence?"

"Yes, sir."

"Why was it necessary to have Jimmy make a second statement?"

"Like I told you, I wasn't one hundred percent sure Troiano was telling me the truth." For the first time, McCready looked straight at Jimmy. Jimmy lowered his eyes and looked away. The detective then went on to explain that at approximately twelve noon, he turned Jimmy over into the custody of Detectives Rodriguez and Amato. It had been decided that photographs of the scene, with Jimmy pointing out the murder site, were needed. Also, they needed Jimmy to show them where Ricky had tossed the murder weapon. Their men were still searching the water off Northport Harbor.

Judge Copertino adjourned the court until Monday.

A few Northport teenagers started wearing shirts saying "Ricky Lives." An unknown teenager painted new graffiti in the gazebo: "Gary Lauwers lives in our hearts." Another hand had added "Death to Troiano."

On the eighth, the deputy medical examiner testified. It was the second day of the trial and the kind of testimony that courtroom watchers and headline writers love. Dr. Stuart Dawson was the M.E.'s name and he gave detailed descriptions of the seventeen-year-old's decomposed body.

Dawson's testimony alternately helped and hurt Jimmy's case. First he told the jury that it may have taken Gary "quite a few minutes to die," which would have given Jimmy time enough to help in the slaughter. But under cross-examination he admitted that if the knife had pierced Gary's heart, the boy could have collapsed within seconds.

"So which is it, Doctor?" Naiburg pounced when it was his turn to examine the medical expert. "If these stab wounds punctured his heart and, what is more probable, his lungs, would he have been able to jump up and run into the woods?"

"I don't know," came the reply.

"What do you mean, you don't know? You said

there were eight verifiable wounds in and around
the spinal column. You said that any one of them—
any *one*—could have severed the nerves, causing
immediate lower-body paralysis. How could the
poor kid have gotten up and run away with those
wounds as well as the knife holes in his heart and
lungs? How?"

Dr. Dawson shook his head. He couldn't answer
that.

"You can't answer that?" Naiburg was almost
shouting now. "You are an expert! An *expert*, Doctor! If any of those wounds had pierced the heart,
Gary would have been *dead*, not just immobilized,
but dead within fifteen seconds."

"I don't know that," the doctor replied softly. "I
don't know how deeply that knife penetrated the
body."

A medical examiner cannot testify to that which
he does not know, that which he cannot demonstrate as fact. Two weeks lying in the bushes, in
the sun, in a shallow grave had reduced Gary
Lauwers's body to something that no one could
make any absolute judgments about. The doctor
had done his best, and now, despite Naiburg's ag-
gressive questioning, he refused to allow himself to
be rattled.

Dr. Dawson testified that it was quite simply impossible to determine how deeply or even how
many times Gary had been stabbed. Knife marks
on Gary's clothes and marks on the bones indicated that he had been stabbed at least thirty-two
times. When pressed, the doctor stated that all

357

twenty-two stab wounds in the victim's back were in a row. That, the doctor said, showed that both the assailant and the victim had not moved during this part of the attack.

That night Jimmy dreamed of Gary for the first time. He, Ricky, and Gary were back at the bonfire. Gary was standing up, smiling. Ricky walked over to Gary and put his hand on Gary's chest. Ricky's hand went into the boy's body, and it stayed there. Ricky wiggled his hand but it didn't come out of Gary's chest. Gary stood there, a big grin on his face.

"Come on, Jim," Ricky laughed. "Get over here. Put your hand in the little bastard too."

"No, man," Jimmy said. "That's okay, you do it. I don't wanna."

"Look, it's easy." Ricky laughed and plunged his other hand into Gary. Gary just stood there, grinning.

Jimmy shook his head. "Not me, man. You do it if you want to. I don't want any part of it."

Ricky started toward Jimmy, dragging the still-grinning Gary along with him, his hands still inside Gary's chest. Jimmy backed up, away from their approach. He looked over his shoulder and saw he was standing on the edge of a cliff. There was a sheer drop-off immediately behind him. He couldn't step back. He turned and Gary's face was right up close to his own, except that it wasn't Gary's face. It was a skull. A skull with only one eye and blood filling up the empty mouth. He started to scream.

He awoke, his nightclothes damp with sweat. Across the cell-block corridor, somebody yelled, "Shut the fuck up, will ya!"

CHAPTER SEVEN

The next day it was Albert's turn. He showed up at the courthouse surrounded by detectives—after all, he was their prize. He was a muscular youth, not too tall, but with long arms and big hands. His dark hair was full and hung over his forehead in thick waves against his olive skin. He wore a light gray suit and a brown tie with a blue shirt. Like Laurie in a skirt, this was the first time Jimmy had ever seen Albert in a suit.

Albert took the stand but couldn't look at Jimmy. Jimmy, however, glared at him with his piercing blue eyes. Here where there had once been a friend was an enemy. Here a one-time dope-smoking buddy stood, ready to send Jimmy to the death house to save his own skin. The traitor gave

Jimmy a bad taste in his mouth, but he knew he wasn't supposed to spit on the carpeted courtroom floor.

Prosecutor Keahon spent some time assuring Albert of his rights. He had agreed to testify for the state, to tell them everything about the case he knew. And for that he was forever immune to prosecution himself in the case. Albert nodded. Jimmy grimaced.

He told his name and how he knew the defendant, told about his home life and his school activities. He said that since the murder his parents had found it wiser to take him out of Northport High and enroll him in Kings Point High. He didn't tell the court that kids in Northport refused to speak to him and that his family received threatening phone calls. He also didn't tell about the time he was badly beaten at a beer party. It was after the grand jury hearing and he was socked and hit several times by boys his own age, not because he testified against Jimmy, but because he didn't stop Ricky from killing Gary. In death, Gary Lauwers had many more friends than when he was alive.

Albert admitted he was a regular drug user. In fact, he had started on drugs in the eighth grade. What did he use? Everything. Was he high on the night of the murder? Well, he had had a little beer and just one hit of mescaline. He didn't know how many hits the other three had taken, three or four at least.

"Do you think your memory is influenced by these drugs?"

"No. I got a good memory."

He explained how they had been at the gazebo and then had gone to Dunkin' Donuts about 10:30 that night and then had headed for the woods. He backtracked a bit to say that Jimmy had stopped at Trinity Church to go to the bathroom. Then they had proceeded into the woods. Finally, he got to the part about the murder.

"When did you first have an idea Ricky Kasso was going to kill Gary?"

"I didn't have an idea. Gary did. He told me when we were around the fire. He said, 'Al, I think Jimmy is going to kill me.' I was surprised."

"Jimmy? Don't you mean Ricky?"

"No, he thought Jimmy was after him, but Jimmy heard that and he said, 'Gary, why should I kill you? I don't have any reason to kill you.' Gary was still worried though."

"Was that before or after they cut the sleeves off Gary's jacket?"

"Before."

"Who cut the sleeves off the jacket?"

"I think Gary cut them off himself. Either that or he cut one and Jimmy cut the other. Gary had taken off one of his socks and thrown it on the fire, but it didn't help much to make it burn. They cut off some of Gary's hair. It didn't make much of a fire either."

"Who cut off the hair?"

"I think Jimmy cut off some and so did Ricky."

"Then what?"

Albert looked at Jimmy. Jimmy was still glaring. "Gary got real nervous. He kept looking at me as if I should do something. I was sitting away from the fire. I didn't know what to do. Then Gary got up and tried to run into the woods. Jimmy tackled him and Ricky ran over and grabbed him."

"Let me interrupt here a minute, Mr. Quinones," Attorney Keahon said. "Prior to Gary's running . . . prior to Gary's running away, had any stabbing occurred?"

"No."

Keahon sighed. "Then what?"

"Gary got off the ground and Ricky jumped on Gary's back and bit him in the neck and bit him in the ear and then Ricky stabbed Gary in the side and then Gary ran into the woods." He glanced at Jimmy, then glanced away. "Then Ricky went after Gary and grabbed him by his jacket and brought him back to the campfire."

"Did Gary say anything at that time?"

"He said, 'I love you, Mom.'"

"That's when he said those words?"

Albert nodded. "Then Jimmy came over and kicked Gary after Ricky threw him on the ground. Then Jimmy handed the knife to Ricky and told Ricky to slice Gary's throat."

"Jimmy told Ricky to kill Gary?"

"Yeah. He kept makin' signs to Ricky like this." Albert drew his forefinger rapidly across his windpipe in a cutting motion. "Ricky started stabbing Gary with the knife. Gary began to yell. Ricky told him, 'Say you love Satan!' but Gary wouldn't do it." Here Albert began to sob. "And Ricky started stabbing him some more. He started stabbing him in the back, started stabbing him in the

363

chest. It was terrible! It gave me nightmares for months afterward."

When he had calmed a bit, Keahon asked, "And where was Jimmy all this time?"

"By the fire," Albert said simply. "Finally, Gary said, 'I love Satan.' Then I guess he was dead. Ricky and Jimmy went over to the body and they started lookin' down at it, sayin', 'There is smoke comin' out of his back.' Then Ricky picked up Gary's hands and Jimmy picked up a leg. I walked over there and I picked up a leg and we started dragging him into the woods. Then all three of us went to my house so Ricky could take a shower and get some clean clothes. Then Jimmy and Ricky left the house, they went someplace. I don't know where. I didn't go. I was too shook up." He started sobbing again. Judge Copertino called for a lunch recess.

That afternoon Defense Attorney Naiburg had his opportunity with Albert. He went easily at first and asked the young man if he "thought his head was messed up by drugs." Albert considered this for a few moments and said, "No."

Naiburg probed. What were the substances the young man in the witness chair had put into his body? Albert answered that he had used LSD, cocaine, mescaline, and something he called "embalming fluid," which turned out to be wood chips rolled into cigarette form.

Naiburg said he was interested in the nightmares Albert said he had had since the murder. Could he elaborate on that?

"One night after the murder," Albert explained,

"I was lying in bed with the windows open and I heard Gary screaming. I wasn't asleep or anything. I was wide awake but I heard Gary's voice and he was screaming. I got scared. I got out of bed and went downstairs and turned on the TV. I stayed up all night."

Naiburg nodded. "Any others?"

"Well, several times I had dreams that I was killing Gary. Not that Ricky was, but that *I* was. They used to wake me up. And another time I was just about to go to sleep when I looked up and there was a skeleton floating over my dresser. I was sure it was Gary. It really freaked me out."

"But you don't think, Mr. Quinones, that drugs have messed up your head?"

Again the pause. "No."

Naiburg started in on the story leading to the murder. He pointed out that Jimmy, in his statement to the police, had said the fight started about 2:00 in the morning, yet Albert said they had started into the woods about 10:30 that night. Why was there this time difference between Jimmy's statement and Albert's testimony? Albert said he didn't know. Naiburg also wondered why Jimmy stated that Albert had told him Ricky was going to kill Gary and yet Albert testified it was Gary himself who told Albert. How did Albert figure that one? Again, Albert didn't know. Maybe Gary "guessed" it. Could Albert recall it in any greater detail?

Albert thought, then spoke. "Awhile later, after we got to the place where they set the fire, Gary said that he had a funny feeling that Ricky was going to kill him. Jimmy started saying, 'Ricky, I'm not going to kill you.' "

"Ricky?" Naiburg interrupted.

"I mean Gary. He said, 'Gary, I'm not going to kill you. I have no reason to kill you.' Then both me and Jimmy said, 'Don't worry, Gary. He's not going to kill you.' I didn't really think Ricky would do such a thing. Then, like a half hour later, forty-five minutes later, Ricky started jumping on Gary and punching him in the face. They just started rolling on the ground. I walked up to Gary and I kicked him in the face. Then I . . ."

Naiburg stopped stock-still. "Wait a minute," he said quickly. "Will you repeat what you just said?"

Albert looked confused at the interruption. "What did I say?"

"The part about you kicking Gary in the face."

"Yeah, okay. While Ricky had Gary down on the ground, I went over and I kicked Gary in the face."

There was a hush in the courtroom. This detail had never been mentioned before. "Why?" asked Naiburg.

"Why? I don't know why. I just did it."

"But that's not what you told the police in your statement," the defense attorney said. Naiburg glanced at the prosecutor, wanting to make sure he had heard it too. "You told the police you had no part in this murder. You said all you did was watch."

Albert shrugged. "I lied," he said simply. "What I told the police wasn't the truth. They beat me up and told me Jimmy had said I kicked Gary. I told them I didn't do anything like that. I wasn't going to get involved in this. Anyway, it was Jimmy the cops wanted to nail. Not me. They wanted Jimmy and Ricky, not me." He went right on with his story, anxious to get it out, get it over with, and get out of that place. "As I said, I kicked Gary in the face. Then I walked back to where I had been sitting and Jimmy ran up to him and kicked him in the ribs and Gary started screaming, 'You broke my ribs! You broke my ribs.' He was screaming real loud." Albert looked at Jimmy. Their eyes locked. Albert looked away. If he had looked instead at Prosecutor Keahon, he would have seen a man in shock.

"So Gary got to his feet and then Ricky grabbed his legs and Gary fell on the ground on his hands and knees and then Ricky held Gary down and Troiano walked over and held Gary down, and Ricky started cutting his hair off with a knife, and then Troiano started cutting his hair off, and Gary started saying, 'Al, stop them. Don't let them kill me.'" Albert looked at Jimmy. Jimmy's eyes were on his hands. "Gary started saying he had five hundred dollars at home and that he would give it to him—give it to Ricky and us. I don't know if he did or not. I don't know where Gary would get that kind of bread. They kept cutting his hair off and then Gary got scared and then he got up and ran into the woods."

He paused, frowned, trying to recall the exact sequence. There was absolute silence in the courtroom. "Then Ricky ran after him. He had the knife in his hand. Then I ran after Ricky, to stop

367

Ricky, to try tripping him so he would fall, but Gary got tangled up into the vines. Ricky grabbed Gary by his jacket and he brought him back to the campfire. That's when Ricky started stabbing Gary."

"Where was Jimmy all this time?"

"By the fire."

"You didn't see Jimmy holding Gary down while Ricky killed him?"

"No."

"In Jimmy's statement to the police, he said he held Gary in a headlock while Ricky Kasso stabbed him."

"It never happened like that," Albert said.

"Then why," asked the defense attorney, "did Jimmy tell the police that it did?"

"I don't know." Albert shrugged. "Ask him."

The reporters crowded around both attorneys when they exited the courtroom that afternoon. Prosecutor Keahon told *The New York Times* that while he acknowledged that Mr. Quinones's statement was riddled by inconsistencies, he did not believe some of his star witness's testimony. "The jury doesn't have to believe everything. It can take some and throw some out. Every witness can lie and tell the truth and many do both." When *Newsday* asked him about the impact of Albert's admission that he had lied about his role in the killing, Keahon refused to comment.

Naiburg was delighted to comment. He noted that Albert had changed important points in the narrative of the killing, and that in previous statements Albert had said Jimmy had helped recapture

Gary and bring him back so Ricky could stab him. "The testimony today bears no relationship to anything he said before. Quinones is so unreliable that you can't believe a word that he says."

"What's wrong with him?" asked a reporter.

"I've been researching this drug thing," the defense attorney said, "and what we have here is a guy who is totally burned out, who doesn't have a brain cell left."

There were several business-law students from Walt Whitman High School in Huntington, Long Island, at court that day. Each year the students take a field trip.

"This year we got lucky and got a good trial," remarked their teacher, Ralph Schneider.

"Yeah, but it is scary," said senior Elizabeth Mastrino. "When I saw Jimmy come into the courtroom wearing handcuffs and with sheriff's officers on each side of him . . . just being in the same court with a murderer made me tingle."

"It was a real surprise to see how young they really looked," put in Gerald Chiddick. "Jimmy is nineteen and Quinones is only seventeen. It makes me wonder how people so young could do something so wrong and ruin themselves for life."

"It's the drugs," Carrie Sinkin added quickly. "In a split second something like this can happen with large quantities of a strong drug in you. When you do drugs like that you don't know what you're doing."

"I don't understand why Albert Quinones was granted immunity," said Wendy Kouvenhaven. "I mean, how can our justice system allow a person who stood by and watched the stabbing of a boy, helped to bury him and gave refuge for the actual murderers, and then lied in statements to the police about his involvement, be granted immunity and be free of any prosecution?"

"Aw, they need somebody to testify and somebody has to pay for the murder," another student said.

"Why is Troiano the only one on trial?"

"Yeah, he shouldn't accept the full blame for the death."

"Yeah, Quinones had just as much to do with it."

"If one goes to jail, then both should go to jail," a senior said. "That's fair."

Quinones returned to the stand the next day but his story didn't. This time he asserted that no one but Ricky had chased Gary through the woods. That it was Ricky who dragged Gary back to the fire. This time he said that Ricky had *not* forced Gary to say "I love Satan." He wasn't even certain when—or whether—Troiano had held Gary.

As the story changed, as Quinones's voice rose and faded, Naiburg asked the boy whether what he saw that night was "real or a trip."

"It's real," Quinones replied. He went on, though, to describe watching the trees bending to touch the ground as he watched.

Defense Attorney Naiburg asked that Suffolk County Detective James McCready be recalled to the stand. The tall, youngish cop, with a shock of black hair over his forehead, was a little surprised when he found himself back in the witness chair. Naiburg assured him that he just wanted to establish some exact time periods. Quickly Naiburg summed up for the jury who McCready was. He had been the officer who had taken Jimmy's first statement. He had also taken Ricky Kasso's statement of guilt. But he was not the officer who took Jimmy's second statement, and it was that second version that had brought Jimmy to trial. After having the detective explain again how the boys were arrested and taken to Yaphank, Naiburg asked if he had taken Jimmy in to see Kasso at 11:45 A.M. that morning. McCready said that was approximately the time.

Naiburg did not add that in his private conversations with Jimmy the boy had said it was the other way around. That Ricky had been taken in to see *him*. Jimmy was the one alone in the room when Ricky came in and said, "I blew it." Naiburg didn't mention it in court. The waters were muddy enough as it was.

McCready testified that day that Jimmy had been quite cooperative, "in fact, almost too cooperative with the police," he said. Jimmy told him, "I always do square business with the cops."

"You turned Jimmy over into the custody of Detectives Rodriguez and Amato and they took him back to the murder site. For some photographs?" McCready agreed that was the way it happened.

"But you started suspecting Jimmy after that?

371

Even though he didn't admit to playing any part in the crime, you began to suspect him?"

"I knew it was unlikely that just one person was involved in the crime," McCready replied. "There were thirty-two stab wounds in the body. That's an awful lot of wounds for just one person to inflict."

"Let me read a couple of parts from Jimmy's first statement." Naiburg went back to the counsel table and picked up two sheets of paper. Jimmy looked up into his face. He wondered where his lawyer was going with this tack. "In Jimmy's first statement he says, and I quote, 'Ricky was stabbing Gary and making him say, "Say you love Satan." ' Then 'Ricky chased Gary when he started running into the woods and dragged him back to the bonfire. He kept stabbing Gary until he was dead.' " Naiburg looked at McCready. The detective just sat there. "Then here, a little farther down, I quote again from Jimmy's first statement—'Ricky told me to help drag Gary's body from the clearing and into the woods. I did this with Ricky and then I saw Ricky bending over Gary, saying something about Satan. As he was saying this, Gary's head moved and Ricky bugged out and started stabbing Gary in the face.' " Naiburg lowered the pages. "That's the statement you took from the defendant."

"It is."

"Now let me read you these same scenes but in Jimmy's *second* statement. In the incriminating one that Detective Rodriguez took." The attorney walked back to the counsel table, put the first pages down, and picked up a set of other pages. He flashed a quick short smile at Jimmy. Jimmy relaxed. "Now here is what Jimmy says in the second version. Here is where Jimmy incriminates *himself.*" His eyes went down the page. " 'All of a sudden I heard Gary say, "I love you, Mom." When I looked, Gary was on his knees and Rick was stabbing him in the back.' " Naiburg's eyes went down a few more lines. " 'Gary managed to run from us and we chased him back into the woods. Rick and I dragged him back and I believe during this time we took turns cutting hair off Gary's head.' " Naiburg ran his finger down the page. " 'I knew that Gary had to be killed or he would rat us all out if he lived. While I held him, Rick also cut some hair off and stabbed him some more. I didn't see Albert Quinones do any of this. I guess he was just watching. I saw Ricky put Gary in a headlock and Gary was saying something like "Please don't kill me." Ricky stabbed him some more. Like I said, I was glad because Gary could not leave those woods alive. Ricky was saying some shit about Satan over Gary's body. He's into things about Satan and the devil. I saw Gary lift his head slightly and Ricky went buggy and started stabbing Gary in the face. I don't have any idea of how many times but it was a lot.' " Naiburg put the pages down and looked at the detective in the chair and then at the jury. "Aside from the dramatic prose, there is quite a difference in dramatic *content* as well from the first statement. Don't you agree?"

Detective McCready agreed.

"One other fact of time I'd like to verify," Naiburg said. "Ricky Kasso began dictating his statement to you at approximately 12:05." McCready nodded. "Jimmy was on his way back to Northport at that time?"

"He was with Rodriguez and Amato. I suppose they were on their way by then."

"And Ricky's statement was completed and notarized by 12:50?"

"I think that's what I said earlier."

"It was," said Naiburg.

On Friday the major witness was Suffolk County Detective Louis Rodriguez. He sat in the witness chair, neatly dressed in a blue suit and striped tie, and explained, when Bill Keahon asked him to, how he had taken Jimmy back to Northport and how Jimmy confessed his part in the murder.

He had been working until almost midnight the night before, he remembered, but he came in before noon at the request of a Sergeant Jensen. Jensen wanted photographs of the site in Aztakea Woods and suggested Jimmy go with Rodriguez to help him pinpoint the location. Photographers had been there the day before and taken over a hundred photographs. Jensen also thought Jimmy could show Rodriguez exactly where in the harbor Ricky had thrown the knife. Rodriguez said he and Jimmy went in one car and Detective Amato went in another. They drove to Northport and checked in at the station house. Then, everybody in one car, they drove to the dock, where they talked with police divers who were searching for the murder weapon. Then it was to Skipper's (one of the village's better restaurants) for lunch. Then Rodriguez made a phone call to Jensen and they got back into the car and drove as close as they could get to the wooded area. It was at that time, Rodriguez said, that Jimmy decided to confess his part in the killing. Jimmy told the detectives that he had helped Ricky bring Gary back when he ran into the woods and he had held him down while Ricky stabbed him. He also told them that when Ricky lost the knife, he handed it back to him.

Then the detective showed some of the photographs that had been taken that day. They were in color and enlarged several times so that the jury could see them from where he sat. They showed Jimmy pointing at the place where the fire had been. They showed Jimmy pointing at the place where Gary's body had been hidden. They showed Jimmy finding clumps of Gary's hair and handing them to the police officers. There were no pictures of Gary's body. It had been removed to the morgue by that time.

In the courtroom, Gary's blond sister, Nicolle, looked impassively on.

Rodriguez told about writing down Jimmy's words and composing his statement. At Prosecutor Keahon's request, the detective read the statement in a slow and carefully modulated voice. "Rick told Gary to repeat 'I love Satan,' which Gary did, even though he was really hurting. . . . I knew that Gary had to be killed or he would rat us all out if he lived. While I held him, Rick also cut some hair

375

off and stabbed him some more." The jury sat silently listening to Jimmy's self-incriminating statement being read aloud one more time. Keahon asked him how Jimmy had told him about his part in the murder.

"It just came to pass," the dark-haired officer replied. "We were about to get out of the car and he told me, 'Ricky did all the stabbing. I held him, but Ricky did all the stabbing.'"

Keahon had a smile on his face when he turned this witness over to Naiburg. Maybe Albert had not been everything the prosecution had hoped for, but here was a *real* witness, a police officer with fifteen impressive years on the force who had no reason to invent things. He wasn't on drugs. He wasn't afraid of reprisals by school friends. He had only been doing his duty. Several reporters thought Keahon had the case in his pocket after Rodriguez's testimony.

Naiburg pounced.

He started by having the photographs shown again. There stood his client, in living color, pointing to a charred patch of earth where a bonfire had been lit. Why was this picture taken? The answer: To have a record of the site. And this one, with Jimmy in Technicolor again, pointing to where the body had been found. Why? Answer: To have a record. But didn't the police already *have* records of the site? Hadn't the officer testified that on the very day before Jimmy was taken back to the woods that police photographers had taken almost a hundred photos of the site? What was the point in taking more pictures? Answer: We needed them.

Who authorized more photographs that day? Answer: Sergeant Jensen. Did Sergeant Jensen tell you to put Jimmy in those photographs? Answer, after a pause: No. You just took it on yourself to put the boy in them? Answer, after a pause: Yes.

"You took the defendant, when he was not even a suspect, and put him in these photos for the sole purpose of eventually showing them to this jury and palming them off as *evidence*. Didn't you? These photos are not evidence of any wrongdoing on the part of the defendant. They merely show that Jimmy knows how to stand still in front of a camera. They prove absolutely nothing else. These photos are totally unnecessary for the investigation of the case. Do you admit that the *only* reason they were taken was so you could come in here and show the jury this *evidence?*"

If looks could kill, Attorney Naiburg would have fallen to the floor in a heap, but all Detective Rodriguez could do was admit, yes, that was the reason behind the photographs.

Naiburg then started in on Jimmy's second statement. The confession. When did Jimmy admit to holding down Gary so Ricky could stab him? Answer: In the car, just before we got out to go into the woods. "And yet," the lawyer argued, "instead of immediately going back to the precinct and writing this new statement, you continued into the woods taking those worthless photographs." The attorney said there was no logic to it. The detective looked as if he didn't care what the attorney thought.

And what about that statement? What about

377

Jimmy's thoughts? Not his actual deeds during the event but his *thoughts*. Naiburg grabbed a copy of the second statement. " 'I knew that Gary had to be killed or he would rat us all out if he lived.' " Naiburg glared at the detective. " 'Like I said, I was glad because Gary could not leave those woods alive.' " Naiburg turned the pages back. "And here, his first *thought*—'I decided I didn't care because Gary should not have taken the dust belonging to Rick.' Did Jimmy Troiano tell you when—exactly when—he had those thoughts? When he related the sequence of events, did he tell you what he was thinking at exactly that moment?"

"No," the detective admitted, "I don't know exactly *when* he had those thoughts. It could have been a day after the murder or two days after, a week after, or two weeks after the Lauwers boy died."

"But you inserted them in his statement where you thought they should go. Isn't that what happened?"

"As I recall they came toward the end of his oral recitation. He just happened to think about them at the time."

"Detective Rodriguez, if the defendant had told you that during any of the events he had seen trees that were melting, would you have included that in his statement?"

"No."

"Why?"

The officer smiled. "It just doesn't make sense."

"Did the defendant display any confusion as to

378

the sequence of those events as he related them to you?"

The detective said Jimmy was confused about whether the hair cutting took place before or after the stabbing. There was some confusion about when the kicking occurred too. No, he never mentioned Albert kicking Gary. Jimmy was also confused about the exact time the fight started. He was only positive about two times: 7:00 P.M. and 2:00 A.M.

"Detective Rodriguez, my client was also confused about when he picked up the knife and handed it to Ricky Kasso. I would like to read the court a portion of some questions and answers that you, sir, gave at a preliminary hearing. I have the official transcript right here." Naiburg knew exactly where on the table the document lay. "The answers are yours, sir." He began to read:

" 'Q: Can you tell me the difference with regard to picking up Kasso's knife?
A: Different as to the sequence, as I recall it.
Q: As to the sequence?
A: Yes.
Q: Can you be more specific?
A: I thought, pardon me, I thought we had some discussion about that because I thought that the picking up of the knife had occurred prior to the . . . or subsequent to the dragging back of the body the first time and I think we kind of straightened that out.'

379

"Straightened that out?" Naiburg's voice rose. "What else did you *straighten out* in Jimmy's statement?" Rodriguez just stared at the lawyer. "Straightened that out? That's all well and good, but . . ." Here he paused, looking first at the jury and then at the spectators and then at Jimmy. "But there's absolutely no indication in Jimmy's statement that he ever picked up the knife and gave it to Ricky. That damning confession has never been a part of your official statements. Neither one of them!"

"We talked about that," Rodriguez said, "but I was afraid he would stop cooperating with us if I put it in the statement. Jimmy told me, 'I don't want to be seen handling the knife.' So I left it out."

"You left it out?" Naiburg's voice rose again and he shook his head. He turned to the jury, hunched his shoulders, and put up the palms of his hands. "Did you hear that? He left it out!"

Bookies taking bets on the outcome of the trial told their clients that the odds had changed.

CHAPTER EIGHT

The first witness for the defense was bearded, middle-aged John Thomas of Northport. He carries mail in the village and has known Jimmy for years. He is an active member of Trinity Episcopal Church and he testified that Jimmy had been to the church twice on the night of the murder—both times to use the bathroom. The second time was just as the church was being locked up for the night and Thomas had to ask Jimmy to leave. "It was about 11:20 P.M. Jimmy went out and joined about six or eight other teenagers and they went off down the street. I didn't think too much about it."

"Are you sure it was the defendant?" Naiburg asked.

"Oh, yes." Thomas smiled. "He was walking the way he always walks, head down and slightly bow-legged. When you've seen Jimmy walk, you've seen Jimmy."

Naiburg had called on Thomas to prove Jimmy was not in the woods at 10:00 P.M., as some earlier police reports had it, but his witness backfired on him when Keahon cross-examined him.

Under mild questioning Thomas admitted that Jimmy seemed normal. That he walked and talked and even waved to some friends "normally." There was no indication that he was high on dope, no apparent modifications of his behavior because of drugs. If the defense was hoping to complete their picture of a doped-up and brain-numb Jimmy who didn't respond normally that night, they missed the boat.

Naiburg's second witness was a toxicologist named Dr. Jesse Bidanset from St. John's University. He was presented as a narcotics expert, and Keahon protested against his taking the stand because of court precedents where experts have been barred from giving generalizations about the effects of drugs. For every different expert, Prosecutor Keahon argued, there is a different opinion. Judge Copertino overruled him.

Keahon needn't have worried. The doctor testified, as was expected, that statements taken from people who were under the effects, or had been under the effect, of hallucinogens were generally unreliable.

Under cross-examination Keahon got him to acknowledge that a person under the influence of such a drug as LSD would accurately remember many details of a murder. "They would tend to recall events correctly even if they changed the sequence."

The day's session had been short and reporters outside asked Naiburg if he was going to call any more of Jimmy's friends from Northport.

"From what I can see, he doesn't have any more friends in that town," he said. "They've already convicted him."

"When are you going to call Jimmy to the stand?"

"I'm not," he said.

"You're not? Why not? Come on, man. The people have the right to hear his side of the story."

"I'm presenting *his* side of the story," the attorney said. "Jimmy's recollection of the events that night are as screwed up and confused as Albert Quinones's are. It wouldn't serve any purpose to have him get on the stand."

"But you know he's guilty as hell," said a woman on the fringe of the crowd. "You don't want him to testify because Mr. Keahon will rip him to shreds."

Naiburg's face flushed. It was rare when he displayed any emotion. "Do *you* know he's guilty, madam?"

"Of course he is," she said.

"Did you see him that night? Were you there?" His face got redder. "If you were there, then you had better get on the stand yourself and tell what you saw up there in the woods." She looked at him, righteous indignation written all over her face. "But if you don't know what you're talking about, I suggest you keep your big mouth shut." He walked quickly away.

"Commie!" she shouted after him.

On Thursday morning the defense called its third witness, Mr. Philip Quinn. He looked only slightly older than the defendant, but Naiburg quickly established his credentials: (1) a former LSD user; (2) director of Topic House, a substance-abuse facility in Plainview, Long Island; (3) he had counseled over one hundred abusers of LSD.

He stated he had studied both statement number one and statement number two that Jimmy had given the police as well as the testimony Albert Quinones gave in court. "None of these boys' recollections are reliable," he told the jury. "What they have sworn is true could only be illusion. Facts and incidents become muddled because the mind of the chronic abuser is already confused. LSD jumbles the mind, changes patterns in the sensory process, and events get reshuffled in the telling. The sequence of events is quite unreliable when you're on LSD.

"LSD creates psychoticlike episodes. Now that doesn't mean the users are insane. The user senses that his mind functions are not normal so he tries extra hard to *appear* normal."

Naiburg was fascinated with this witness. "So what you are saying is that even while they are high, they are attempting to cover it up so others won't know."

"Exactly," Quinn replied. "I've known abusers

who have appeared normal yet they have been so high they were hallucinating out of control. What they do is attempt to put things in order, to make things seem logical. They try to fill in the blanks, as it were, in their own mental gaps. They supply answers when, in reality, there *are* no answers."

"So they become liars," said Naiburg.

"No," Quinn replied. "Not liars, because what they tell you they believe. They believe that things that come to the surface of their minds are true and they tell them for the truth."

"But their stories can change?"

"Oh, yes, and they *do* change. The story can change with each retelling and time is not important here. A story can change over a matter of minutes or hours or days. It is not so much what the abuser is saying that is important, but rather his own emotional need to have his thoughts be in some way rational and orderly."

"How long does the effect of the drug last?" Naiburg asked. "If an abuser didn't have LSD for a couple of days, would he be back to normal?"

Quinn shook his head. "I wish it was that simple. It would make my job much easier. No, chronic abusers can remain under a drug's influence for more than seven months after their last fix."

"Seven months?" The defense attorney made sure the jury got that. Jimmy was smiling and nodding with the information. Of anyone in the courtroom, he knew exactly where the witness was coming from. "Then how open is the drug abuser's mind? I mean, how susceptible are they?"

"You can plant something in somebody's mind very quickly and very easily," Phil Quinn testified. "Their mind is wide open to a lot of suggestion."

"And then once that suggestion is planted, they are unable to distinguish if it is reality or not?" Naiburg said.

"Correct. Suggestions, stories, even snatches of conversations get all mixed together when an abuser is high. The trouble always comes when he tries to sort them out."

"So if the police had told Jimmy he had helped kill Gary, and they told him that while he was still under the influence of drugs, he would believe it to be a fact?"

"Yes, I suppose so."

"And if the police had told him he ran after Gary and he and Ricky brought him back to the campfire, he would believe them?"

"Yes, I suppose so," said Quinn. "You have to remember that policemen are authority figures. Chronic users like Jimmy become highly suggestible, especially if the person is an authority figure. Very often in trying to impress this authority figure with how reliable and straight they themselves really are, they'll make something up. They don't want to appear foolish."

"Your witness, Mr. Keahon."

The prosecutor spent very little time with Phil Quinn. After all, here was a man who was testifying to exactly what the defense had said was happening in Jimmy's mind all along. And in Albert Quinones's mind as well.

386

"Is it possible that Jimmy Troiano was telling the truth when he admitted helping Ricky Kasso?"

"Yes," replied Quinn. "It is possible. I have never met or talked with Jimmy Troiano and all I can tell you is what I've observed with my own clients. I know what the abuse of LSD can do to a memory. I know what this drug can do to brain cells. With the mass of confusion in this case, I wouldn't bet on anything."

Keahon said he had no more questions for the witness.

"Mr. Naiburg," Judge Copertino said, "you may call your next witness."

"I have no other witness, your honor. The defense rests."

"That's it?" Jimmy asked his attorney. "That's all the witnesses? A mailman and two drug counselors? Jesus Christ, Naiburg. The other side hit me with Laurie and that fucker Albert and half the cops on Long Island! You only have those three?"

"That last witness, Phil Quinn, was the best possible witness we could have had. The jury listened to him. He told it like it was. He didn't have an ax to grind or a reputation to uphold. Relax, Jimmy, I know what I'm doing."

"I sure as hell hope so," Jimmy sighed. "I've got the rest of my life riding on you."

CHAPTER NINE

The attorneys' summations to the jury took place on the next Monday. Naiburg, for the defense, went first. He spoke for two hours, his voice calm except when he was berating the police work in the case. He paced back and forth, making some of the jurors feel he was getting his exercise while he worked.

After reminding the jurors that they had to throw out everything they might have heard in the media about this case and everything they might think about capital punishment, he said, "Your considerations can only be and should only be whether or not the guilt of that young man has been proven beyond a reasonable doubt.

"Root if you will for my position. Likewise, I

388

urge that you give Mr. Keahon the same consideration during his closing remarks. There will be ample opportunity for you, during deliberation, to dispassionately analyze both positions. Everything each of us has done during the course of this trial, every question we have asked, every witness we have called, was leading up to the next few hours. We will both be trying to make sense of what we have presented . . . to tie it all together . . . to show why we have done what we have done and what we believe it all means.

"I will argue that there remains a reasonable doubt, in fact, much more than a reasonable doubt, as to what is real and what is not . . . and to what is truth and what is not, as to what is believable and what is not. There were four young men in Aztakea Woods that horrible night. One was savagely attacked and killed. Another, the attacker, has taken his own life. The third was presented here as an eyewitness to the guilt of Jimmy Troiano . . . and the fourth is sitting behind me on trial for one the most heinous crimes known to man . . . murder in the second degree. I submit to you that Albert Quinones does not know, did he ever know, nor will he ever know what happened the night Gary Lauwers died. I submit to you that James Troiano does not know, did he ever know, nor will he ever know what happened the night Gary Lauwers was killed. I submit to you that *we* do not know and, unfortunately, will never know what happened the night Gary Lauwers was killed. Any person of conscience and sound moral judgment must inevitably harbor a sense of deep frustration because of what we do know happened that night and because of what we do not know about that night."

He paused in his pacing and stared directly at one of the women jurors. "From the day the body of Gary Lauwers was discovered, this case was publicized here, and around the world, as a cult murder . . . a Satanic ritual. There *was* a devil in this case and its name is LSD. It's not that LSD caused the death of Gary Lauwers, although it might have, but rather, it has stolen the minds of the young men who worshiped it. The devil has taken from them, and therefore from us, the ability to determine what is real and what is fantasy, what can be believed and what cannot, and what is truth and what is not.

"We have learned that this devil drug creates audio, visual, and sensory hallucinations. It destroys the ability to determine and relate concepts of time and order. It nurtures paranoia and suggestibility. Most of all, it takes from the user the ability to determine what is real and what is not. With chronic users like Albert Quinones and Jimmy Troiano, the effects are all the more devastating.

"As Phil Quinn said, the LSD user believes, probably to protect his own sanity, that what he is saying at any given time is *true*. The fact that the story might change in a matter of minutes is not important to him.

"The evidence is overwhelming to support the contention that Albert Quinones falls into the category of the chronic user. This contention is supported by his own admissions, his recurring flashbacks, his visions of skeletons over his dresser, of his ability to determine what is real and what is not."

"Only two of the boys who were in the woods that night are still alive. In deliberating the facts of this case, it is the testimony and statements of Albert Quinones and the statements by James Troiano that you must turn to and rely on, *if they are reliable,* for the answers."

Naiburg started to tear apart the testimony Albert had given. "Albert testified he had no idea Ricky was going to kill Gary. In fact, Ricky and Gary had fought so many times in the past that I'm sure neither Jimmy nor Albert paid it much heed. To be guilty Jimmy would have to *know* and share a community of purpose with the thing Ricky was intending to do. If Jimmy cutting Gary's hair and Jimmy kicking Gary, if they occurred, were not designed to assist Ricky in the murder, then they have no value in your deliberations.

"Albert's statement reports that at some point Jimmy handed Ricky the knife and said, 'You better kill him.' There is no report in Jimmy's statements that he ever handed Ricky Kasso a knife. With regard to the words 'You better kill him,' Albert, in his testimony, categorically denied that they were ever said. I can just picture some homicide detective saying to Albert Quinones, 'I guess Jimmy said he'd better kill him' and Albert answering, 'Yeah, I guess he did.' And now it is evidence against Jimmy Troiano."

The defense attorney then went down a list of seventeen places where Albert's testimony differed

391

from Jimmy's statements. Naiburg emphasized the last two:

"Number sixteen. Jimmy says that he held Gary while Ricky stabbed him. Albert says it never happened."

"Number seventeen. Jimmy says that Ricky had Gary in a headlock while he was stabbing him. Albert never mentioned it.

"I have learned during this trial"—Naiburg put the pages he had been holding back on his table—"that absolutely nothing a chronic user of LSD reports can be believed. I wouldn't leave my umbrella at home if Albert or Jimmy called me and said it wasn't raining. Certainly, I would not convict a nineteen-year-old boy of murder on anything they said."

He paused long enough to take a sip of water. "Before I start my analysis of Jimmy Troiano's second statement, there are a few things I want to get off my chest. There are things which are bothering me about the way the police investigated this case, and the manner in which they presented it here at the trial.

"The police take Jimmy from Yaphank to the scene of the crime for some unknown reason. At the scene they take a series of photographs which are totally unnecessary for the investigation of the case. Photographs of him pointing to things which they already knew existed, and things which they had taken over one hundred photographs of the day before. The only reason they did it, and Detective Rodriguez so admitted, was so they could come in here, turn to this jury and say to you"—

his pointed index finger swept across the twelve jurors—'look, Jimmy Troiano is guilty. We have pictures.'

"I am also offended by the fact that a homicide detective of fifteen years, like Detective Rodriguez, pulled something as shabby as intentionally making mistakes on a statement just so he can come in here and say to you, look, you see, the defendant was actively participating in the taking of this statement. I am offended because if a detective would falsify his testimony about something like that, then what are we to believe about the rest of his testimony?"

Naiburg started down the list of things in Jimmy's second statement that he didn't believe Jimmy had known he was admitting to. "Rodriguez not only wrote and ordered this statement to show some sequence of rational thought, but he intentionally doctored it so that Jimmy Troiano would be convicted of murder. If I had not questioned him about it, how vile, how totally misleading those inclusions would have been. I only pray that I asked all the questions I should have asked. How many other things did Rodriguez place conveniently in that statement other than the defendant's thought process and the time of the cutting of Gary's hair?"

He put the statement back on the table and turned again to the jury. "I'm also bothered by something I sensed developing during the presentation of this case. When I am trying a case and I have a gut feeling something is wrong, I keep looking. Something was bothering me during this case and I'm still not sure whether or not I have found the answer. I am going to present it to you because sometimes twelve minds are better than one.

"I first became bothered when Rodriguez testified that he arrived at Yaphank at eleven o'clock in the morning, having worked since midnight the night before. This wasn't Rodriguez's investigation nor was it his *team*. Jimmy was supposedly a cooperating witness at that time. Yet, Sergeant Jensen tells Rodriguez to take Jimmy back to Northport for *two* reasons. The *first* is so that he can show Rodriguez where Ricky Kasso threw the knife. They knew, however, that Jimmy's information was only secondhand and they *certainly* didn't need Jimmy to show them where the Northport Harbor was! Rodriguez also reported that Jensen asked him to have Jimmy walk him through the scene and point out the various locations and have photographs taken. I asked Rodriguez if Jensen told him to put the defendant in those photographs, he said no. We heard that over one hundred photographs had been taken the day before. If the sole purpose was to transport Jimmy back to Northport, Jensen could have used any police squad car to accomplish that. There was no apparent reason for the request and no apparent reason why Detective Rodriguez didn't express some concern about his task. After all, he is a homicide detective with fifteen years seniority who had been working for twelve hours. At the very end of my cross-examination of Rodriguez, it began to dawn on me and I began to ask some questions in the hope of solving this riddle.

"Rodriguez claims that it was about 11:45 when McCready took the defendant out of the room for a brief time and then he left with the defendant and Amato at 12:00. The presence of Amato is *also* troublesome. Here is another detective who was not working on this investigation, who was not the regular partner of Detective Rodriguez, who, I would assume, had his own cases to investigate. Yet he is put *together* with Rodriguez for the important task of taking Jimmy Troiano to Northport for absolutely no reason at all. Homicide detectives are the *elite*, they are not used as chauffeurs!

"You are probably wondering why Detective McCready was recalled for some extended cross-examination. It was only to establish a couple of times. I established that he took the defendant in to see Kasso at 11:45. I also established that Kasso's statement was completed and notarized by 12:50. On redirect examination, McCready explained that Kasso told them he would give them a statement but did not actually begin to talk until 12:05, *after* the defendant had already left. To be perfectly honest, it doesn't make sense. McCready had testified that he wasn't one hundred percent sure the defendant had told him the truth. Jimmy was the only one who might be able to verify some of the things Kasso *would* say. If Kasso had a change of heart and refused to talk, Troiano could again be used to motivate him. But they sent him to Northport to perform a useless task. It doesn't make sense.

"Add to that the serious *illogic* of the Kasso statement being completed in *only* forty-five minutes!

395

This guy was the murderer, this guy was the guy who wielded the knife, this guy was supposedly the primary target at that time. McCready claims that he immediately reduces Kasso's statement to writing without first trying to make sense or order of Kasso's declarations. It is not conceivable that taking a statement from Kasso would have been any *easier* than taking a statement from Troiano or Quinones. Even if they went directly to the written statement, there was time taken in advising him of his rights and securing a waiver of those rights, taking the statement in question and answer form, writing it out by hand and having it signed and notarized. All this took place in forty-five minutes. It doesn't make sense.

"Ladies and gentlemen, I don't claim to have the answer to this mystery, but the only thing I can fathom is that someone is lying. The times or the sequence has been orchestrated by someone. It all leads me to only one logical conclusion . . . and that is this. McCready *blew* it. After Troiano's statement was reduced to writing, he was immediately taken in to Kasso and told Ricky to tell all. I make an *assumption* that Ricky said something which made them question if Jimmy was more involved than his statement indicates. What to do now? Call in the best they've got. Call in the guy who can get a statement from a stone wall. Call in the guy who is fifteen years on the job and has taken hundreds of confessions. Send him out with Jimmy Troiano for the *sole and exclusive purpose* of getting a statement from that young boy.

"I assume the ends of justice require pushing,

396

twisting an arm, berating a guy to get a confession. Unfortunately, we are not dealing here with a normal situation or a normal boy. We are dealing here with a young man that can be molded like a piece of clay. The slightest suggestion, the slightest instigation can motivate him to say anything an experienced detective wants. Rodriguez is more than an experienced detective . . . he is a clever man who knows just where in a defendant's statement to put the defendant's thought processes, no matter when they were thought.

"Can you imagine what it would be like, how easy it would be, how suggestible would be the defendant if he were *under the influence* of LSD or angel dust when he was *being questioned?* We know that LSD and angel dust were found in the defendant's car. We know that Ricky Kasso had traces of angel dust in his body when he died and he was *with* Jimmy at the arrest. We know that he was a heavy and regular user. Knowing what we know about this case, it must have been almost laughable watching Rodriguez trying to get an orderly account of events from the defendant. To say nothing of putting it in an order which would be most effective on you, the jury."

"I submit that there was absolutely nothing James Troiano was sure about or could relate with any certainty to the detective. If called upon to repeat that statement ten minutes after it was reduced to writing, the statement would have been, had to be, totally different. Unfortunately, for us, there is no tape recording or video tape of the interview which resulted in this statement."

397

It was time for another drink of water and a pause to let his vocal cords relax. He started in again, Prosecutor Keahon watching and listening and unsmiling.

"Dr. Dawson testified that there were eight reportable wounds in and around the spinal column with four of them just grazing the column. He admitted that if any one of them severed the nerves, it would have caused immediate lower-body paralysis and prevented Gary from running. We have no way of determining if that occurred, but it is as equally possible as not. This would support the contention that the running took place before and not *after* the stabbing.

"Dawson also testified that at least ten of the twenty-two wounds in the back could have pierced the heart or the major artery. When we consider the size of the blade and the size of the cuts, we know that the knife moved from side to side when it was in the body. If *any of those wounds*—and there could have been multiple stab wounds the first time—pierced the heart, Gary would have been dead, much less immobilized, within fifteen *seconds*. You must also keep in mind that they had been fighting for quite a while and that Gary had ingested LSD, both of which increase the heart rate and the speed of bleeding.

"At a minimum, according to Dawson, the lung would have had to be punctured. Again, how many times it was punctured is something we will never know. Even if it was only punctured *once*, Gary would still have died within minutes. Would Gary have been able to *run* with one, two, or three or more punctures to the lung? I suggest not. The running away from Ricky must have taken place *prior* to the stabbing.

"Detective Rodriguez claims that he would not put something in a statement that did not make sense. However, he now reports that Ricky was saying things about Satan over Gary's body when all of a sudden Gary lifted his head and Ricky stabbed him in the face. Ladies and gentlemen, that poor boy had a minimum of twenty-two stab wounds in the back, all of which could have proved fatal, in any place between fifteen seconds and three minutes, and yet, he was still alive?"

Attorney Naiburg walked over to the counsel table and stood behind Jimmy. He put his hands on the boy's shoulders. "Did Jimmy Troiano really believe he was telling the truth to Detective McCready that morning? I submit he did. I am sure Mr. Keahon will argue that the defendant lied because he just wanted to get out of there and get to California. But that doesn't really test. Would a defendant who wanted to get out of there so he could cut to the West Coast do something which would inspire Kasso to say something that would be contradictory to what the defendant had already told the police officer? I submit he would not. I submit that Jimmy believed he was telling the truth and I submit that McCready believed that it *was* the truth. Would a defendant, as McCready indicated Jimmy did, supply the names of other people who knew about the crime if he believed he was lying or, for that matter, involved at all? Ladies and gentlemen, Jimmy had no motive to lie and unlike Ricky Kasso *no motive to kill Gary Lauwers.*"

Naiburg walked back to the jury box. When he started speaking his voice was low. The jurors had to strain to hear his words. "Ladies and gentlemen, I humbly and respectfully submit that only God Almighty knows or will ever know what happened that night, and I humbly and respectfully submit that if Jimmy Troiano or Albert Quinones deserve to be punished, it is the *Almighty* who must make that decision. In this case, like no other case I have ever seen, man alone will never do. *We cannot,* no matter what our frustration, no matter what churns in our gut, do anything other than, by man's law, acquit James Troiano. That is all we are capable of doing.

"I can say and do no more. I can only pray that you have the strength to do what is just. Convicting that boy of this crime is no less an injustice, no less a horror, than the death of Gary Lauwers. May God guide your deliberations."

As the people in the courtroom filed out for lunch, Naiburg sat at his table, his face in his hands.

The afternoon belonged to Prosecutor William Keahon.

Unlike Defense Attorney Naiburg, Keahon didn't play the gallery, didn't pace like a panther. He gave the opposite of the morning's performance. It was almost as if he didn't have to exert himself. The scuttlebutt in the corridors and in the press room was that that little fucker Troiano was on his way to the penitentiary. There was nothing that could save him. Keahon had brought up big guns from police and medical departments. They had pictures and they had two signed statements. The little scumbag had admitted holding down Gary while that other creep, Kasso, knifed him. The whole thing was a waste of time and the taxpayers' money. Even the public was getting tired of it. They had been fascinated when the story first broke, but now that it was a certainty Troiano would be locked up for the rest of his life, it didn't sell papers.

Keahon started by reading large portions of testimony, things he wanted the jurors to remember. He asked the jury to understand that even though Jimmy had been high on drugs, he was lucid enough to recall the murder for his friends. "Before the police ever talked with Jimmy Troiano, he was able to tell it all to Laurie Walsh. So where's the loss of memory? Where's the confusion?"

He had only good things to say about the police cooperation in the case. The Suffolk County police and the detectives had put little pieces together and brought a blatant criminal to justice. That's what police were for. That's why taxpayers want them out there doing their job. "There was nothing mysterious or surreptitious about their methods," he said. "They did an expert job. Anyway, Troiano had first tried to put all the blame for the murder on Ricky Kasso. Of course Kasso was guilty, but Troiano knew *he* was just as guilty. He lied on the first statement, hoping to hoodwink the police into letting him go free, letting him out the front door so he could get all the way out to California. Well, it didn't work. The very police methods that Mr. Naiburg decries were the ones that enabled society to bring this depraved young man to justice. He didn't care that Gary was about to be killed. He said if you take Ricky's drugs, then it's okay if you kill him."

He went over Albert's testimony, finding lucid bits in the morass of contradictions and half-truths. Yes, he supposed that drugs did play tricks on an abuser's memory, but all memories are not the same, all minds don't function alike. Albert had testified that Jimmy had picked up the knife and handed it back to Ricky so Ricky could finish the job. That is what being an *accomplice* to a murder is all about.

"That was a pretty sick night," he said in his low-keyed way. "That was a bizarre night. That was a brutal night, a sadistic night. But details show it was *real*, not a fantasy."

He went through all the details of the killing, from the first words that tipped Gary off as to what Ricky's intentions were to the final scene when Ricky and Jimmy looked down at the body and thought there was smoke coming from the corpse's back. "Can you imagine what that boy was feeling?" he asked the jury. "And that boy over there"—he pointed at a stony-faced Jimmy—"that boy over there showed absolutely no remorse."

He ended by asking them for a verdict of guilty of murder in the second degree.

*   *   *

On Tuesday, April 23, Judge John Copertino gave the jury its instructions, emphasizing that they were to weigh all the evidence and to ignore the emotions and the rhetoric that had clouded the case. He asked them not to bring in any outside influences, to forget what they had read in the newspapers or heard on television. He also told them to weigh their decision on the facts presented, not on their instincts or feelings about the defendant or the death penalty.

"I was lying in my cell," Jimmy recalls. "It was the night before the jury came in with their verdict. I had been trying to sleep but I know I *wasn't* asleep. Sleep had been pretty hard for me those last few days of the trial. Anyway, I was lying there, the lights were out, someplace down the corridor a con was snoring. Maybe that's why I couldn't sleep, I don't know. Anyway, there was this kind of glow from one corner of the cell, by the back wall, like someone had turned on a very weak and fuzzy flashlight and beamed it at the wall. I stared at it and then there was Ricky! I mean there he was, standing there in that weak light and lookin' at me. I wasn't frightened. I knew he was dead. Ricky didn't scare me while he was alive, so why should I be afraid now that he was dead? I think I said out loud—or it might have only seemed that it was out loud—'Rick, what the fuck are you doin' here?'

" 'Came for you, old buddy,' he says, and he's got that shit-eatin' grin on his face.

" 'I ain't goin' anywhere with *you!*' I said. 'I'm gonna get out of here, I'm gonna go to California.'

"He put his hands up around his chest, makin' out like he was bustin' a gut with laughin', and he says, 'You're not goin' anywhere but over here with me. Those assholes got it all set up, man. They're gonna throw you in prison and some guy with a big knife is gonna get you. Shit, they got it all set up. You're not gonna have more than six weeks in that prison until they rub you out.'

"I guess I was too annoyed to be scared. I asked him, 'Who are *they?*'

" 'The people in Northport,' he says. 'They're layin' for you. They got *me*, didn't they? One way or another, they're gonna get you. They got themselves a list and it says Jimmy Troiano right at the top of it.'

"Like hell it does, I started to say to him but he vanished. I stayed for about an hour waiting for him to appear again, but he didn't. I must have fallen asleep because a jailer woke me up and told me it was time for breakfast."

On Thursday afternoon they came for Jimmy. He was ready for them, wearing his plaid shirt and dungarees. When they led him into the courtroom and over to the counsel's table, he looked at his mother and father in the front row. He grinned at them. What else could he do? He sat beside Attorney Naiburg. Jimmy was unable to read anything in his face.

Then the jurors filed in. Jimmy got nothing

404

from their faces either. They were somber and emotionless.

"Ladies and gentlemen of the jury," the judge said, "have you reached a verdict?"

"We have, your honor," said the foreman, Claire Maturo.

"Will the defendant please rise?"

Jimmy stood up. All eyes went from the jury over to Jimmy and then back to the jury.

"We find the defendant," said the foreman, "not guilty."

There was a shout from the audience. Vincent Troiano, who had sat impassively all through the trial, lowered his head to his chest. Then he closed his eyes tightly and raised his head back toward the ceiling. "Thank you," he whispered.

Jimmy's mother let out a cry: "Oh, my God . . . thank God." She started sobbing and hid her face on her husband's shoulder.

Jimmy stood there for a moment, wavering on his feet, then he sat back onto the chair. He closed his eyes and didn't care if people saw the tears.

Immediately after the verdict county officers rushed the jurors from the courthouse. The idea was to keep what was, for most, an unpopular verdict low-keyed in the press stories that were bound to come. It didn't work.

"We all had a job to do and we did it well," one of the jurors said.

"We took all the factors into account. We just couldn't come up with enough proof," said another.

405

"I don't think the state presented us with enough facts to convict him of second-degree murder. Maybe assault, kicking him, burying the body or something . . . but in my mind, I don't think they proved he actually contributed to the death."

"None of the jury members ever voted to convict Troiano," a woman recalled. "In our first tally we voted five for acquittal and the other seven were not sure."

It was obvious that Prosecutor Keahon was shaken by the verdict. He left the courthouse, declining any comment to reporters.

A delighted Defense Attorney Naiburg was only too happy to stop and talk. "There's proof of the defendant's guilt, but also reasonable doubt. I don't think anybody but God knows what really happened that night. The prosecutor and I both gambled. We both threw the dice. It happened that I won."

As in Mudville when the Mighty Casey struck out, there was no joy in Northport when Jimmy Troiano was found not guilty. The entire town had discussed the case for months. They had offered opinions to one another, had enlarged upon what few facts they knew, and had invented details to fill in the gaps. They had tried Jimmy and had found him guilty and had banished him from the village limits forever.

Jimmy was condemned not for what he might have done to Gary, but for what the murder and the resultant bad publicity had done to Northport.

CHAPTER TEN

Lisa was born and raised in Northport. She is slim and attractive and it wasn't too long ago that she herself was running with kids and doing dope. Now she's the mother of two and is on welfare.

"There's nothing for kids to do around here. We had a place here a long time ago called the Hole in the Wall. It was a teenage dancing place and it didn't serve no alcohol. One night the guy what owned it had all the kids come wearing bandannas. They had a big brawl and one kid killed another kid. Slammed his head in a car door. There weren't any drinks. They were just kids hanging out.

"Down at the gazebo they had this shit on the walls—'Gary lives in our hearts' and 'Ricky lives!' Well, when the kids were working to clean it off, on the day of Gary's funeral, a nearby public phone rang and a voice said, 'Satan lives!' And they hung up.

"When I was a kid I used to come down here to the yacht basin and swim. Now it's filthy and polluted. Look at that water! Who could swim in that? Now the town is full of people and tourists. My father says that wherever it's pretty, people want to go. Well, they want to go here and look what they've made of it.

"The people who've lived here for a long time don't like it so much. It's kinda nice that Northport got this kick in the ass to knock them back a bit.

"I know all about dope. I've tried it. I know what it can do. When you get high there is no right and wrong. You just do whatever you want. My son, he's fourteen, used to skip school and go with some other kids his age to the house of one of his girlfriends. Her mother was there but she was drinking most of the day. The kids came there, she gave them booze and they gave her marijuana cigarettes.

"This Satan stuff. I think that all kids at that age start to think about good and bad and the devil. Then, too, all these Jesus freaks are all over the place and they would make anybody start admiring Satan.

"Nobody paid any attention to the Rickys and the Jimmys and all of a sudden somebody got killed and then we were forced to pay attention to these kids, forced to listen to them as they cried out for help.

408

"There used to be a guy here who was a 'Nam vet. His name was Pat, the kids called him 'Pat Pagan.' He was only in his late thirties, but he had long white hair from the time he was shell-shocked over in 'Nam. He dressed like a bum and had an altar in his house and everything. I used to see him standing around on corners talking with young kids. One time I saw him with about twelve kids and they were hanging on to every word he said. Well, when the cops found Gary's body, they brought this Pagan guy into the station and grilled him about it. He said he didn't know anything about it. Probably didn't. Then a little while after that he jumped in front of a train and killed himself. Right there, on the railroad tracks.

"That Kasso kid was a good-looking boy, I'm sure he had all the girls he wanted. But he didn't have any*body*, know what I mean? He wasn't in school, he had no job, he had nothing. All that he had was in his head, this wild idea, this idea he could do anything he wanted and take anybody with him. So when he sat down with a bunch of other kids, they looked at him and listened to him and paid attention to what he said. And, of course, he supplied the dope. I can't believe that all those kids were Satan worshipers. Not all of them and not all the time. You can't get a handful of *adults* together who believe all in one thing. But kids have to run with a pack. If you're not part of an *in* group, then there's something wrong with you.

"Why did Ricky hang himself? Because he had come down off his high and got no support. They grabbed him when he was high, and let him come down off that high in jail. Then like an animal he wakes up in a cage, and then he's upset and then he thinks 'What the hell am I gonna do?' And not thinking too clearly, he says 'The hell with it.' What gives him a will to live anyway? He's just murdered somebody. He's been caught. Why should he live on and let the good citizens of Northport punish him for something he probably only vaguely remembered doing? So he hung himself.

"When he died my husband and a bunch of other bums went down to the park with clubs and baseball bats to chase the kids out. Like a damned vigilante committee. They should have shown some interest before Gary was killed. The bums!

"I had a boyfriend who was a junkie and he used to take pride in telling people 'I'm a junkie' because, at least, he *was* something. He was still living with his mother and she was nuts and he didn't have anything else. So now this Kasso guy goes around saying 'I am a Satanist.' Why not? It got him attention. People noticed him. What should he have done, gone around saying 'I follow Christ'? What attention is that going to get him?"

And in the gazebo a young kid sits strumming a guitar and singing the words to a street song that caught on after *Rolling Stone* printed it:

> "Hey, Ricky, you're so fine,
> Why doncha stab me one more time?
> Do-de-do, do-de-do.
> Hey, Ricky, you're a nice guy,

Why doncha stab me in the eye?
Do-de-do, do-de-do.
Hey, Ricky, you're so swell,
Why you hangin' in your cell?
Do-de-do, do-de-do,
Do-de-do, dah, dah."

MINE TO KILL
by David St Clair

On Wednesday, 28th August, 1878, Esther Cox, a plain, unassuming girl from the town of Amherst in Nova Scotia rode out on a buggy on her first date. Storm clouds lowered on the horizon; later there was lightning and torrential rain. Esther returned at nightfall, soaked through and too distraught to speak to her family: her innocent trip had turned into the beginning of a personal nightmare.

At first there were rustlings in her bedroon at night, then unseen hands gouged a terrible message on her wall: ESTER COX, YOU ARE MINE TO KILL!

On the third night, Esther leapt from her bed. 'Oh, my God', she screamed, 'I'm dying! Please dear God! I'm dying!'

This is the chilling story of a girl's possession by malevolent spirits. Like CHILD POSSESSED (also available in Corgi paperback), everything in this book actually happened.

0 552 12587 3

CHILD POSSESSED
by David St Clair

This is a true story. Nothing has been added in the interests of sensationalism. What happened in the small town of Watseka, Illinois, between the years 1865 and 1878 may strain credibility, as well as shock. But it did happen.

Mary Roff, a gentle, unassuming 19 year old girl, died suddenly on the morning of July 5th, 1865, in the town of Watseka, Illinois. Her death was strange, but her life had been stranger. For several years she had been subject to sudden, unaccountable "fits" – But her death brought to an end her sad and disturbing case . . .

Thirteen years later, in 1878, Mary Roff reappeared – in the living body of Lurancy Vennum . . .

0 552 11132 5

THE DEVIL ROCKED HER CRADLE
by David St Clair

Mary Lawrence was a Catholic girl brought up to be pious, meek and hardworking and whose only ambition was to become a nun. Yet in 1928 Mary Lawrence was the subject of one of the most protracted and harrowing exorcisms carried out this century: *an exorcism where the priests in attendance seriously doubted whether in this particular instance, good would triumph over evil.*

David St Clair has gone back to the original sources and to eyewitnesses and uncovered for the first time the background behind Mary's possession: how her father was himself possessed by demons having left his own father for dead after a brawl; how her mother was poisoned by her aunt and died while her father and aunt made love in the room next to the death chamber; how Mary's ambitions to become a nun were frustrated by her father, and how she began to speak in tongues at Mass, outraging the priests with her obscenities, whilst Satanic voices filled her head and human excrement was found smeared on the walls of her house.

Thirty years later Mary Lawrence was a shadow of her former self, and close to death. Only one man, the greatest exorcist of his day, Father Theophilus Reisinger, could save her. So it was that they met in the small convent in Earling, Iowa where one of the most titanic struggles between good and evil of all time was about to take place . . .

0 552 12705 1

BLOODLINE
by David St Clair

HE WAS JUST SIX YEARS OLD . . .
and her only child, yet after the shocking kidnapping and
even the horrible identification of his small tortured body,
Lois refused to believe her son was dead – *really* dead.

Plagued by strange psychic premonitions and disturbing wide
awake visions, Lois became more and more convinced that
her child was being held captive somewhere – for some unknown reason – and she was the only one who could save
him.

And then the framed engraving arrived . . . the one with the
old manor house and the weird little man who moved
effortlessly under the glass. He led her to Scotland . . . and a
family . . . and the unspeakable horror of her BLOODLINE.

0 552 13323 X

A SELECTED LIST OF HORROR TITLES AVAILABLE FROM CORGI AND BANTAM BOOKS

THE PRICES SHOWN BELOW WERE CORRECT AT THE TIME OF GOING TO PRESS. HOWEVER TRANSWORLD PUBLISHERS RESERVE THE RIGHT TO SHOW NEW RETAIL PRICES ON COVERS WHICH MAY DIFFER FROM THOSE PREVIOUSLY ADVERTISED IN THE TEXT OR ELSEWHERE.

☐	09156 1	The Exorcist	*William Peter Blatty*	£2.99
☐	13034 6	Come Down into Darkness	*Clare McNally*	£2.99
☐	12691 8	What About the Baby?	*Clare McNally*	£2.99
☐	12400 1	Ghostlight	*Clare McNally*	£2.99
☐	11652 1	Ghost House	*Clare McNally*	£2.50
☐	11825 7	Ghost House Revenge	*Clare McNally*	£2.99
☐	13033 8	Somebody Come and Play	*Clare McNally*	£2.50
☐	13323 X	Bloodline	*David St Clair*	£3.99
☐	12705 1	The Devil Rocked Her Cradle	*David St Clair*	£2.99
☐	12587 3	Mine to Kill	*David St Clair*	£2.99
☐	11132 5	Child Possessed	*David St Clair*	£2.99
☐	17255 7	Hellfire	*John Saul*	£2.95
☐	17171 2	Brainchild	*John Saul*	£2.50
☐	17466 5	Nathaniel	*John Saul*	£3.50
☐	17387 1	All Fall Down	*John Saul*	£3.50
☐	17564 5	The Unloved	*John Saul*	£3.50
☐	17462 2	The Unwanted	*John Saul*	£2.95
☐	10471 X	Full Circle	*Peter Straub*	£2.99
☐	13466 X	Still Life	*Sheri S. Tepper*	£2.99

All Corgi/Bantam Books are available at your bookshop or newsagent, or can be ordered from the following address:
Corgi/Bantam Books,
Cash Sales Department,
P.O. Box 11, Falmouth, Cornwall TR10 9EN

Please send a cheque or postal order (no currency) and allow 80p for postage and packing for the first book plus 20p for each additional book ordered up to a maximum charge of £2.00 in UK.

B.F.P.O. customers please allow 80p for the first book and 20p for each additional book.

Overseas customers, including Eire, please allow £1.50 for postage and packing for the first book, £1.00 for the second book, and 30p for each subsequent title ordered.

NAME (Block Letters) ....

ADDRESS ....

....